NEW CASTLE COUNTY

Critical Essays on Edward Albee

Critical Essays on Edward Albee

Philip C. Kolin
and
J. Madison Davis

G. K. Hall & Co. • Boston, Massachusetts

Library of Congress Cataloging in Publication Data

Critical essays on Edward Albee.

(Critical essays on American literature)
Includes index.
1. Albee, Edward, 1928-   — Criticism and
interpretation. I. Kolin, Philip C. II. Davis,
J. Madison. III. Series.
PS3551.L25Z63 1968   812'.54   86-12112
ISBN 0-8161-8875-0

This publication is printed on permanent/durable acid-free paper
MANUFACTURED IN THE UNITED STATES OF AMERICA

CRITICAL ESSAYS ON AMERICAN LITERATURE

This series seeks to anthologize the most important criticism on a wide variety of topics and writers in American literature. Our readers will find in various volumes not only a generous selection of reprinted articles and reviews but original essays, bibliographies, manuscript sections, and other materials brought to public attention for the first time. This volume on Edward Albee by Philip C. Kolin and J. Madison Davis is a welcome addition to the program. It contains thirty-nine essays and reviews, including several translated from German for the first time. Among the reprinted selections are essays by John Gassner, Walter Kerr, Clive Barnes, Brendan Gill, Jack Kroll, Brian Way, John Kenneth Galbraith, and Anne Paolucci. In addition to an extensive introduction, which provides the most comprehensive bibliographic essay ever published on Albee, there is an interview with Edward Albee, Matthew C. Roudané's article on *The Man Who Had Three Arms* (the first published essay on that play), and Lea Carol Owen's bibliography of interviews with Albee. We are confident that this volume will make a permanent and significant contribution to American literary study.

JAMES NAGEL, GENERAL EDITOR

Northeastern University

To Colby H. Kullman:
Friend and Scholar

CONTENTS

INTRODUCTION

The plays of Edward Albee have aroused controversy from the beginning of his career some twenty-five years ago. Each Albee play since *The Zoo Story* has served as a lightning rod attracting an extraordinary range of reactions and interpretations. Critics have extravagantly praised Albee as the hope of the American theater or condemned him as a charlatan; yet they interpret his works in such different ways that they might appear to be condemning or praising not just different playwrights, but dramatists from widely opposed theatrical or political camps.

Some critics place him in the mainstream of major theatrical traditions; others attack the multiple implications of his plays as theatrical posturing. Critics have identified numerous and diverse influences, from Unamuno to Strindberg to *The Tatler* to Tennessee Williams to medieval moralities to vaudeville to piano pieces by Satie to humorous sketches by Thornton Wilder. Albee himself has contributed to the critical controversies through his numerous interviews (more than eighty to date), articles, and counterattacks. Often his comments have inspired new rounds of speculation based upon interpretation of the playwright's remarks. Much of the firestorm of discussion around both plays and playwright may yet prove to be the result of forcing interpretation upon works that essentially are constructed to defy it, as was true of so many literary and artistic works since the 1960s. But for Albee one conclusion is inescapable: he is one of the most controversial playwrights of our time. The criticism has poured out in an avalanche unequal to that devoted to other contemporary writers, the volume of which is indicative of Albee's importance, certainly in his own lifetime, if not (as some have argued) in the future of American and world drama. Liked or disliked, excoriated or glorified, original or imitative, Albee is undeniably *the* major playwright in the United States in the last quarter century.

Organizing this criticism so that one can grasp the many directions critical theory on Albee has taken is nearly as difficult as selecting the most significant, well written, and provocative commentaries on Albee's work. Within the limits of this volume, however, we have provided a representative selection of significant reviews and criticism on most of Albee's plays, emphasizing those items which illuminate his work as a whole. We have also printed, for the first time, a translation of the German reviews of Albee's first production of *The Zoo Story* and his later *Death of Bessie Smith*, a new interview with Albee, an annotated bibliography of Albee interviews, and the first critical article on Albee's *The Man Who Had Three Arms*.

RESEARCH TOOLS FOR ALBEE SCHOLARSHIP

Robert A. Wilson's checklist is the first descriptive bibliography of Albee's work,[1] possibly the only one; there is no complete listing of Albee's primary work, however, and one must piece it together from James E. White's "An Early Play by Edward Albee"[2] and Philip C. Kolin's article proving that two (not one, as Richard Amacher and others had stated) Albee poems had been published in *Kaleidoscope*, a now-defunct Texas magazine.[3] Albee's poetry for *The New Yorker* and his ephemeral pieces also underscore the need for an up-to-date, complete bibliography of primary works. The Atheneum publication of Albee's complete plays in four volumes has done scholars a great service in making the plays readily available and may encourage the use of a consistent text.[4]

Currently, the most useful bibliography of secondary sources is included in Kimball King's *Ten Modern American Playwrights: An Annotated Bibliography*.[5] It devotes over one hundred pages to editions, criticism, and reviews. *Edward Albee: An Annotated Bibliography, 1968–1977* by Charles Green[6] covers commentary in English only, and was designed to be a supplement to Richard E. Amacher and Margaret Rule's *Edward Albee at Home and Abroad*, which annotates books and articles, though not reviews.[7] As a supplement to Green the bibliography by Michael D. Reed and James L. Evans in *Edward Albee: Planned Wilderness; Interview, Essays, and Bibliography*[8] is not entirely adequate. Philip C. Kolin's classified checklists in the *Serif*[9] have been praised in Charles Carpenter's "American Drama: A Bibliographic Essay," which provides a brief though valuable critical overview of Albee criticism and bibliography.[10] Lea Carol Owen's bibliography of interviews and topical index (in this volume) should also be useful to Albee scholars.

BOOK-LENGTH STUDIES ON ALBEE

As Carpenter points out, Albee is the most absorbing postwar American dramatist, ranking second only to O'Neill as a subject for critical exegesis.[11] Since the 1960s, over fourteen booklength studies of Albee have appeared in the U.S. and abroad (excluding more than fifty doctoral dissertations), many attempting to connect the disparate elements of his plays to provide an overview of his drama. C. W. E. Bigsby's *Albee* (1969),[12] *Edward Albee: A Collection of Critical Essays* (1975),[13] a chapter in *Confrontation and Commitment: A Study of Contemporary American Drama* (1966),[14] and the extensive assessment in the second volume of his survey of American drama since 1900 (1984)[15] have established him as one of the most perceptive Albee scholars. His collection of criticism, the first gathering of essays on Albee, was an important contribution to Albee studies. Bigsby takes a broad and balanced view of Albee's career, seeing in it an intertwining of various traditions and influences, and thereby avoids the common tendency to overestimate any particular element in the plays. He recognizes, for instance, that while Albee adopted many techniques from the Absurdists he also recognized the insufficiency of their vision. Limited in depicting human existence as meaningless, the Absurdists found themselves at a dead end and merely reveled in their linguistic and theatrical skills. Albee, however, goes beyond the dead end to an existentialist's commitment to intimacy through the stripping of illusion. The playwright, says Bigsby, has thus formulated an alternative to both illusion and despair.

While Bigsby's commentaries admit Albee's social criticism, psychological insight, and technical mastery, they emphasize Albee's concern with the metaphysical position of humanity. "Albee creates a hero who is crushed, not, like the protagonist of the naturalistic novel, by environment and heredity, nor, like the anti-hero of Beckett's plays, by the sheer weight of an indifferent universe, but by his own conscious submission."[16] Bigsby's erudition and ability to entwine the various strands in the plays without excluding others lead to a balanced and fulfilling reading of Albee.

Belgian critic Gilbert Debusscher has a view similar to Bigsby's in claiming that Albee's "work constitutes a synthesis of a European and an American tradition."[17] His *Edward Albee: Tradition and Renewal* (1967)[18] is a meaty little book sharing the erudition and broad view which makes Bigsby's criticism so incisive. Debusscher provides a thorough analysis of Albee's work up to 1966, including the adaptations *Malcolm* and *The Ballad of the Sad Café*. He traces the relationships between Albee and such playwrights as Jean Genet, Tennessee Williams, Samuel Beckett, and Eugene Ionesco. Hailing Albee as the major American playwright of the 1960s and the most important source of a renewal confronting the inhibited conservatism of the Broadway stage, Debusscher avoids ascribing too much importance to any one source of influence or thematic concern, and yet offers firm opinions, as exemplified by his blunt statement on *The Sandbox*: "The essential purpose of this short play is to decry accepted ideas, stereotyped attitudes, convenient sentiments — in brief, the clichés of daily life and language. The two idols Albee attacks are the family and death."[19] *Edward Albee: Tradition and Renewal* is essential reading for those wishing to see Albee on the larger stage of world and American drama.

Another excellent overview is provided in Anne Paolucci's *From Tension to Tonic: The Plays of Edward Albee* (1972).[20] According to her introduction, her book is "the summary of a long, brooding enjoyment of Albee's plays. . . . For this reason, I have pursued no theses or formal patterns of criticism—though I believe Albee's plays are substantial enough in content and form to withstand the most rigorous varieties of critical analysis." She does, however, build many of her observations upon an affinity she sees between Dante and Albee. "Albee," she asserts, "has done more than any other recent author to revive the glorious tradition of polysemous writing, in a modern vein."[21] She is thus primarily concerned with Albee's exploitation of language, a talent which even his harshest detractors are willing to concede. Calling Albee "a master of dialogue," she traces his development from the early plays through *Box* and *Quotations from Chairman Mao Tse-Tung*. Like the work of Debusscher and Bigsby, *From Tension to Tonic* is straightforward, yet profound. It lacks the scope of the works discussed earlier but presents compelling interpretations.

Ruby Cohn, who coined the term "Albeegory," also focuses on Albee's talent for dialogue in *Edward Albee* (1969),[22] and in her chapter in *Dialogue in American Drama* (1971).[23] Albee, writes Cohn, has tried to dramatize the reality of the human condition, "but whereas Sartre, Camus, Beckett, Genet, Ionesco, and Pinter represent that reality in all its alogical absurdity, Albee has been preoccupied with illusions that screen man from reality." Albee, unlike the Europeans, does not strip away the illusions, however: ". . . illusion is still present, and the action often dramatizes the process of collapse, so that we, the audience, arrive at a recognition of the reality behind the illusion."[24] In *Dialogue in American Drama*, she successively analyzes the progression of Albee's native gift for language as it developed through the plays up to *Box*, concluding that Albee is "the most skillful composer of dialogue that America has produced." Cohn suspects, however, that his very craftsmanship may dampen the genuineness of his artistic search: ". . . just because his verbal craft *is* so fine, one longs for the clumsy upward groping toward art."[25]

Many critics, however, would object to Cohn's view that Albee's content may have been obscured by his ingenuity, finding a constant upward groping toward art, which often fails in such "obscure" plays as *Tiny Alice, Box-Mao-Box*, or *The Lady from Dubuque*. A provocatively thesis-oriented study is Michael Rutenberg's *Edward Albee: Playwright in Protest* (1969),[26] which bears the virtues and vices of its decade by fitting Albee into the social protest environment of the 1960s. Though Rutenberg's thesis may seem forced on occasion, Albee, like all other playwrights, must be considered a product of the social milieu, and his coming to prominence in that troubled time has considerable bearing on the motives behind his drama. Albee, indeed, has frequently been at odds with the New York theater establishment: ". . . there is no hiding," a reviewer wrote in 1962, "he does have something of the preacher in him, something of a modern young Savonarola preaching to the corrupt

Florentines."[27] More recently, Albee himself reestablished the importance of social criticism in his work by saying, "The fact that I keep writing, sending semaphore signals so to speak, must mean I'm still engaged."[28]

"Edward Albee," Rutenberg asserts, "writes reformist plays of social protest which unflinchingly reveal the pustulous sores of a society plagued with social ills."[29] In interpreting the plays through *Box*, Rutenberg explores the background of social issues which each play articulates. For example, Rutenberg investigates the possibility that the names George and Martha in *Who's Afraid of Virginia Woolf?* might derive from George and Martha Washington and symbolize America.[30] Rutenberg considers *A Delicate Balance* to be Albee's greatest achievement, because of its multiple levels of social protest overlooked by the critics. However interesting and provocative *Playwright in Protest* is, however, one is hard-pressed to accept social reform as *the* primary unifying factor in Albee's work.

Like most of the other rewarding studies of Albee, Foster Hirsch's *Who's Afraid of Edward Albee?* (1978)[31] is a short book with an interesting thesis and a compelling argument. Hirsch's title has more than paronomasic interest: "The question to ask now, at this diminished moment in the career of an enormously gifted writer is 'Who's afraid of Edward Albee?'; and the answer, in the evidence of his progressively claustrophobic and indirect plays, from which his own biography is carefully omitted, is— Albee himself."[32] Hirsch finds Albee's work generally and personally evasive, as, for example, when the playwright avoids facing up to the implications of homosexuality, adoption, and other important biographical influences. We might compare this view with Cohn's uneasiness over Albee's craftsmanship and the need for the artist's groping toward art—a Romantic view of the artist harrowing the hell of his own soul to reach truth. Hirsch, however, considers *Who's Afraid of Virginia Woolf?* and *A Delicate Balance* to be among the best modern plays, assuring Albee's place in the history of drama. In other plays he finds considerable power, such as the early short plays and *Tiny Alice*, but in most of the later plays—*Seascape, Counting the Ways*, and particularly the three adaptations (*Malcolm, The Ballad of the Sad Café*, and *Everything in the Garden*)—Hirsch faults Albee for putting more elaborate obfuscations between himself and his work: the magician disappears, as it were, and only the tricks remain. Though Hirsch's premise may leave things unexplained, his analyses are clear, perceptive, and thought-provoking.

Other booklength Albee studies take various critical stances. Anita Maria Stenz's *Edward Albee: Poet of Loss* (1978)[33] devotes a chapter to each play through *Seascape*. Primarily interested in the characters and how Albee unravels human interrelationships, she tries to discover the meanings of the plays without reference to the context of dramatic literature or movements, and thus relies upon descriptions of original performances. Certainly, her assertion that too many attempts have been made to pigeon-hole the playwright—still alive and evolving—has great validity. "Consistently, almost stubbornly," Stenz remarks, "the author's intense preoccupation with the ways people waste their lives has been overlooked. Albee focuses on twisted human relationships which can evolve within the establishment, on the results of materialism and parasitism, and on the deceptive nature of ambition."[34] Albee protests against an establishment that changes or crushes the finer elements of the human spirit. A stern moralist, Albee is nonetheless sympathetic to those who have allowed themselves to be absorbed into the immorality. Stenz's critical stance, among all the other analyses, thus helps to remind us that not only is the performance crucial to understanding a play, but that the engaging quality of any play does not lie exclusively in symbols, themes, and wit. The characters and their conflicts must also strike a chord that harmonizes with the audience's sense of what it means to be human.

Richard E. Amacher's *Edward Albee* (1969),[35] containing much biographical information to shed light on each play, points out perceived relationships to Greek tragedy. Some of Amacher's interpretations seem forced, though his identification of major themes is helpful. Liliane Kerjan's highly praised *Le théâtre d'Edward Albee* (1971)[36] views Albee as a social critic, and, like much foreign criticism, attempts to place him in the larger context of world drama. Nelvin Vos's brief *Eugene Ionesco and Edward Albee: A Critical Essay* (1968)[37] explores the philosophical aspects of Absurdism in Ionesco and records similarities and differences in Albee's treatment of Absurd themes; however, the playwrights are most often discussed separately, denying readers a more integrated view.

"ABSURDISM" AND ALBEE

In the early part of his career, Albee's plays *The Zoo Story*, *The Sandbox*, *The American Dream*, and *The Death of Bessie Smith* were often linked to the Theater of the Absurd, though *Zoo Story* and *Bessie Smith* are obviously quite different from most plays in that tradition. Martin Esslin's famous *The Theatre of the Absurd* (1961), for example, was the first work to identify Albee's indebtedness to this tradition: ". . . Edward Albee comes into the category of the Theatre of the Absurd precisely because his work attacks the very foundations of American optimism."[38] Esslin praises *American Dream* for its masterly use of American clichés in the same vein as Ionesco's use of French platitudes and Pinter's use of English nonsense dialogue. Esslin further sees elements of Absurd theater in *Who's Afraid of Virginia Woolf?* in the "killing" of the imaginary child and the "Genet-like ritualistic element in its structure" of three rites.[39] *Tiny Alice* was allegorical, argues Esslin, and *A Delicate Balance*, though realistic in setting, was redolent with mystery. *Box-Mao-Box* was a more blatant return to Absurdist techniques. In later works, we might also note such Absurdist elements as the intelligent lizards of *Seascape*, the comic lack of communication in *Counting the Ways*, the identity of the mother in *The Lady from Dubuque*, and the third arm of *The Man Who Had Three Arms*.

Whether Albee has truly been influenced by specific literary works or whether such perceived resemblances are implicit is an ongoing critical debate. Since no single "source" explains any one of Albee's plays, critics who can integrate the tangled web of influences, such as Bigsby and Debusscher, seem to offer a better understanding of the oeuvre than those readers hooked on a single thread. As Albee himself remarked, "I've been influenced by everybody, for God's sake. Everything I've seen, either accepting or rejecting it."[40] Indeed, placing Albee's works in any particular tradition provides obvious difficulties because of the differences between plays. At first glance, Albee's plays seem as varied as if they were written by a number of playwrights: the Southern Gothic of *The Death of Bessie Smith* contrasts with the Absurdism of *The Sandbox*; the naturalism of *Who's Afraid of Virginia Woolf?* contrasts with the Symbolist qualities of *All Over*. Responding to such diversity, Robert Brustein repeatedly criticizes what he considers Albee's wholesale borrowing from other playwrights, be they Ionesco, Strindberg, Pirandello, Dürrenmatt, or Ibsen. "Under certain circumstances, such distinguished models might provide distinguished drama, but Albee generally exploits the work of other writers in order to invest his own with unearned significance. To be blunt about it, Albee has nothing particularly urgent to communicate."[41] Brustein is not entirely negative. He admits the power of many of the plays, Albee's use of language, his ability to create excitement, and the consistency in the sexual pathology of the plays, but sees Albee overreaching his talents and producing "empty profundities" in *Tiny Alice*.

Other critics link Albee's promise to the fate of Absurdism, and depending on their ideology, condemn or praise the expression of it in his plays. In a print debate with Faubion Bowers in *Theatre Arts* in 1962, Glenn M. Loney argued that Theater of the Absurd was only a fad, but found Albee, "The most talented and significant contributor to the literature . . . of the Absurd . . ." and emphasized the planning and purpose in his plays, noting that *Zoo Story, Bessie Smith*, and *Virginia Woolf* are essentially realistic, though many had seen Absurdism in them. Loney praised Albee for being the least Absurd of the Absurdists, incorporating techniques from a fad which will "wear thin," yet promising to develop beyond it. Curiously, Faubion Bowers, who argued that the Theater of the Absurd was "here to stay," implied that Albee, although pelting the theatergoer with a harsh dose of truth in *Virginia Woolf*, had written plays of lasting worth, exactly because of their Absurdism.[42] W. L. Turner accuses Albee of having "a bad case of absurditis," but lauds *Zoo Story* for its dialogue and *American Dream* for a "feeling for clichés not unlike Ionesco's." He concludes, however, that Albee, along with Jack Richardson, Arthur Kopit, and Jack Gelber has yet to produce a significant play. He dismisses *Virginia Woolf* with the notorious remark ". . . if college professors behave that way, I've been sadly out of touch with my colleagues."[43]

Robert H. Deutsch compares *Zoo Story* with Ionesco's *The Bald Primadonna* (*La Cantatrice chauve*) and admits Albee employs only "a slight distortion from expected reality"; however, he still places Albee firmly within the Absurdist tradition, arguing that the Theater of the Absurd is no longer avant-garde, now that such able writers are maturing in it.[44] Robert Mayberry finds Albee, Pinter, and Beckett use a similar technique for "duping" audiences into exposing themselves to reality; these playwrights break the traditional coherence of sight and sound in theater and construct plays on the principle of dissonance. The discord created by what the spectator sees and hears creates a mental pressure to relieve it, so that the play actually takes place in the mind. Albee and Pinter, however, have not been as persistent as Beckett in pursuing new forms, says Mayberry, for *Box-Mao-Box* remains Albee's sole effort in this direction.[45] In defining and exploring this subcategory of Absurd theater, then, Mayberry labels Albee more of a dabbler than a convert. In one of the most insightful analyses of Albee's relationship to Absurdism, Brian Way (in this volume) sees Albee as torn between the "apparent security of realism and the temptation to experiment." Linking Albee's seeming Absurdism to his social criticism, Way convincingly argues that Albee uses Absurdist techniques to demonstrate the invalidity of "the American Way of Life"; yet, Albee does not fully accept the underlying premises of Absurdists such as Ionesco, Pinter, or Beckett. The entire universe is not revealed as absurd, only the American corner of it. By trying to have it both ways, absurd and realistic, Albee cannot muster the poetic power of these playwrights.[46]

THE ZOO STORY

Albee's first play, *The Zoo Story*, proved that a playwright is not a prophet in his own land. The world premiere took place on 28 September 1959 in Berlin (translations of two of the German reviews—the first reviews Albee ever received—appear for the first time in this volume). When the play was produced in America at the Provincetown Playhouse, critical response was generally enthusiastic. Donald Malcolm, for example, wrote that *Zoo Story* "is the work of a hitherto unknown young playwright," but ended his review with these promising words: "The merit of the piece lies in its acute observation of two authentic and interesting types, and one is encouraged to expect many more good things from Mr. Albee."[47]

The most frequent critical approach to the forty-minute play, particularly in the 1960s, related it to the Absurdism which would become much more overt in *American Dream* and *Sandbox*. Often, however, *Zoo Story* is interpreted as a parable of humanity in modern society, though William

Force warns that critics may be reading too much into a play that may not be entirely coherent, or "pretentious where it seeks to be profound."[48] Richard Kostelanetz also finds too much eisegesis in the interpretations and argues that once "the critical veil" is lifted, "*The Zoo Story* describes an unsuccessful homosexual pass."[49]

Kafka's "A Hunger Artist" is considered *Zoo Story's* thematic predecessor by Fred D. White, who finds Jerry symbolic of the artist and Peter symbolic of "the banality, unimaginativeness, and worst of all, the esthetic dictatorship of the masses." As artist, Jerry's role is to reveal the underlying falsehood of so much human thought, but Jerry only succeeds in reaching Peter through his own death,[50] a point also made by Rutenberg, who adds that Jerry thereby forces Peter into insights he would otherwise simply flee.[51] Similarly, Robert S. Wallace believes ". . . basically he [Albee] is attacking the fictions which North American society has developed to escape the alienation and discord which he views as modern urban realities." The "attack on fiction as a substitute for life is developed . . . in such a way that the audience will come to understand not only Peter's dependence on fiction, but its own as well." Jerry's words only add to his isolation, however, and physical contact becomes the only communication.[52] In documenting the social criticism in eight Albee works, Peter Wolfe finds that the play uncovers the problems of relationships across class barriers.[53] The play is often approached as a secular salvation story: Jerry's death saves Peter, opens his eyes, shakes him from the complacency which is integral to his illusory, bureaucratic life-style. Though he considers *Zoo Story* to be Albee's best play before *Virginia Woolf*, Gerald Weales asserts that Jerry forces Peter to kill him, "presumably because his need to make contact . . . can only be filled through death, and Peter can only be a man worth contact when the act of murder assures Jerry that 'he is not really a vegetable,' but 'an animal.' " Weales, however, is incredulous that Albee really believes this, and, if he does, then it is a theme far too weighty for the play to bear,[54] possibly echoing a sentiment voiced by Brooks Atkinson that the ending is "conventional melodrama."[55]

Finding no such problem, Rose Zimbardo provocatively examines the use of symbolism in Jerry's self-sacrifice. Beneath a naturalistic surface, she argues, lies traditional Christian symbolism. She points to Jerry's use of biblical language in his parable of the dog and likens various facets of Jerry's character to Christ. Peter has similarities to his Biblical namesake, especially when he denies the dying Jerry.[56] Bigsby also finds Jerry's role Christ-like and chastises critics like Charles Lyons, Debusscher, and Esslin, who brand *Zoo Story* a pessimistic play about the inevitability of isolation, when the text does not justify such an interpretation.[57] Shanta Acharya agrees, and sees Albee using techniques of Absurdism but refusing to accept the underlying metaphysics.[58] Martin Brunkworst discusses Albee's early plays in the context of Absurdism and compares *Zoo Story* to *Krapp's Last Tape*, a play with which it shared its Off-Broadway debut.[59]

C. N. Stavrou notes the religious overtones and compares the encounter to the struggle between Christianity and Islam, seeing a bond, however tenuous, formed between the conflicting forces.[60]

Analyzing the play in ritualistic terms, Mary Castiglie Anderson regards Jerry's confrontation as a way of moving Peter to maturity by making him face the reality of death. Peter, however, is not initiated into society, as in most primitive rites, but instead retreats into autonomy. To create a new, more consciously formed personality, Peter must reject inherited patterns (fictions).[61] Anderson's interpretation is similar to the French Existentialists' demands that an individual must create his or her own essence, making Jerry a kind of Existentialist Christ who awakens Peter to an acceptance of his responsibility. As Paolucci observes, this recognition leads to an awareness of Existential despair similar to the ending of No Exit.[62] Allan Lewis, who denies that the play is a search for communication, writes, "Peter, who lives, is forced to face a continuing anguish, roused from his cultured complacency to awareness of the destructiveness below the surface of comfortable living," but, "The play gives no answers."[63]

Nor does Mary M. Nilan grant Jerry a heroic role, arguing instead that Jerry is incapable of forging a normal I / Thou relationship and he therefore perverts it into the murderer / victim bond. "Albee leaves unanswered the final question: Is such a perversion of love the only method left whereby modern man can bridge the gap, unite with another, communicate?"[64] Similarly, Robert B. Bennett speculates it is too easy to sentimentalize Jerry's death or to see it as Christ-like. Jerry brings his death upon himself.[65] Debusscher (in this volume), who also questions the "altruism" in Jerry's sacrifice, opines that Jerry's life has been a failure: "His last words do not express the jubilation of a victor but the humble thanks of a wounded animal put out of his misery at last." For Debusscher the primary purpose of the play is to attack bourgeois complacency — it can be understood without the symbolic implications with which Albee has larded it.[66]

Identifying sources and analogues of The Zoo Story have helped a number of readers to make sense of Albee's modern parable. Lucina P. Gabbard compares O'Neill's The Hairy Ape and Zoo Story, characterizing Albee as a social critic decrying the lack of communication between classes.[67] Mordecai Levine suggests that the play's success in Germany may have been at least partly due to its resemblance to a Thomas Mann short story.[68] The influence of a McCullers story, as well as The Secret Sharer and Heart of Darkness, has been advanced. Even Hamlet has been dragged in.[69] Perhaps the most illuminating exchange on the subject of Albee's influences occurs in the Spielberg / Macklin debate. Peter Spielberg argued that the principal source for the play was Coleridge's Rime of the Ancient Mariner — citing how a mysterious speaker forces himself on a stranger and the confrontation between mariner and albatross, Jerry and dog. He concluded that modern man bears an albatross around his neck and remains separated from the rest of mankind. This interpretation was evidently too much for Anthony Macklin who attacked the comparison as irresponsible. Spielberg then rebutted Macklin.[70] The confrontation is perhaps more interesting for illustrating a recurrent problem with each Albee production: to what extent is Albee's work derived from earlier sources? All too often, the links seem tenuous, the result of a critic's cleverness with analogy. Since Albee raises questions that bear on the ultimate ambiguities of human existence, it is inevitable that his work is subject to multiple interpretations, many of which may be grasping for answers when only questions exist.

THREE SHORT PLAYS

The American Dream and its companion *The Sandbox* seemed to fulfill the promise of *Zoo Story*. During the 1960s they were among the most frequently performed plays on college campuses, and helped establish Albee's career, though he had yet to write a full-length play. Most of the criticism centered on the Absurdist elements of *American Dream* and *Sandbox*. Harold Clurman wrote that there was "no harm in a young writer's being influenced . . . But there is a certain literalness in *The American Dream* . . . which makes me suspect the French influence is not helpful."[71] Like Clurman, most reviewers compared these plays to the works of Ionesco and Beckett, often ignoring subtle but important Albee distinctions. The social satire in *American Dream*, for example, seems more pertinent to the American way of life than to all of anxious existence. Wendell V. Harris (in this volume) remarks that the *American Dream* "is a satire directed against the emasculated men and domineering women, the heartlessness, the glitteringly hollow goals and ideals which Albee seems to see on every side in contemporary America." Later, however, Harris (as does Paolucci in her compelling analyses of the early Albee plays[72]) observes that the satire is not entirely limited to a criticism of American life.[73] *The American Dream* also invites interesting biographical comparisons with the playwright's past,[74] and reveals Albee's consistent interest in theatrical innovation. As Henry Popkin wisely observed, ". . . Albee is one of the few dramatists who are not afraid to undertake a variety of styles."[75]

Paul Cubeta's analysis of *The Sandbox* is one of the best, most concise introductions to this brief play.[76] Ruby Cohn (in this volume) points out the influence of Ionesco's techniques of dialogue on *American Dream* and *Sandbox* and analyzes the "thrust-and-parry exchanges" containing "the clichés of middle-class America."[77] As indicated earlier, Brian Way's essay on Absurdity in Albee is also one of the most revealing assessments on these plays.

Like *Zoo Story*, *The Death of Bessie Smith* opened in Berlin, but its American premiere was not as well received as *American Dream* and

Sandbox, perhaps because the play is not as easy to categorize. As we find in *Zoo Story* and *Virginia Woolf*, *Bessie* lies somewhere between realism, naturalism, social satire, and perhaps several other critical spheres. It has been praised for its chilling portrayal of racial bigotry and fulminating spite by critics, such as Rutenberg, Hirsch, and Luke M. Grande,[78] who were sensitive to the element of social protest, but the play has been faulted for its unclear or nonexistent structure. Paolucci, for example, claimed that "the death of Bessie Smith is in every sense peripheral to the main action of the play,"[79] and Paul Witherington (in this volume) judged several parts of the play to be "thematically irrelevant."[80] The different worlds of the play are, however, thematically fused, as, for example, each character searches for fulfillment through escape. The need for escape can be linked to existentialism, and commentators have found Absurdist elements despite the ostensible naturalistic setting.[81] Also, the metaphysical issues which recur throughout Albee's work are prominent.

Bigsby's analysis is one of the best on *Bessie Smith*. Arguing that the play is not the racial protest some critics have made it, he finds it reflects Albee's concerns about the decline of society in general: "Thus a declaration made by the intern in the sixth scene can be taken as an accurate description not only of the theme of this play but also of the faith which has animated Albee in all of his work from *The Zoo Story* to *A Delicate Balance*: 'I am not concerned with politics . . . but I have a sense of urgency . . . a dislike of waste . . . stagnation.' "[82] Debusscher, however, finds the play preoccupied with racism, the sexual metaphor of implicit incest and the war between the sexes (which Debusscher thinks Albee may have inherited from Strindberg), and illusion, or the "life-lie." These themes foreshadow much of Albee's later work. The final message in *Bessie* is one of existential despair: no one in the play can extract meaning from the death of Bessie Smith. "It is obvious," concludes Debusscher, "that this is not a well-made play . . . the schematic characterization, the cinematographic cutting, the suggested setting, the symbolic lighting, bring this play closer to German expressionistic theater." He nonetheless sees the play as part of Albee's continuous development.[83]

WHO'S AFRAID OF VIRGINIA WOOLF?

Who's Afraid of Virginia Woolf?, Albee's most acclaimed play, illustrates the range of critical responses to Albee and his work. As the first full-length Albee play to be performed on Broadway, *Virginia Woolf* generated extraordinary critical interest and, despite many stinging reviews, became the cause célèbre of the 1962 dramatic season, especially after W. D. Maxwell resigned from the Pulitzer committee to prevent the prize's being awarded to Albee. "It need not be liked, but it must be seen," wrote Walter Kerr.[84] "It may not be everyone's bowl of 'Wheaties,' " wrote Stanley Richards, "but I challenge anyone to dismiss it."[85] Richard Gilman sardonically commented, "He [Albee] makes Lillian Hellman seem like the recording secretary of a garden club."[86] It was inevitable that such strong reactions to a major production would be followed by an avalanche of criticism.

Because of the earlier plays, a number of critics attempted to look beneath the ostensibly realistic framework of the play to find Absurdism in it. Elizabeth Phillips, for example, uses Esslin's definitions to argue that it properly belongs in the Theater of the Absurd, along with *Zoo Story*, *Bessie Smith*, *Sandbox*, and *American Dream*, and that Albee has more kinship with European playwrights than with American.[87] In an important article (in this volume), Wendell V. Harris counters much of the early critical theory by seeing *Virginia Woolf*, "not only in its presuppositions and implicit philosophy the most cheering and morally hopeful of Albee's plays, but [one] which contains much more assurance of the possibility of meaningful choice than has generally been offered by recent drama."[88] Elemér Hankiss reaches similar conclusions in his animated article in *New Hungarian Quarterly*. A few years ago, he writes, we would have dismissed Albee as a nihilist or pessimist, but *Virginia Woolf* has caused "lively and open discussions . . . about ourselves and our aesthetic principles." Though it is a "devil-spawned" play for Hankiss, it causes mixed feelings, for it "actually has an effect—and a positive one, too." He asserts that the play is more intricate than those of O'Neill, Beckett, and Ionesco, particularly in its network of tensions, and that it rises above mere naturalism by "protesting against the senselessness and impunity of life." Hankiss concludes that *Virginia Woolf* achieves not only the avant-garde protest against the existing order, but "has transformed the oppressive whirl of events into a fascinating human vision." The play, "though gloomy is yet full of hidden and radiating lights."[89]

Numerous commentators, both pro- and anti-Albee, have investigated the theme of illusion and reality, obviously an important clue in determining Albee's Absurdist or non-Absurdist intentions. A. Choudhuri, who devotes a chapter to *Virginia Woolf* in *The Face of Illusion in American Drama*, begins by linking Albee's attacks on American civilization to a larger criticism of sterility in modern life. The characters in Albee's plays are filled with vague fears and deep insecurities that derive from a culture which increasingly forces people to live in, through, and for illusion. *Virginia Woolf*, observes Choudhuri, substantiates the significance and impact of illusion on American culture much more powerfully than any of his other plays, but it never satisfyingly resolves the question of whether it is possible to live without illusions. George and Martha are closer at the end of the play, but it is unclear whether they will find facing the stark world together either positive or tolerable.[90]

Daniel McDonald takes a less traveled path in arguing that one can become too involved in the symbolism spied in the play. *Virginia Woolf*, he asserts, "is not an allegory about Godot, Good Deeds, or The American

Dream; it is a story of real people and their illusions." Despite the problematic nature of the word "real," McDonald reminds us that it is too easy to get caught up in the game of fabricating a symbology that is, in the ultimate impact of the play, less important than the emotions and actions of the characters in conflict. He sees the play as a contrast between the "idealistic promise of youth and its subsequent failure." McDonald admits that allegorical symbolism reinforces the theme, but avers that pursuing it exclusively causes one to miss the point of this human portrait.[91] It is, however, the difficulty of distinguishing truth from illusion that Albee is emphasizing, argues Ruth Meyer, who retorts that McDonald overlooks the deliberate ambiguities of the play's language. Albee is engaged in a "comedy of concealment," she argues; the clichés spoken by the characters simultaneously reveal personality, yet protect them from exposing their real identities. No clear line exists between truth and illusion in the play; therefore, though an illusion is exorcised, "there is no truth revealed in its place."[92]

Thomas P. Adler disagrees, and by closely examining the roles of Nick and Honey attempts to resolve the question of whether Albee was defending the necessity of illusion or the necessity of stripping it away. Adler concludes that the ending is basically optimistic, and that once the illusion is exorcised, the characters are free to move to new levels of creativity and fecundity.[93] Bigsby is not as sure about the positiveness of the ending, but sees it as generally optimistic. Driven "from humiliation to humility," the characters at the end have a possibility of hope because of their direct confrontation with reality. Bigsby likens this process to Goethe's *Faust*, as well as to Arthur Miller's *After the Fall*, and calls *Virginia Woolf* a "modern secular morality play," though it lacks the precise parallels that make *Zoo Story* a near allegory.[94]

Max Halperen addresses the general problem of "What Happens in *Who's Afraid . . .?*" by asserting that the play is brilliant, "a dramatic experience that cannot be chop-logiced out of existence," yet it is also obscure in scope, meaning, and even action.[95] Diana Trilling, on the other hand, finds the message of the play utterly clear: it "couldn't be more terrible: life is nothing, and we must face our emptiness without fear." A riddle exists, however, in the audience's positive reception of it. Unlike *Long Day's Journey into Night*, it does not truly "shake" the theatergoer, nor inspire true pity and terror; indeed, for many people it seems to induce a reassurance. Trilling idiosyncratically attributes this to a delight that an audience has in seeing professors, a class perceived "to have some moral as well as intellectual advantage over the rest of the population," speaking filthy and behaving in a manner that is anything but ideal.[96] John Kenneth Galbraith (in this volume) comments on this atmosphere of academic failure, but defines failure as a universal theme, and not merely something by which a nonacademic audience is reassured.[97] Madeleine Armstrong attacks the "problem" of the play's popularity by relating it to Albee's earlier, more avant-garde *American Dream*. She concludes that Albee makes his characters familiar to the audience, raises social issues, and suggests improvements.[98] She thus sees a more positive intention in the work than does Trilling. Frederick Lumley, however, finds nothing significant other than "the wholesale destructive or at any rate disruptive insight into the hypocritical way of life and the sterility of the society it engenders."[99]

Albee's role as social critic has elicited a large measure of the criticism of *Virginia Woolf*. Rutenberg characteristically sees Albee turning his attention from the oppressed elements in our society to the corrupt, hypocritical, sterile class "whose job it is to shape and guide the tastes and morals of this country's next generation.[100] Lee Baxandall also focuses on the social ramifications, seeing the early plays as revealing the moral degeneration of American society. Although *Virginia Woolf* offers "the ghoulish spectacle of our decline and collapse," Albee presents no real diagnosis of society's collapse and has only limited solutions.[101] Sidney Finkelstein is more specific in relating *Virginia Woolf* to social evils. In his *Existentialism and Alienation in American Literature* (1965), he links the domestic disturbances in the play to the political situation of the cold war. George and Martha attack each other because they have lost their integrity under pressure — "sold out" — and they know it. Though the play does not make it explicit, "This is the intellectual 'deep freeze' of the 'cold war,' which has congealed the spirit of free inquiry and debate of ideas, and brought many of the institutions of higher learning in the country into a new ice age."[102]

Dan Ducker views the play in terms of communication and the attempts by the four characters to express themselves. Because *Virginia Woolf* echoes existentialist philosophy, many people have tried to force it into Absurd theater; however, Ducker finds patterns of comedy shaping *Virginia Woolf* — a couple struggles "to achieve that blissful kingdom of middle life, namely marriage."[103] Other critics have also associated *Virginia Woolf* with the comic, among them David Pryce-Jones, who called it a "modern drawing-room comedy, which is to say a comedy in the death cell"; using a popular phrase of the age, Henry Hewes branded it "a neo-naturalistic horror comedy."[104] In one of the finest essays on Albee and humor, Sharon Spencer (in this volume) associates him with the "Sick" comics of the 1960s, thus integrating the satire, social protest, and black humor of his work.[105]

The existentialism perceived by Finkelstein and Ducker is elaborated in Eugene H. Falk's comparison of the play and Sartre's *No Exit*. Falk finds "common roots which link these materially different and seemingly unrelated works." Both "show how man depends on the willing acceptance by others of the illusions he harbors about himself." Both show characters unable to transcend their situations, to take hold of the freedom they need to create an essence not forced upon them by circumstance and preexisting condition. Freedom comes only with the anguish of choice, which Sartre's and Albee's characters are not willing to face.[106] Even the "killing" of the child is not sufficient, Falk seems to imply, to enable George and Martha to escape the hell they have created. Assisted by Albee's own acknowledged familiarity with Spanish existentialist Miguel de Unamuno's novels, Duane R. Carr compares the story "Saint Emmanuel the Good, Martyr" with *Virginia Woolf* to identify thematic resemblances. He sees both works examining the necessity of illusions, with the play recognizing that George and Martha's illusions were false and that they can now go on building other illusions that are less false. "Although Albee [unlike Unamuno] does not conclude that an ultimate victory is in store for George and Martha, they do achieve . . . a 'hint of communion' which should allow them to face the truth of existence together."[107]

Sartre and Unamuno are at the top of a long list of authors whose works, themes, or techniques have been linked to *Virginia Woolf*. Such comparisons call to mind Jorge Luis Borges's remark that an artist creates a tradition when he or she brings a new work into existence. These "influences," then, may be perceived as predecessors that Albee deliberately tapped for some artistic effect, predecessors who may have influenced Albee subconsciously, or of whom Albee gives no acknowledgement, despite provable resemblances. No critic (not even Albee himself) could distinguish between the latter categories, especially since Albee is so obviously well read, so that assessing the merits of many of the arguments for influence depends mostly on assessing the quality and strength of the resemblances. A sensible approach is to grant a wide range of influences, direct and indirect, which have been integrated, with greater or lesser success, into *Virginia Woolf*. This is the critical stance of Bigsby, as well as of Allan Lewis, who mentions *Medea*, the Christ story, *Hedda Gabler*, Mother Earth, and the comic vein of Beckett, Ionesco, and Giraudoux, though he does not explicate the connections completely.[108]

Emil Roy identifies a variety of influences (in this volume) and asserts that *Virginia Woolf* is "another of the great culminating compositions which integrate a tradition and, to an extent, exhaust its vitality." Albee, he maintains, fuses naturalism, existentialism, and the Theater of the Absurd in a uniquely original way and predicts a period of frustrating experimentation or of "a slow hardening into self-imitation ending in an embrace of the values he so bitterly castigates."[109] Indeed, after *Virginia Woolf*, many critics have seen Albee following exactly this course. In 1963 Catherine Hughes warned that, despite Albee's mastery of the technical aspects of theater, he had yet to write a consistently successful play: "From *Zoo Story* to *Virginia Woolf*, the flashes of brilliance are accompanied by moments of improbable mediocrity, descents to a kind of inverted self-romanticism and pseudo-significance."[110] *Tiny Alice*, in particular, would later raise accusations similar to Hughes's and Roy's, though more aggressively.

Many critics see in *Virginia Woolf* vestiges of nineteenth-century realism and naturalism. Randolph Goodman, a playwright himself, lists "astonishingly numerous" similarities between *Virginia Woolf* and *Hedda Gabler*, though he finds Ibsen's play a "subtler exploration of character, deeper psychological insights, muted ironies, and the tantalizing ambiguities of human drives and desires." Goodman, however, believes *Virginia Woolf* has a "Strindbergian spirit . . . transmitted through the medium of Ibsen" and muses whether Strindberg's, Ibsen's, or O'Neill's portrait "hangs above Mr. Albee's desk."[111] Terry Otten points out similarities to Ibsen's *Little Eyolf*. Each play is "a realistic presentation of psychological frustration and a 'religious' play in which ritual provides a metaphysical perspective." The central symbol in both plays is the child, "who is [in *Virginia Woolf*] both the means by which George and Martha compensate for their meaningless lives and, paradoxically, the means of their salvation — however limited that salvation may be."[112] Many critics also compare *Virginia Woolf* and Strindberg's works, particularly *The Dance of Death*; Manfred Treib's 186-page monograph is devoted to such a study.[113] Martin Gottfried used such resemblances to attack Albee, finding the two plays so similar "as to raise questions of plagiarism."[114] Brustein makes a similar accusation, intoning again his belief that Albee borrows so extensively because he has nothing original to say.[115]

Naturally, Albee's title has invited comparison with works by Virginia Woolf herself. Gretl Kraus Fischer holds that "consciously or subconsciously, Albee was inspired by Virginia Woolf's writings, especially by one of her short stories, 'Lappin and Lappinova,' " about a young couple pretending to be rabbits. The wife alone is secure in the illusion, and the husband, annoyed with it, announces that "Lappinova" (the wife's rabbit name) has been trapped and killed, thus destroying the couple's relationship. Viewing the killing of the imaginary son in *Virginia Woolf* in a similar light, Fischer admits that the play has a much more complex ending, but attributes it to Albee's attempt to make a more universal statement about human experience.[116]

Other interesting influences have been proposed. Douglas Cole calls attention to echoes in the marital battle in *Virginia Woolf* to Richard Steele's *Tatler*, No. 85, in which a game entitled Snap-dragon is compared to the contentions between many a man and wife.[117] Additional influences include King Vidor's film *Beyond the Forest*,[118] Bertolt Brecht,[119] *The Taming of the Shrew* (along with the legend of St. George, Oedipus, and Virginia Woolf's writings),[120] G. B. Shaw's *Heartbreak House*,[121] Harold Pinter's *The Lover*,[122] and Noel Coward's *Hay Fever*.[123]

Nor have larger archetypal concerns been neglected. Paul Witherington develops a meticulous case to argue that Albee's canon is a modern expression of the Gothic. His plays react against the perceived flaws in contemporary society through satire and contain the three Gothic elements of reduction, inversion, and recognition.[124] James P. Quinn, on the other hand, perceives elements of the romantic quest in the structure of *Virginia Woolf*: "the *agon* or conflict, the *pathos* or death struggle, and the *anagnorisis* or discovery, the recognition of the hero." *Virginia Woolf*, however, parodies the romantic myth, as, for example, in the conclusion: "The typical close of the romantic quest is the wedding of hero and heroine suggesting the restoration of fertility and order for the new society. In Albee's play, we have a symbolic death and a parody of the Requiem mass, suggesting the sterility of a barren future."[125] Rictor Norton believes the play "occurs within the framework of the concepts of *Dies Irae*, Easter, and The Birthday . . . It is a ritual of purgation and purification, a Dionysian revel . . . a 'tragedy' in the original sense of the term — a 'goat song.' " Accordingly, he explicates allusions to the nursery rhyme parodied in the title, and to Virgina Woolf, hypothesizing that the conclusion of the play is indeed a rebirth, and its theme is positive. "Albee's play demonstrates the cathartic principle that destruction and violence are not ends in themselves, but purge both the actors and spectators, and prepare the way for rebirth."[126]

The popularity of Eric Berne's *Games People Play* (1964) led to several attempts to fit the "Fun and Games" of *Virginia Woolf* into Berne's psychological theory. Joy Flasch finds numerous examples that fit Berne's categories, such as "Blemish," "Sweetheart," "Man-Talk," and many others. She does not believe, though, that George and Martha's attempt to face reality at the end of the play will necessarily lead to a better relationship; even though Berne would argue that the "good life" could be well worth giving up the complex of games in which George and Martha engage.[127] Applying Berne's ideas to an interpretation of the play, Louis Paul finds the same ambiguities voiced by Joy Flasch, though he emphasizes the "emptiness, anxiety, and cold despair" in the ending.[128] Morsberger analyzes the use of the "movie game" at the beginning of the play and compares its use in Mart Crowley's film *The Boys in the Band*.[129] Perhaps motivated by the often repeated (though often denied by Albee) assertion that *Virginia Woolf* was actually written for two male couples, Donald M. Kaplan discussed homosexuality in relation to George and Martha in a psychoanalytic view of American theater.[130]

Other articles on *Virginia Woolf* are worth study. L. Howard Quackenbush documents the play's important influence on such Latin American dramatists as René Marqués, José de Jesús Martínez, Virgilio Pinera, and Maruxa Vilalta. According to Quackenbush, the influence is primarily that of one Absurdist upon others.[131] June Schlueter identifies George and Martha as metafictional characters.[132] Finally, one of the most interesting articles on *Virginia Woolf* is Leonard J. Leff's description of how screenwriter Ernest Lehman, director Mike Nichols, and producer Jack Warner turned the play into the most lucrative film of 1966. Leff examines Lehman's drafts and correspondence underscoring Nichols's intention to cling as closely as possible to the original intentions of the playwright.

Leff's study illuminates the various aesthetic and practical decisions made by these men on such matters as the importance of the obscenity in Albee's work or the setting of specific scenes. Often this description of the give-and-take so common in the making of a film is more useful in gaining an overall understanding of the play than much of the criticism since it helps one see why the film turned out as it did.[133]

TINY ALICE

Tiny Alice invites even more explication than Virginia Woolf simply because of the abstract, mystical quality of Albee's 1964 drama. More commentary can be found on Tiny Alice than on any two of Albee's other plays combined, excluding Virginia Woolf, of course. The critical approaches to Tiny Alice are similar to those taken toward Virginia Woolf, although the hue and cry of dissatisfaction was far louder for Albee's later play. In short, Albee's detractors had a field day with Tiny Alice. Many of the first reviewers were concerned they could not adequately describe what took place.[134] Wrote John McClain: "He [Albee] told somebody in an interview that he hoped critics wouldn't reveal the surprises in the plot and he is on safe ground with me. I couldn't possibly tell you what goes on for most of the almost three-hour evening."[135] Bigsby appropriately quotes Albee's reply to a confused John Gielgud (who was about to play Julian and who had refused to deliver a soliloquy in Act III), "I know you want to know what the play is about, John, but I don't know yet, so I can't say."[136] In contrast, Albee further remarked that the play was "a perfectly straightforward story, dealt with in terms of reality and illusion, symbol and actuality. It is the very simplicity of the play that had confused so many."[137] If critics were uneasy with the earlier plays, they were downright baffled and belligerent with this one. Many who had hailed Virginia Woolf as a masterpiece condemned Tiny Alice as a piece of theatrical knavery.

Philip Roth vehemently attacked Albee for wanting to "seem deep" by emphasizing metaphysics, while he actually wrote a play with a simple-minded homosexual theme. "Why Tiny Alice is so unconvincing, so remote, so obviously a sham—so much the kind of play that makes you want to rise from your seat and shout 'Baloney'—is that its surface is an attempt to disguise the subject on one hand, and to falsify its significance on the other." According to Roth, the subject of Tiny Alice is merely the gay male's terror of being seduced and destroyed by a woman: "It has about as much to do with Christ's Passion as a little girl's dreaming about being a princess locked in a tower has to do with the fate of Mary Stuart."[138]

The suspicion of homosexual content in Albee's plays has produced much critical squeamishness, and it surfaced blatantly with Tiny Alice. One recalls Martin Gottfried's statement, "If right-wing critics and audiences had not missed the homosexuality in *Who's Afraid of Virginia Woolf?* they probably would have condemned it out-of-hand for violation of traditional morality," as well as the persistent rumor that George and Martha were actually intended to be a homosexual couple, something Albee has vehemently denied, but which Gottfried has made central to his criticism. When Gottfried turns to *Tiny Alice*, he calls it Albee's "most important work to date," but apparently does not intend it in a positive sense: "The play is ridiculous, a hodgepodge of philosophical and metaphysical pretensions. It is endlessly talky and lined with homosexuality." He agrees with Roth that the play is really about "the maternal seduction of virginal Christlike homosexuals." Gottfried then argues, however, that though it had neither the derivative surrealism of his early plays, "nor the neo-Strindberg naturalism of *Virginia Woolf*, it struck an honest note for Albee."[139]

Interestingly enough, when *Tiny Alice* was revived five years after its debut by William Ball's American Conservatory Theater it was much better received, though Albee himself accused the performance "of being fagged up, rewritten, distorted."[140] Leonard Probst of NBC seized upon the contemporaneity of the production: "Now it's breezy, even campy at times . . . the lines in the text are not treated as scripture . . . There's more romp and less pomp . . . She [*Tiny Alice*] hasn't grown in stature. But she's more fun to look at in this San Francisco version."[141] A soliloquy that John Gielgud had refused to deliver in the first production was reinstated, but, alas, did nothing to clarify the play according to most commentators. "Camp" was "in" by 1969 and whatever message the play might have was of less consequence than the flamboyance of the production. Even Gottfried had a more favorable view of the revival. In his opinion, the original production failed to exploit the theatrical opportunity as did the ACT production, which "made an honest man of the playwright."[142]

Few critics believe that *Tiny Alice* is an unqualified success. Richard Alan Davison argues it is reasonably successful, mostly for its theatricality, and William F. Lucey writes it is "not an immediate success as entertainment," but "is a notable contribution to the American stage."[143] John Stark (in this volume) almost alone asserts that the obscurity of the play is one of its deliberate virtues. Since "readers have come to accept the creation of obscurity as a literary technique," one should not object to it in a play. He develops his opinions from Susan Sontag's concept of "Camp" art. *Tiny Alice* is art about art, or metadrama, and should be considered an experiment.[144]

Often critics saw the philosophical and metaphysical aspects of the play as "ambition" or "pretension." Those who consider the play "pretentious" fault it for using mumbo-jumbo to conceal superficiality. Brustein calls *Tiny Alice* "a huge joke on the American culture industry."[145] Catherine Hughes asserts that "Although Albee has claimed that the critics are to blame for imposing on *Tiny Alice* things he never intended, he is mistaken. It is a bad, and a pretentious play."[146] Robert Skloot curiously called *Tiny Alice* an important play, then "not a very good play" (because of its inconsistency): ". . . it might well have been written by a hip Plato smoking pot."[147] Frederick Lumley thought ". . . the themes and the ideas are so abstruse, the symbols so vague and elusive, that we feel we have here more the notebooks for a play Albee has in mind to write one day . . .," but Lumley did concede that it is Albee's most ambitious play.[148]

When critics call *Tiny Alice* "ambitious," they soon announce that Albee has merely failed to make his meaning clear, despite his protestation (and director Schneider's) that it is perfectly clear. Bigsby, for example, quotes Ignazio Silone's opinion that words have become divorced from reality, and hears Albee saying that illusion and reality have become confused. Language, therefore, is inadequate to communicate on the level on which Albee would like it to. "[I]n many ways Albee has lost command of the dramatic medium itself."[149] Henry Hewes asks whether Albee "would have been pleased if someone had called *Tiny Alice* 'a play that unfolds with great skill, whatever the hell it is choosing to say.' "[150] Bernard F. Dukore argues that the play cannot be understood except as symbolic, yet even then its themes are unclear, its meanings inconsistent and clouded by homosexual slang.[151]

Those who judge that Albee's theme is difficult, but accessible, often strive to ferret out the playwright's intention. James E. White countered Dukore, Brustein, and others in claiming that *Tiny Alice* "probes deeply into the paradox and irony of man's institutions," and, that through it, though Albee deliberately withholds his judgment of Julian's search, expresses a metaphor for seeking the ideal.[152] Mary Elizabeth Campbell claims *Tiny Alice* is primarily allegorical, with a structure similar to that of the medieval and Tudor moralities. Julian succumbs to false gods, accepting "the values of materialism as replacement for his hard-achieved and daily nurtured spiritual values." At the end he repudiates these false values, though he is martyred. The obscurity derives, says Campbell, from the multiple facets of the characters. Their imagery, language, and apparent naturalistic qualities are so intriguing that they eclipse the meaning.[153] In another article, Campbell analyzes three characters (Lawyer, Miss Alice, and the Butler) as allegorical figures. She compares the entire play to "The Struggle of the Vices and Virtues," and Act III to *Everyman*. The Lawyer is likened to Dante's Satan; Miss Alice is the Flesh, and the Butler offers the material comforts of the World. Campbell repeats her assertion that materialism is the point of the play, brooding over it, "like old Covetousness on his scaffold-throne in *The Castle of Perseverance*."[154]

Stanley Romaine Hopper also sees *Tiny Alice* as a mystery / morality play, but concludes it ultimately fails because of the disjunction of its medieval form with its modern themes.[155] Dorothy Tolpegin argues the characters represent abstract qualities (the Butler, for example, is "technology") but each has a potential for a second, more idealized, quality ("service to mankind" for the Butler), and the play revolves around the tension between these qualities.[156] Paolucci also defines *Tiny Alice* in allegorical terms, and views it as a natural evolution from elements in earlier plays going all the way back to *Zoo Story*. Albee, she contends, has perfected the technique of reducing the confusion of reality to symbolic essentials. She does not, however, find the play an allegory. The symbolism is not static; "and although the temptation to find exact correspondences is irresistible, the illusion of realism is equally demanding." The play's "chief impact lies in the surrealistic telescoping of real and imagined, past and present, apparent and actual, true and false." Like *Virginia Woolf*, *Tiny Alice* portrays the stripping of illusory faith.[157]

The play has also been seen as a commentary on the loss of faith in a scientific age. For Alice Mandanis, J·lian represents the agnosticism of our scientific age and is sacrificed to a worn out "remnant of the anthropomorphic image of the Divine presence." "It is possible," she concludes, "that Albee's vision is too dishonestly disguised and falsified by the baroque surface of neo-Platonism, homosexuality, masturbation, and prurience," but that *Tiny Alice* "compels consideration" as a provocative play.[158] The mystery of Miss Alice herself is the focus of William Willeford's carefully argued essay, particularly in his response to the mouse imagery and its relation to concepts of God. Alice is simultaneously mouse, woman, and God: Albee "does not make specific allusions to myth and legend but tries to suggest the blurred outlines and shadows of such forms."[159] A sensible linking of *Tiny Alice* to the Adamic fall is provided by N. S. Pradhan, who notes thematic correspondences in other American literature, such as the loss of innocence and the New World as garden.[160]

Interpreting *Tiny Alice* as a dream-play or fantasy is a frequent approach, because, as Thomas B. Markus comments, confusion results from trying to make sense of the play on a strictly literal level. The ambiguities are essential to the play's essence. Markus calls the play a tragedy, because it evokes pity and terror,[161] and one indeed might compare the ritualistic, unreal qualities to similar qualities in classical tragedy, as did Paolucci. Rutenberg hails *Tiny Alice* "a metaphysical dream play," one which can be compared to Dürrenmatt's *The Visit*, a fact which he believes led critics to misunderstand and misinterpret *Tiny Alice* from a realistic point of view.[162] Stenz sees Albee "demonstrating how faith, when it is confused with a passion for the absolute, can become a substitute for full participation in life."[163]

A provocative psychological reading is Leighton M. Ballew's, which holds that the entire play takes place in Julian's mind and is thus intended to reveal the existential problem of absurdity in human existence.[164] V. De Ruyter also identifies the play as Julian's dream vision, with the Lawyer as God, Miss Alice as the Virgin Mary, the Butler as the Holy Ghost, the Cardinal as the Catholic church, and Julian as Christ.[165] Mary Castiglie

Anderson follows Julian on an "odyssey *through* the looking glass on a quest for self-discovery," and interprets the play as a revelation of spirituality based on a subconscious carnality. If this were the only theme, the play would simply be a statement against religion, but Anderson believes Albee uses the pattern of allegorical romance, along lines suggested by Northrop Frye, with Miss Alice representing an archetypal Anima.[166] *Tiny Alice*, though, ultimately resists being treated as an allegory, writes Leonard Casper, because its message is "the persistence of mystery." He asks us to suppose that "*Tiny Alice* is a tribute to finite man's terrifying instinct for infinity" and then postulates various explanations, which he finds adequate and inadequate in various ways. "*Tiny Alice*," he concludes, "is a dramatization of all that must remain tantalizingly beyond the mind's reach."[167]

As with many Albee works, *Tiny Alice* lends itself to psychobiographical interpretations. Jules Glenn explores the relevance of Albee's life as an adopted child to the action of *The American Dream*, in which adoption is openly portrayed, and to *Tiny Alice*, in which it is disguised. Julian is in a position similar to that of the adopted child and is plagued with similar problems. Adopted children "project various superimposed representations of their several families onto those about them. The confusion many viewers felt about the play undoubtedly is the result of the intense reality with which symbols are treated."[168] Psychoanalyst Abraham N. Franzblau advises that *Tiny Alice* ought to be judged from the logic of the unconscious, and notes that the play examines problems that have always troubled humanity. When Julian dies, "The scene echoes Freud's queries about whether all religious dogma does not stem from man's unwillingness to accept mortality, to recognize the rapacious cruelty of nature, or to sacrifice some of his libidinous gratifications for the help he needs from his fellow men." Albee has no answers; however, he still is fascinating: ". . . using the mysterious escalators of the unconscious, [he] reaches the citadels of our private certainties and shoots them full of question marks."[169]

A DELICATE BALANCE

A Delicate Balance won Albee his first Pulitzer Prize, though the play did not receive widespread plaudits from reviewers. The Broadway portrayals of Tobias by Hume Cronyn, Agnes by Jessica Tandy, and Claire by Rosemary Murphy were frequently praised while, ironically enough, the lack of action and emphasis on dialogue disturbed many commentators. John Simon, for example, found that the characters "speechify" and the situations present "rank improbability," and concluded that *A Delicate Balance* is a "posturing play."[170] Wilfrid Sheed brutally proclaimed that the play is driven apart "by lead-weights of preachment and unearned poetry."[171] Accusing Albee of borrowing from T. S. Eliot, Brustein faulted

Albee for his inappropriate use of language: "characters discuss their relationships in a lapidary style as far from modern speech as the whistles of a dolphin."[172]

Such remarks seem to ignore the possibility that the inaction and formal language constitute a thematic purpose in themselves. On one level, Albee has achieved a delicate balance between American realism and French surrealism, and thus the play might more satisfactorily be seen as practicing the aesthetic theories of postmodernism, or metadrama, which would become more pronounced in the 1970s. The themes arise from the closed circle created by the language and reveal how people are trapped by their language. When Gerald Weales described the setting as "a mansion in the suburbs of hell,"[173] and Walter Kerr observed the play was staged "in amber void,"[174] they appropriately responded to the claustrophobic world of the play. Virginia I. Perry has wisely written that "it is precisely because the play *does* disturb one's sense of well-being that critics have judged it so harshly, not recognizing that A Delicate Balance is intended to point out the fragile nature of that illusion of security by exploring the ill-defined boundaries which separate sanity from madness."[175]

The reviewer for *Time* acknowledged Albee's gift for language if not the power of his thought: Albee is seen as "a lover of English whose sentences curl with the involuted beauty of a sea shell, but when he puts on his thinking cap, he is a poseur."[176] An unusual facility with language is required to be successful in turning language in on itself, and Albee's linguistic abilities have brought him praise throughout his career. Many readers have commented on Albee's use of language in A Delicate Balance. E. G. Bierhaus, Jr. examines the meanings implied by the characters' names, as well as the significance of the cat story and the "surprising permutations of the characters,"[177] and Ronald Hayman is critical of the literary inflexibility of the language.[178] Witherington mentions language in relation to the Gothic elements he perceives in Albee's work,[179] and Terence Brown explores the different levels upon which the language functions.[180] M. Patricia Fumerton, however, attempts a detailed analysis of the play's language, asserting that the characters are "conscious manipulators of their language: a frightened people who use language in an attempt to control or simply survive fearful realities." By the end of the play, language has become a "protective device . . . a thick layer of skin."[181]

John J. Von Szeliski also establishes the significance of the language in A Delicate Balance and reviews the critical controversy surrounding its production. Von Szeliski considers A Delicate Balance a major drama, "a brilliant and highly significant play," and finds that its style and content are the keys to the play's greatness. The reviewers' negative responses, Von Szeliski argues, were caused by such things as its apparent realism overlaying an essentially surrealistic nature. One tries to believe in the characters, for example, as individuals, yet finds them "more than real." Offering little direct action, A Delicate Balance forces the spectator to concentrate on its thematic concerns; the play's strength lies in its interplay of ideas about contemporary American existence.[182] In response to Albee naysayers, M. Gilbert Porter (in this volume) argues that the emptiness at the center of the play, which may be translated as the pointlessness in and of the characters' lives, is actually significant and basic to the play's strength. He finds a circularity in the play in which characters reverse roles and change commitments in a "Dantesque dance," ending where they began in a loveless void, facing Nothingness.[183] Ruby Cohn claims that the play lacks the "lethal dialogue that has become Albee's trademark" and is "ascetically sparing of vivid imagery and dazzling dialogue," though the reason for it seems to be "that a drama with emptiness at its center, must echo in hollowness."[184] Robert M. Post similarly uncovers the layer of fear at the center of the play.[185] Carol Sykes notes the similarity of Tobias's cat story to Jerry's dog story in Zoo Story and concludes both are really about the weakness of most human relationships.[186] Laura Julier's discussion of the women in A Delicate Balance illuminates the themes of the play by primarily focusing on Agnes and her ability to confront the existential choices that life forces on everyone.[187]

BOX-MAO-BOX

Box and Quotations from Chairman Mao Tse-Tung, Albee's insepara-ble companions, is a dense work, highly unconventional, though, in many ways, very much a product of the 1960s. Bigsby, who may have written the best analysis of the play, points out that over half of it consists of lines not actually written by Albee himself, but borrowed from the "Little Red Book" of Chairman Mao and a poem by Will Carleton.[188] In many ways the work anticipates the interest in "deconstructing" language which would become influential in American criticism in the 1970s, and thus encourages an analysis of its use of language. Anthony Hopkins points out that, despite its apparent difference from the previous plays, Box-Mao-Box actually is consistent in theme and technique with earlier Albee works.[189] Calvin Rand finds the play can only be judged from the standpoint of its total dramatic impact after more than one viewing, but even then it repeats the usual themes about the decline of the West.[190] Paolucci and Rutenberg also provide helpful commentaries of this challenging work in their books.[191] Perhaps a world of explication lies ahead for readers confronting Box.

SEASCAPE AND ALL OVER

Seascape (1975) and All Over (1971) have often been considered companion plays, because the former ends on the word "Begin," and the latter on "All over." The major Broadway production of Seascape with

Barry Nelson, Deborah Kerr, Maureen Anderman, and Frank Langella ended Albee's hiatus from the theater in the early 1970s and earned him his second Pulitzer Prize. Although negative criticism greeted Albee over the play's vitality and even its language, many reviewers praised him for these same characteristics.[192] Thomas P. Adler (in this volume) argues that the play is the "reverse mirror image" of A Delicate Balance, a truer companion piece than All Over, and hears many echoes of Thornton Wilder's positive philosophy.[193] Samuel Bernstein sees Albee employing the techniques of Absurdism in order to make the most positive statement of his career, a personal statement antithetical to those of Pinter and Beckett. Bernstein remarks, ". . . the models of realism and Absurdism appear like two hovering presences, essentially distinct, yet capable of intertwining, disengaging, and intertwining once more."[194] Linking the play with Bruno Bettelheim's definition of a fairy tale as "a work of art which teaches about inner problems through the language of symbols," Lucina P. Gabbard argues that the play's principal concern is the awareness of death that comes with middle age. She further relates the play to Jungian initiation theories. "Thus," she concludes, "through the language of symbols, Albee speaks to his major theme — acceptance of death is transcendence."[195]

As Clive Barnes has observed, if Seascape is a rose play, its earlier companion All Over is a black play.[196] The death that pervades the play, argues Robbie Odom Moses, refers not only to "those who have died," and "those who are dying," but to "those who are dead to life." Though the dying man is not portrayed on stage, he has more life in him than those waiting for him to die. Paradoxically, death becomes a metaphor for the quality of life. Moses applies this theory to other Albee plays as well, concluding that Albee finds the transcendence of death-in-life only through love.[197] Nelvin Vos also links the manifest themes of death in All Over to other Albee works. The existential problem of facing Being and Nothingness at death is what interests the playwright, and it recurs in all his plays.[198]

James Neil Harris (in this volume) identifies many similarities between the life and work of Maurice Maeterlinck and All Over. Arguing that All Over can be usefully understood as a Symbolist drama, Harris offers another convincing argument of Albee's close affinity to European theater traditions and thus encourages others to explore Albee's dramas in relation to Symbolism.[199] Paolucci finds the characters in All Over reminiscent of those in A Delicate Balance, though for her All Over is more static and less suggestive. "All Over is the dying breath of an exhausted past. There is no meaningful future ahead, only the heightened immediacy of the present moment. . . ." She calls it, however, one of the best dramatic conceits in Albee's repertory, and concludes, ". . . this monotonous, subdued skirting of psychological reality may have been exactly what the dramatist intended; the death vigil is the unmistakable sign of impotence."[200]

THE MOST RECENT WORKS

Perhaps because theatergoers have become so jaded to the kinds of theatrical shocks that contributed to Albee's controversialness in the 1960s and early 1970s, his most recent plays have not provoked the violent reactions of the earlier works. *Counting the Ways* and *Listening* opened on stage in 1977 in Hartford, Connecticut to enthusiastic reviews in the *Hartford Courant*, but their subsequent performance in New York elicited mostly negative reactions.[201] Clive Barnes pronounced the plays "meticulously directed" by Albee himself, but gave them a checkered review at best.[202] The London opening, not directed by the playwright, was attacked as a "Sixty-minute, second-rate doodle."[203] The most common reaction was that the plays were baffling. Thomas P. Adler's review (in this volume) happily accepted *Counting the Ways* on its own terms, admitting it was bound for neither commercial nor critical success but conceding that "this 'diversion' . . . can delight with its considerable charm and wit and occasional beauties of language."[204]

Philip C. Kolin offers the only full-scale critical study of *Counting the Ways*, analyzing it as a theatrical experiment modulating a vaudevillian structure. Kolin explains the significance of the number "two," explores the structural parallels between He and She, studies the use of language (including the "empty allusions"), and explicates the love tests in the plays. Kolin contrasts Albee's play with *The Glass Menagerie* to illuminate differences between Williams's "theatre of the heart" and Albee's absurd arena of love. "As a result of Albee's manipulation of the convention of the past affectionately remembered, lost affection is comic and absurd in *Counting the Ways* while it is moving and tragic in *The Glass Menagerie*." Kolin's essay may prompt further studies of Albee's response to Williams in terms of dramatic technique and symbolism.[205]

The Lady from Dubuque, staged in 1980, received very few positive reviews, though Gerald Clarke asserted it was Albee's best work since *Who's Afraid of Virginia Woolf?* Douglas Watt called it "compelling," and Clive Barnes found the play's strength in "the irony and coarseness of the writing, the verbal clarity, the ivory turn of phrase, and, most important of all, in Albee's bone-dry, distilled-ice-cold compassion for human frailty."[206] Ethan Mordden offered a more typical response in saying that *Lady* "offered two hours of pointless and pretentious wordplay."[207] Other reviewers accused Albee of not creating characters who were human enough and of repeating himself,[208] though Albee repeating himself is usually more interesting than most playwrights' new plays (as critics had observed of *A Delicate Balance*). John Simon harshly wrote, "[it is] one of the worst plays about anything, ever."[209] Few critical articles on the play have appeared. In her essay on *Lady* June Schlueter argued that the problem with the play was not Albee's repeating his themes — Beckett has done it for years — "but simply that, in dramatic terms, he has not said it effectively."[210] Matthew C. Roudané has analyzed the theme of waste in *The Lady from Dubuque* and reached a conclusion similar to Robbie Odom Moses's about *All Over*: the character who is dying (in *All Over*, dead) is more alive than the others, who are wrapped up in themselves, turned off, and unaware of the many choices they have made.[211]

The Man Who Had Three Arms opened in 1982. After receiving mixed reviews in Chicago, it was brutalized by the New York critics. Several commented that what they had seen was not a play at all. Himself, the main character, verbally assaults the audience from a podium, recounting his sudden rise to fame because he had freakishly grown a third arm out of his back. Working from galleys of the play, Matthew C. Roudané has written the first critical article on it; his study was expressly commissioned for this collection. Roudané examines the Pirandellian aspects, the theme of instant media celebrity, and the connections with Artaud's Theater of Cruelty.[212] He concludes that the play does not entirely achieve its goals. For Albee those goals are clear-cut — the play is a parable about the fate of cult leaders and demagogues.

CONCLUSION

In outlining the many approaches Albee criticism has taken, one is immediately struck by the plenitude of it: Albee means many things to many people. One is also struck by how often the variety of styles and techniques in Albee's works are turned against the playwright, as if he should abandon his restless experimentation and drop into a convenient pigeonhole carved out for him by critics. Consistent themes can be found in the plays, but they are more often raised in the form of questions than pat answers. Albee employs recurrent imagery and dramatic techniques as well. Yet, the major consistency and strength of his drama is a constant searching, changing, and evolving to find new modes of expression. Criticizing him for changing is like damning Picasso for not remaining a Cubist or attacking Joyce for not sticking with short stories. As Albee himself commented, "Why go on repeating yourself? Why do that? Do what interests you. Poor Tennessee, he was criticized . . . for writing the same play over and over again. So he wrote something different called *Camino Real* and then they criticized him for breaking away from what he did so well!"[213]

Inevitably, the artist who places a value on innovation may seem inconsistent, since some attempts will be more successful than others. He or she may also miss commercial success unless society's quest for satisfaction coincides with the artist's vision. Albee became a "star" playwright very early in his career in part since his work expressed the quintessence of the early 1960s. If society had not been ready to accept the critique of language and range of subject in the motion picture of *Virginia Woolf*, for example, how bowdlerized might the film version (which most people would see) have become? Ten years later, society had changed and Albee had moved on to different subjects, styles, dramatic forms, and far less critical and commercial success. Yet, it is too easy to equate critical and commercial success with artistic success. Albee is an experimenter, and though he might wish that each play be a "hit," he is remarkable in not being satisfied with duplicating the successes of the past or pandering to the whims of public fashion. As Bigsby observes, if Albee's radical experimentation "has on occasions proved somewhat disastrous, as with *Malcolm* and, perhaps, *Tiny Alice*, that is a small price to pay for renewed vigour in a theatre which a decade ago was fading into insignificance."[214] Albee probes the "eternal verities," as Faulkner called them, and persists in his search for art and his quest for truth. The praise his works have garnered indicates his importance to the theater in our time, just as do the vehemence of the attacks against him. But more significantly there exist his plays — consummately crafted, daring, and explosive — and they alone, in all their complexity, assure Albee's place as a major American and world dramatist.[215]

PHILIP C. KOLIN   J. MADISON DAVIS
University of Southern Mississippi   *Pennsylvania State University*

Notes

1. Robert A. Wilson, "Edward Albee: A Bibliographical Checklist," *American Book Collector* 5 (March-April 1983):37–42. Also of interest to Albee bibliographers is the *Author Price Guide* on Albee (Stock number 002, available from Author Price Guides, 7649 Old Georgetown Road, Bethesda, Maryland 20814), which offers "a facsimile of the author's signature, a brief biographical sketch; an up-to-date list of the author's first editions (American and British) with entries for limited and trade editions; numbers of copies (if available); how to identify the first edition; and estimated prices." For some illustrations of Albee's first editions see Karen Rood, "Edward Albee," in *First Printings of American Authors: Contributions toward Descriptive Checklists*, ed. Matthew J. Bruccoli et al. (Detroit: Gale, 1978), 3:1–9.

2. James E. White, "An Early Play by Edward Albee," *American Literature* 42 (1970):98–99.

3. Philip C. Kolin, "Two Early Poems by Edward Albee," *Resources for American Literary Study* 5 (Spring 1975):95–97.

4. Edward Albee, *The Plays*, 4 vols. (New York: Atheneum, 1981–82).

5. Kimball King, *Ten Modern American Playwrights: An Annotated Bibliography* (New York: Garland, 1982), 1–108.

6. Charles Green, *Edward Albee: An Annotated Bibliography, 1968–1977* (New York: AMS Press, 1980). For an assessment of Green's work, see Floyd Eugene Eddleman's review in *Modern Drama* 25 (Winter 1982):585–86.

7. Richard E. Amacher and Margaret Rule, *Edward Albee at Home and Abroad* (New York: AMS Press, 1973); Rule had previously published an unclassified bibliography: "An Edward Albee Bibliography," *Twentieth Century Literature* 14 (April 1968):35–45.

8. James L. Evans and Michael D. Reed, "Edward Albee: An Updated Checklist of Scholarship, 1977–1980," in *Edward Albee: Planned Wilderness*, ed. Patricia De La Fuente, Donald E. Fritz, Jan Seale, and Dorey Schmidt (Edinburg, Tex.: Pan American University Press, 1980), 121–29.

9. Philip C. Kolin, "A Classified Edward Albee Checklist," *Serif* 6 (September 1969):16–32; "A Supplementary Edward Albee Checklist," *Serif* 10 (Spring 1973):28–39.

10. Charles Carpenter, "American Drama: A Bibliographic Essay," *American Studies International* 21 (October 1983):37–39. For a collection of Albee interviews see the forthcoming *Conversations with Edward Albee*, ed. Philip C. Kolin (Jackson, Miss.: University Press of Mississippi).

11. Carpenter, "American Drama," 37.

12. C. W. E. Bigsby, *Albee* (Edinburgh: Oliver and Boyd, 1969).

13. C. W. E. Bigsby, *Edward Albee: A Collection of Critical Essays*, Twentieth Century Views series (Englewood Cliffs, N.J.: Prentice-Hall, 1975).

14. C. W. E. Bigsby, *Confrontation and Commitment: A Study of Contemporary American Drama* (Columbia, Mo.: University of Missouri Press, 1968).

15. C. W. E. Bigsby, "Edward Albee," in *A Critical Introduction to Twentieth-Century American Drama: Tennessee Williams, Arthur Miller, Edward Albee* (New York: Cambridge University Press, 1984), 2:249–329.

16. Bigsby, *Albee*, 111.

17. Ibid., 115.

18. Gilbert Debusscher, *Edward Albee: Tradition and Renewal* (Brussels: Center for American Studies, 1969).

19. Ibid., 30.

20. Anne Paolucci, *From Tension to Tonic: The Plays of Edward Albee* (Carbondale: Southern Illinois University Press, 1972).

21. Ibid., xiii.

22. Ruby Cohn, *Edward Albee*, University of Minnesota Pamphlets on American Writers 77 (Minneapolis: University of Minnesota Press, 1969).

23. Ruby Cohn, *Dialogue in American Drama* (Bloomington: Indiana University Press, 1971), 130–69.

24. Cohn, *Albee*, 6.

25. Cohn, *Dialogue in American Drama*, 168–69.

26. Michael Rutenberg, *Edward Albee: Playwright in Protest* (New York: DBS Publications, 1969).

27. Tom Prideaux, "Coward, Flop, Pig: Marital Sweet Talk on Broadway," *Life*, 14 December 1962, 110.

28. William Glover, "Albee Not on a Soapbox, But. . . ," *New Orleans Times-Picayune*, 30 January 1977, sec. 2, 11. See also Roudané interview in this volume.

29. Rutenberg, *Edward Albee*, 8. An interesting perspective on Albee's social intentions is provided by Soviet critic Maria Koreneva who sees Albee in the tradition of O'Neill, as an exponent of "organic" drama, which develops according to the artist's inner need: "Edward Albee and the Development of Modern Drama," *Hungarian English Studies* 14 (1981):47–55.

30. L. E. Chabrowe suggested this in "The Pains of Being Demystified," *Kenyon*

Review 25 (Winter 1963):145–46. Also see Lee Baxandall, "Theatre and Affliction," *Encore* 10 (May-June 1963):12.

31. Foster Hirsch, *Who's Afraid of Edward Albee?*, Modern Authors Monograph Series 4 (Berkeley, Calif.: Creative Arts Book Co., 1978).

32. Hirsch, *Who's Afraid?*, 3.

33. Anita Maria Stenz, *Edward Albee: Poet of Loss*, Studies in American Literature, vol. 32 (The Hague: Mouton, 1978).

34. Ibid., 3.

35. Richard E. Amacher, *Edward Albee* (New York: Twayne, 1969, rev. 1982).

36. Liliane Kerjan, *Le théâtre d'Edward Albee* (Paris: Seghers, 1978).

37. Nelvin Vos, *Eugene Ionesco and Edward Albee: A Critical Essay*, Contemporary Writers in Christian Perspective (Grand Rapids, Mich.: W. B. Eerdmans, 1968).

38. Martin Esslin, *The Theatre of the Absurd*, rev. ed. (Garden City, N.Y.: Anchor, 1969), 267. For a very recent assessment of Albee and Absurdism, see Anne Paolucci's "Albee and the Restructuring of the Modern Stage," *Studies in American Drama, 1945–Present* 1 (1986): 3–23.

39. Ibid., 268–69.

40. "Talk With the Author," *Newsweek*, 29 October 1962, 52–53.

41. Robert Brustein, "The New American Playwrights," in *Modern Occasions*, ed. Philip Rahv (New York: Farrar, Straus & Giroux, 1966), 124–27. See also *Seasons of Discontent* (New York: Simon and Schuster, 1965), 28–29, 46–49, 145–48, 155–58, and 304–11.

42. Faubion Bowers, "Theatre of the Absurd: It's Only a Fad," *Theatre Arts* 46 (November 1962):20, 22, 24, 66–69; "Theatre of the Absurd: It's Here to Stay," *Theatre Arts* 46 (November 1962):21, 23, 24, 64–65.

43. W. L. Turner, "Absurdist Go Home!" *Players Magazine* 40 (1964):139–40.

44. Robert H. Deutsch, "Writers Maturing in the Theatre of the Absurd," *Discourse* 7 (Spring 1964):181–87.

45. Robert Mayberry, "A Theater of Discord: Some Plays of Beckett, Albee, and Pinter," *Kansas Quarterly* 12 (1980):7–16.

46. Brian Way, "Albee and the Absurd: *The American Dream* and *The Zoo Story*," in *American Theatre*, ed. John Russell Brown and Bernard Harris, Stratford-Upon-Avon Studies 10 (New York: St. Martin's Press, 1967), 189–207; rpt. *Edward Albee*, C. W. E. Bigsby, ed. Twentieth Century Views (Englewood Cliffs, N.J.: Prentice-Hall, 1975),26–44.

47. Donald Malcolm, Review of *The Zoo Story*, *New Yorker*, 23 January 1960, 76.

48. William Force, "The 'What' Story? or Who's Who at the Zoo?" *Studies in the Humanities* 1 (Winter 1969):47–53.

49. Richard Kostelanetz, "The Art of Total No," *Contact* 4 (October / November 1963):62–70.

50. Fred D. White, "Albee's Hunger Artist: *The Zoo Story* as a Parable of The Writer Vs. Society," *Arizona Quarterly* 39 (Spring 1983):15–22.

51. Rutenberg, *Edward Albee: Playwright in Protest*, 36–37.

52. Robert S. Wallace, "*The Zoo Story*: Albee's Attack on Fiction," *Modern Drama* 16 (June 1973):49–54.

53. Peter Wolfe, "The Social Theatre of Edward Albee," *Prairie Schooner* 39 (Fall 1965):248–62.

54. Gerald Weales, "Off-Broadway: Its Contribution to American Drama," *Drama Survey* 2 (June 1962):20.

55. Brooks Atkinson, "Village Vagrants," *New York Times*, 31 January 1960, sec. 2, 1.

56. Rose Zimbardo, "Symbolism and Naturalism in Edward Albee's *The Zoo Story*," *Twentieth Century Literature* 8 (April 1962):10–17; rpt. in Bigsby, *Edward Albee*, 45–53.

57. Bigsby, *Albee*, 15–16.

58. Shanta Acharya, "*The Zoo Story*: Alienation and Love," *Literary Criticism* 12 (1978):27–36.

59. Martin Brunkworst, "Albee's Frühwerk in Kontext des absurden Theaters: Etappen der Deutungsgeschichte," *Literatur in Wissenschaft und Unterricht* 12 (1979):304–18.

60. C. N. Stavrou, "Albee in Wonderland," *Southwest Review* 60 (Winter 1975): 46–61.

61. Mary Castiglie Anderson, "Ritual and Initiation in *The Zoo Story*," in *Edward Albee: An Interview and Essays*, ed. Julian N. Wasserman, Joy C. Linsley, and Jerome A. Kramer (Houston: University of St. Thomas, 1983), 93–108.

62. Paolucci, *From Tension to Tonic*, 43.

63. Allan Lewis, "The Fun and Games of Edward Albee," *Educational Theatre Journal* 16 (March 1964):29–39; rpt. in *American Plays and Playwrights of the Contemporary Theatre* (New York: Crown, 1965), 81–98.

64. Mary M. Nilan, "Albee's *Zoo Story*: Alienated Man and the Nature of Love," *Modern Drama* 16 (June 1973):55–60.

65. Robert B. Bennett, "Tragic Vision in *The Zoo Story*," *Modern Drama* 20 (1977):55–66.

66. Debusscher, *Edward Albee: Tradition and Renewal*, 12–21.

67. Lucina P. Gabbard, "At the Zoo: From O'Neill to Albee," *Modern Drama* 19 (1976):365–74.

68. Mordecai Levine, "Albee's Liebestod," *College Language Association Journal* 10 (March 1967):252–55.

69. James Missey, "A McCullers Influence on Albee's *The Zoo Story*," *American Notes & Queries* 13 (April 1975):121–23; Elsa Rael, "Joseph Conrad, Master Absurdist," *Conradiana* 2 (Spring 1969–70):163–70; Roger Ramsey, "Jerry's Northerly Madness," *Notes on Contemporary Literature* 1 (September 1971):7–8.

70. Peter Spielberg, "The Albatross in Albee's Zoo," *College English* 27 (April 1966):562–65; Anthony Macklin, "The Flagrant Albatross," *College English* 28 (October 1966):58–59; Peter Spielberg, "Reply: The Albatross Strikes Again!" *College English* 28 (October 1966):59.

71. Harold Clurman, Review of *The American Dream*, *Nation*, 11 February 1961, 125–26.

72. Paolucci, *From Tension to Tonic*, 26–36.

73. Wendell V. Harris, "Morality, Absurdity, and Albee," *Southwest Review* 49 (Summer 1964):249–56.

74. See Jules Glenn, "The Adoption Theme in Edward Albee's *Tiny Alice* and *The American Dream*," in *Lives, Events, and Other Players: Directions in Psychobiography*, ed. Joseph T. Coltrera (New York: Jason Aronson, 1981), 255–69. See also Hedwig Bock, "Die 'Mom' als Typus und Archetypus im Werk von Edward Albee," in *Die amerikanische Literatur in der Weltliteratur: Themen und Aspekte*, ed. Claus Unlig and Volker Bischoff (Berlin: Schmidt, 1982), 437–47.

75. Henry Popkin, "Theatre Chronicle," *Sewanee Review* 61 (Spring 1961):342–43.

76. Paul Cubeta, "Commentary," in *Modern Drama for Analysis*, 3d ed. (New York: Holt, Rinehart and Winston, 1962), 598–602.

77. Cohn, *Dialogue in American Drama*, 137–40. Also see Kathleen R. Shull, "Albee's

Humanistic Enterprise: *The Sandbox* and *The American Dream*," *North Dakota Quarterly* 51 (Fall 1983):116–28, for a telling discussion of the theme and structure in these two plays.

78. Rutenberg, *Edward Albee: Playwright in Protest*, 79–94; Hirsch, *Who's Afraid of Edward Albee?*; Luke M. Grande, "Edward Albee's 'Bessie Smith': Alienation, the Color Problem," *Drama Critique* 5 (1962):66–69. For a discussion of the interrelationships of the white and black plots, see Philip C. Kolin, "Cars and Traveling in *The Death of Bessie Smith*," forthcoming in *College Language Association Journal*.

79. Paolucci, *From Tension to Tonic*, 19–20.

80. Paul Witherington, "Language of Movement in Albee's *The Death of Bessie Smith*," *Twentieth Century Literature* 13 (July 1967):84.

81. Bigsby, *Albee*, 21–27.

82. Debusscher, *Edward Albee: Tradition and Renewal*, 21–30.

83. Walter C. Daniel, "Absurdity in *The Death of Bessie Smith*," *College Language Association Journal* 8 (September 1964):78–80. For a discussion of Albee's changing sense of character accompanying and controlling his shifting dramatic techniques, see Mary Susan Yates, "Changing Perspectives: The Vanishing 'Character' in Albee's Plays," *College Language Association Journal* 28 (December 1984):210–29.

84. Walter Kerr, Review of *Who's Afraid of Virginia Woolf?*, *New York Herald Tribune*, 15 October 1962; rpt. *New York Theatre Critics' Reviews, 1962*, 252.

85. Stanley Richards, Review of *Who's Afraid of Virginia Woolf?*, *Players Magazine* 39 (December 1962):85.

86. Richard Gilman, Review of *Who's Afraid of Virginia Woolf?*, *Commonweal*, 9 November 1962, 176.

87. Elizabeth Phillips, "Albee and the Theatre of the Absurd," *Tennessee Studies in Literature* 10 (1965):73–80.

88. Harris, "Morality, Absurdity, and Albee," 249.

89. Elemér Hankiss, "Who's Afraid of Edward Albee?" *New Hungarian Quarterly* 5, no. 15 (1964):168–74.

90. A. Choudhuri, "*Who's Afraid of Virginia Woolf?*: Death of an Illusion," in *The Face of Illusion in American Drama* (Atlantic Highlands, NJ: Humanities Press, 1979): 129–43. Saying that one must face reality is obvious and elementary argues Donald Schier, who sees it as the play's sole, insignificant theme. "Who Cares Who's Afraid of Virginia Woolf?" *Carleton Miscellany* 5 (Spring 1964):121–24.

91. Daniel McDonald, "Truth and Illusion in *Who's Afraid of Virginia Woolf?*" *Renascence* 17 (Winter 1964):63–69.

92. Ruth Meyer, "Language: Truth and Illusion in *Who's Afraid of Virginia Woolf?*" *Educational Theatre Journal* 20 (March 1968):60–69.

93. Thomas P. Adler, "Albee's *Who's Afraid of Virginia Woolf?*: A Long Night's Journey Into Day," *Educational Theatre Journal* 25 (March 1973):66–70.

94. Bigsby, *Confrontation and Commitment*, 87–88.

95. Max Helperen, "What Happens in *Who's Afraid. . . ?* in *Modern American Drama*, William E. Taylor, ed. (Deland, Fla.: Everett / Edwards, 1968), 129–43.

96. Diana Trilling, "The Riddle of Albee's *Who's Afraid of Virginia Woolf?*, in *Claremont Essays* (New York: Harcourt, Brace & World, 1964); rpt. *Edward Albee*, ed. C. W. E. Bigsby, 80–88.

97. John Kenneth Galbraith, "The Mystique of Failure: A Latter-Day Reflection on *Who's Afraid of Virginia Woolf?*," *Show*, May 1964, 112.

98. Madeleine Armstrong. "Edward Albee and the American Dream," *Quadrant* 9 (March 1965):62–67.

99. Frederick Lumley, *New Trends in 20th Century Drama* (New York: Oxford University Press, 1972), 330.

100. Rutenberg, *Edward Albee: Playwright in Protest*, 95.

101. Lee Baxandall, "The Theatre of Edward Albee," *Tulane Drama Review* 9 (Summer 1965):19–40.

102. Sidney Finkelstein, *Existentialism and Alienation in American Literature* (New York: International Publishers, 1965), 234–42. See also James G. Martin, "The 'Two Cultures' Theme in Albee's *Virginia Woolf*," *Notes on Contemporary Literature* 12 (January 1982):2–5.

103. Dan Ducker, " 'Pow!' 'Snap!' 'Pouf!': The Modes of Communication in *Who's Afraid of Virginia Woolf?*" *College Language Association Journal* 26 (June 1983):465–77.

104. David Pryce-Jones, Review of *Who's Afraid of Virginia Woolf?*, *Spectator*, 14 February 1964, 214; Henry Hewes, Review of *Who's Afraid of Virginia Woolf?*, *Saturday Review*, 27 October 1962, 29.

105. Sharon Spencer, "Edward Albee—The Anger Artist," *Forum* [Houston] 4 (Winter-Spring 1967):25–30.

106. Eugene H. Falk, "*No Exit* and *Who's Afraid of Virginia Woolf?*: A Thematic Comparison," *Studies in Philology* 67 (July 1970):406–17.

107. Duane R. Carr, "St. George and the Snapdragons: The Influence of Unamuno on *Who's Afraid of Virginia Woolf?*," *Arizona Quarterly* 29 (1973):5–13.

108. Lewis, "The Fun and Games of Edward Albee," 29–39.

109. Emil Roy, "*Who's Afraid of Virginia Woolf?* and the Tradition," *Bucknell Review* 13 (March 1965):27–36.

110. Catherine Hughes, "Edward Albee: Who's Afraid of What?" *The Critic* 21 (February / March 1963):16–19.

111. Randolph Goodman, "Playwriting with a Third Eye: Fun and Games with Albee, Ibsen, and Strindberg," *Columbia University Forum* 10 (Spring 1967):18–22.

112. Terry Otten, "Ibsen and Albee's Spurious Children," *Comparative Drama* 2 (Summer 1968):83–93.

113. Manfred Treib, *August Strindberg und Edward Albee: Eine vergleichende Analyse moderner Ehedramen (Mit einem Exkurs über Friedrich Dürrenmatts Play Strindberg)*. Europaische Hochschulschriften Reihe 18. Vergleichende Literaturwissenschaft, Bd. 23 (Frankfurt-am-Main: P. D. Lang, 1980).

114. Martin Gottfried, *A Theater Divided: The Postwar American Stage* (Boston: Little, Brown, 1967), 265.

115. This is repeated in much Brustein criticism of Albee. Other critics who have mentioned or explored the influence of Strindberg are Lewis, "The Fun and Games of Edward Albee," 89; John Gassner, "Broadway in Review," *Educational Theatre Journal*, March 1963, 77–80; Rutenberg, *Edward Albee: Playwright in Protest*, 95–96; Paul Goetsch, "Edward Albee: *Who's Afraid of Virginia Woolf?*" in *Das Amerikanische Drama*, ed. Paul Goetsch (Dusseldorf: August Bagel Verlag, 1974), 295–318; Anthony Channel Hilfer, "George and Martha: Sad, Sad, Sad," in *Seven Contemporary Authors: Essays on Cozzens, Miller, West, Golding, Heller, Albee, and Powers*, ed. Thomas B. Whitbread (Austin: University of Texas Press, 1966), 119–39; and Marion A. Taylor, "Edward Albee and August Strindberg: Some Parallels Between *Who's Afraid of Virginia Woolf?* and *The Dance of Death*," *Papers on Language and Literature* 1 (Winter 1965):59–71; "A Note on Strindberg's *The Dance of Death* and Edward Albee's *Who's Afraid of Virginia Woolf?*" *Papers on Language and Literature* 2 (Spring 1966):187–88.

116. Gretl Kraus Fischer, "Edward Albee and Virginia Woolf," *Dalhousie Review* 49 (Summer 1969):196–207. The similarity to "Lappin and Lappinova" was first suggested by Martha A. Johnson, "Note on a Possible Source for *Who's Afraid of Virginia Woolf?*" *Radford Review* 21 (1967):231–33. See also Jenijoy La Belle, "Albee's *Who's Afraid of Virginia*

Woolf?" Explicator 15 (Fall 1976):8–9. Jeffrey Loomis discusses the relevance of Woolf's *Between the Acts* in "After the Acts: Destructive Illusion or Restorative Allusion in *Who's Afraid of Virginia Woolf?" Notes on Contemporary Literature* 14 (January 1983):7–8. Abigail Ann Hamblin argues that Albee and Woolf emphasize similar themes—loneliness, suffering, and the anguish of heightened perception: "Edward Albee . . . and the Fear of Virginia Woolf," *Trace* 2 (1968):198–203.

117. Douglas Cole, "Albee's *Virginia Woolf* and Steele's *Tatler," American Literature* 40 (March 1968):81–82.

118. Leonard J. Leff, "Albee's *Who's Afraid of Virginia Woolf?* and *The Boys in the Band," Costerus: Essays in English and American Language and Literature* 8 (1973):89–99.

119. Charles R. Lyons, *Bertolt Brecht: The Despair and the Polemic* (Carbondale, Ill.: Southern Illinois University Press, 1968), 5, 25; Charles R. Lyons, "Two Projections of the Isolation of the Human Soul: Brecht's *Im Dickicht der Staedte* and Albee's *The Zoo Story," Drama Survey* 4 (Summer 1965):121–38.

120. John A. Byars, "*The Taming of the Shrew* and *Who's Afraid of Virginia Woolf?" Cimarron Review* 21 (October 1972):41–48. For another fruitful discussion of Albee and Shakespeare see Hugh Richmond's chapter "Shakespeare and Modern Sexuality: Albee's *Virginia Woolf* and *Much Ado*" in his *Shakespeare's Sexual Comedy: A Mirror for Lovers* (Indianapolis: Bobbs-Merrill, 1971), 177–96. Recognizing that Albee's work contains calculated echoes of Shakespeare and others, Richmond admits Albee is no slave to convention. His comparison of *Virginia Woolf* and Shakespeare's comedy "shows that Shakespeare's conception of sexual relations can be plausibly transposed into modern terms" (196).

121. D. C. Coleman, "Fun and Games: Two Pictures of Heartbreak House," *Drama Survey* 5 (Winter 1966–67):223–36.

122. Steven H. Gale, "Breakers of Illusion: George in Edward Albee's *Who's Afraid of Virginia Woolf?* and Richard in Harold Pinter's *The Lovers," Vision* 1 (1979):70–77.

123. Terry Otten, " 'Played to the Finish': Coward and Albee," *Studies in the Humanities* 6 (1977):31–36. See also Tetsuo Kishi, "Coward to Albee," *Eigo Seinen* 114 (1968):308–9.

124. Paul Witherington, "Albee's Gothic: The Resonances of Cliché," *Comparative Drama* 4 (Fall 1970):151–65.

125. James P. Quinn, "Myth and Romance in Albee's *Who's Afraid of Virginia Woolf?" Arizona Quarterly* 30 (1974):197–204.

126. Rictor Norton, "Folklore and Myth in *Who's Afraid of Virginia Woolf?" Renascence* 23 (Spring 1971): 159–67; see also Grace Stewart Wurster, "Albee's Festival Chant: *Who's Afraid of Virginia Woolf?" Michigan Academician* 9 (Summer 1976):61–67.

127. Joy Flasch, "Games People Play in *Who's Afraid of Virginia Woolf?" Modern Drama* 10 (December 1967):280–88.

128. Louis Paul, "A Game Analysis of Albee's *Who's Afraid of Virginia Woolf?*: The Core of Grief," *Literature and Psychology* 17 (1967):47–51. A game analysis of *Zoo Story* is offered by Cynthia B. Thomiszer, "Child's Play: Games in *The Zoo Story," College Literature* (1982):54–63.

129. Robert E. Morsberger, "The Movie Game in *Who's Afraid of Virginia Woolf?* and *The Boys in the Band," Costerus* 8 (1973):89–100.

130. Donald M. Kaplan, "Homosexuality and American Theatre: A Psychoanalytic Comment," *Tulane Drama Review* 9 (1965):25–55. See also H. P. Blum, "A Psychoanalytic View of *Who's Afraid of Virginia Woolf?" Journal of the American Psychoanalytic Association* 17 (1969):888–903.

131. L. Howard Quackenbush, "The Legacy of Edward Albee's *Who's Afraid of Virginia Woolf?* in Spanish American Absurdist Theatre," *Revista/Review InterAmericana* 9 (1970):51–71.

132. June Schlueter, "Albee's Martha and George," in *Metafictional Characters in Modern Drama* (New York: Columbia University Press, 1979), 79–87.

133. Leonard Leff, "Play Into Film: Warner Brothers' *Who's Afraid of Virginia Woolf?*, *Theatre Journal* 33 (December 1981):453–66. See also Leff, "A Test of American Film Censorship: *Who's Afraid of Virginia Woolf?* (1966)," in *Hollywood As Historian*, ed. Peter C. Rollins (Lexington, Ky.: University Press of Kentucky, 1983), 211–29. For a lively, urbane account of the genesis of Albee's play on Broadway, see Alan Schneider's "Who's Afraid" (excerpted from his book *Entrances: An American Director's Journey* [New York: Viking, 1986] in *American Theatre*, 2, no. 11 (February 1986):4–9, 40–41. Schneider, who was the first one to direct *Virginia Woolf*, gives an insider's account of the problems and achievements in financing, casting, rehearsing, and performing Albee's magnum opus on Broadway in that fateful October of 1962. Leff's works and Schneider's comments are required reading for anyone interested in the production history of *Virginia Woolf*.

134. Walter Kerr, Review of *Tiny Alice*, *New York Herald Tribune*, 30 December 1964, and Richard Watts, Jr., Review of *Tiny Alice*, *New York Post*, 30 December 1964 – rpt. *New York Theatre Critics' Reviews*, *1964*, 96–98.

135. John McClain, Review of *Tiny Alice*, *New York Journal American*, 30 December 1964.

136. R. S. Stewart, "John Gielgud and Edward Albee Talk About the Theater," *Atlantic*, April 1965, 67–68.

137. Quoted in Louis Calta, "Albee Lectures Critics on Taste," *New York Times*, 23 March 1965, 33.

138. Philip Roth, "The Play That Dare Not Speak Its Name," *New York Review of Books*, 25 February 1965, 4; rpt. Bigsby, *Edward Albee*, 105–9.

139. Gottfried, *The Theater Divided*, 268–71. See Gerald Weales's discussion of the homosexual issue in "Edward Albee: Don't Make Waves," in *The Jumping-Off Place* (London: Macmillan, 1969), 41–45. See also George M. Sarotte's analysis of the homosexual content of Albee's plays from *Zoo Story* to *Malcolm*: "Edward Albee: Homosexual Playwright in Spite of Himself," in *Like a Brother, Like a Lover: Male Homosexuality in the American Novel and Theater from Herman Melville to James Baldwin*, trans. Richard Miller (Garden City, N.Y.: Doubleday/Anchor, 1978), 134–49; Tom F. Driver, "What's the Matter with Edward Albee?" *The Reporter*, 2 January 1964; rpt. *American Drama and Its Critics*, ed. Alan S. Downer (Chicago: University of Chicago Press, 1965), 240–44.

140. Martin Gottfried, Review of American Conservatory Theater's production of *Tiny Alice*, *Women's Wear Daily*, 30 September 1969; rpt. in *New York Theatre Critics' Reviews*, *1969*, 256.

141. Leonard Probst, Review of A.C.T.'s production of *Tiny Alice*, NBC-TV, 29 September 1969; rpt. in *New York Theatre Critics' Reviews*, 257.

142. Gottfried, *The Theater Divided*, 270.

143. Richard Alan Davison, "Edward Albee's *Tiny Alice*: A Note of Re-examination," *Modern Drama* 9 (1968):54–60; William F. Lucey, "Albee's *Tiny Alice*: Truth and Appearance," *Renascence* 21 (Winter 1969):76–80, 110. Lucina P. Gabbard examines the play in "The Enigmatic *Tiny Alice*," *Journal of Evolutionary Psychology* 6 (March 1985):73–86.

144. John Stark, "Camping Out: *Tiny Alice* and Susan Sontag," *Players* 41 (April-May 1972):116–19.

145. Robert Brustein, "Tiny Alice," *New Republic*, 23 January 1965, 33–36.

146. Catherine Hughes, "Edward Albee," in *American Playwrights 1945-75* (London: Pitman Publishing, 1976), 58.

147. Robert Skloot, "The Failure of *Tiny Alice*," *Players Magazine* 43 (February/March 1968):71–81.

148. Lumley, *New Trends in 20th Century Drama*, 330–31.

149. Bigsby, *Confrontation and Commitment*, 89–90.

150. Henry Hewes, "The *Tiny Alice* Caper," *Saturday Review*, 30 January 1965, 38–39, 65; rpt. *Edward Albee*, C. W. E. Bigsby, ed., 99–104.

151. Bernard F. Dukore, "Tiny Albee," *Drama Survey* 5 (Spring 1966):60–66.

152. James E. White, "Albee's *Tiny Alice*, an Exploration of Paradox," *Literatur in Wissenschaft und Unterricht* [Kiel] 6 (1973):247–58.

153. Mary Elizabeth Campbell, "The Statement of Edward Albee's *Tiny Alice*," *Papers on Language and Literature* 10 (Winter 1968):85–100.

154. Mary Elizabeth Campbell, "Tempters in Albee's *Tiny Alice*," *Modern Drama* 13 (1970):22–33.

155. Stanley Romaine Hopper, "How People Live Without Gods: Albee's *Tiny Alice*," *American Poetry Review* 2 (March–April 1973):35–38.

156. Dorothy Tolpegin, "The Two-Petaled Flower: A Commentary on Edward Albee's Play, *Tiny Alice*," *Cimarron Review* 14 (January 1971):17–30.

157. Paolucci, *From Tension to Tonic*, 65–104.

158. Alice Mandanis, "Symbol and Substance in *Tiny Alice*," *Modern Drama* 12 (May 1969):92–98.

159. William Willeford, "The Mouse in the Model," *Modern Drama* 12 (September 1969):135–45. See also Dennis Grunes, "God and Albee: *Tiny Alice*," *Studies in American Drama, 1945-Present* 1 (1986): 61–71.

160. N. S. Pradhan, *Modern American Drama: A Study in Myth and Tradition* (New Delhi: Arnold-Heinemann, 1978), 48–51.

161. Thomas B. Markus, "*Tiny Alice* and Tragic Catharsis," *Educational Theatre Journal* 17 (October 1965):225–33.

162. Rutenberg, *Edward Albee: Playwright in Protest*, 119–36.

163. Stenz, *Edward Albee: Poet of Loss*, 57–70.

164. Leighton M. Ballew, "Who's Afraid of *Tiny Alice*?" *Georgia Review* 20 (Fall 1966):292–99.

165. V. De Ruyter, "*Tiny Alice*," *De Vlaamse Gids* 51 (February 1967):86–91.

166. Mary Castiglie Anderson, "Staging the Unconscious: Edward Albee's *Tiny Alice*," *Renascence* 32 (1980):178–92.

167. Leonard Casper, "*Tiny Alice*: The Expense of Joy in the Persistence of Mystery," in *Edward Albee: An Interview and Essays*, 83–92.

168. Jules Glenn, "The Adoption Theme in Edward Albee's *Tiny Alice* and *The American Dream*," 255–69.

169. Abraham N. Franzblau, "A Psychiatrist Looks at 'Tiny Alice,'" *Saturday Review*, 30 January 1965, 39; rpt. *Edward Albee*, Bigsby, ed., 110–11. See also John W. Clarkson, "*Tiny Alice*: Edward Albee's Negative Oedipal Enigma," *American Imago* 23 (Spring 1966):3–21 and Edward Lipton, "The *Tiny Alice* Enigma," *Saturday Review*, 20 February 1965, 21.

170. John Simon, Review of *A Delicate Balance*, *Hudson Review* 19 (Winter 1966–67):627–29.

171. Wilfred Sheed, Review of *A Delicate Balance*, *Commonweal*, 14 October 1966, 55–56.

172. Robert Brustein, "Albee Decorates a New House," *New Republic*, 8 October 1966, 35–36.

173. Gerald Weales, Review of *A Delicate Balance*, *The Reporter*, 20 October 1966, 52.

174. Walter Kerr, Review of *A Delicate Balance*, *New York Times*, 23 September 1966;

rpt. in *New York Theatre Critics' Reviews, 1966,* 294.

175. Virginia I. Perry, "Disturbing Our Sense of Well-Being: The Uninvited in *A Delicate Balance,*" in *Edward Albee: An Interview and Essays,* 55–64.

176. Review of *A Delicate Balance,* "Whiskey Before Breakfast," *Time,* 30 September 1966, 88.

177. E. G. Bierhaus, Jr., "Strangers in a Room: *A Delicate Balance* Revisited," *Modern Drama* 17 (1974):199–206; Leonard R. N. Ashley has also explored Albee's use of names in "The Names of the Games and the Games of the Names: The Onomasticon of Edward Albee's Plays," *Names* 30 (September 1982):143–70.

178. Ronald Hayman, *Edward Albee* (New York: Ungar, 1973), 98–115.

179. Paul Witherington, "Albee's Gothic: The Resonances of Cliché."

180. Terrence Brown, "Harmonic Discord and Stochastic Process: Edward Albee's *A Delicate Balance,*" *RE: Arts and Letters* 3 (1970):54–60.

181. M. Patricia Fumerton, "Verbal Prisons: The Language of Edward Albee's *A Delicate Balance,*" *English Studies in Canada* 7 (Summer 1981):201–11.

182. John J. Von Szeliski, "Albee: A Rare *Balance,*" *Twentieth Century Literature* 16 (April 1970):123–30.

183. M. Gilbert Porter, "Toby's Last Stand: The Evanescence of Commitment in *A Delicate Balance,*" *Educational Theatre Journal* 31 (October 1979):398–408.

184. Cohn, *Dialogue in American Drama,* 156–63.

185. Robert M. Post, "Cognitive Dissonance in the Plays of Edward Albee," *Quarterly Journal of Speech* 55 (February 1969):54–60.

186. Carol Sykes, "Albee's Beast Fables: *The Zoo Story* and *A Delicate Balance,*" *Educational Theatre Journal* 25 (1973):448–55.

187. Laura Julier, "Faces to the Dawn: Female Characters in Albee's Plays," in *Edward Albee: Planned Wilderness,* 34–44.

188. "*Box* and *Quotations from Chairman Mao Tse-tung:* Albee's Diptych," in *Edward Albee,* ed. Bigsby, 151–64.

189. Anthony Hopkins, "Conventional Albee: *Box* and *Chairman Mao,*" *Modern Drama* 16 (September 1973):141–48.

190. Calvin Rand, "Albee's Musical Box-Mao-Box," *Humanist* 29 (January-February 1969):27.

191. Paolucci, *From Tension to Tonic,* 123–34; Rutenberg, *Edward Albee: Playwright in Protest,* 201–28.

192. Clive Barnes, "Albee's *Seascape* Is Major Event," *New York Times,* 27 January 1975; Douglas Watt, "*Seascape:* The Lizard Has the Lines," *New York Daily News,* 27 January 1975; Martin Gottfried, "Edward Albee's Latest," *New York Post,* 27 January 1975; Edwin Wilson, "Disturbing Creatures From the Deep," *Wall Street Journal,* 28 January 1975; Howard Kissel, *Seascape, Women's Wear Daily,* 27 January 1975; John Beaufort, "New Albee Comedy on Broadway," *Christian Science Monitor,* 30 January 1975 — all are reprinted in *New York Theatre Critics Reviews, 1975,* 368–71.

193. Thomas P. Adler, "Albee's *Seascape:* Humanity at a Second Threshold," *Renascence* 31 (1979):107–14.

194. Samuel Bernstein, *The Strands Intertwined: A New Direction in American Drama* (Boston: Northeastern University Press, 1980), 113–35. See also Mathew C. Roudané's positive reading of the play, "Animal Nature, Human Nature, and the Existentialist Imperative: Edward Albee's *Seascape,*" *Theatre Annual* 38 (1983):31–47.

195. Lucina P. Gabbard, "Albee's *Seascape:* An Adult Fairy Tale," *Modern Drama* 21 (September 1978):307–17. Philip C. Kolin discusses the jet noises in *Seascape* as warnings of approaching death and compares these sounds with the "Booms" in Tennessee Williams's *The*

Milk Train Doesn't Stop Here Anymore in "Of Jets, Milk Trains, and Edward Albee's *Seascape*," *Notes on Modern American Literature* (forthcoming).

196. Barnes, "Albee's *Seascape* Is Major Event."

197. Robbie Odom Moses, "Death as a Mirror of Life: Edward Albee's *All Over*," *Modern Drama* 19 (1976):67–77.

198. Nelvin Vos, "The Process of Dying in the Plays of Edward Albee," *Educational Theatre Journal* 25 (March 1973):80–85.

199. James Neil Harris, "Edward Albee and Maurice Maeterlinck: *All Over* as Symbolism," *Theatre Research International* 3 (1978):200–8.

200. Paolucci, *From Tension to Tonic*, 122.

201. Mark Boyer, "Premier Albee: Irresistible Rhythms, Unnatural Acts," *Hartford Courant*, 9 February 1977, 19, 26; Douglas Watt, "A Long Night of Albee," *New York Daily News*, 5 February 1977, rpt. in *Newsbank (Performing Arts)* 11 (January/February 1977):B10; Julius Novick, "Doing His Best," *Village Voice*, 21 February 1977, 99.

202. Clive Barnes, "Stage: Double Bill by Albee," *New York Times*, 4 February 1977, C4.

203. Irving Wardle, "Sixty-minute, Second-rate Doodle," *London Times*, 7 December 1976, 11.

204. Thomas P. Adler, "*Counting the Ways* by Edward Albee," *Educational Theatre Journal* 29 (October 1977):408.

205. Philip C. Kolin, "Edward Albee's *Counting the Ways*: The Ways of Losing Heart," *Edward Albee: An Interview and Essays*, 121–40. Kolin also discusses Albee's risqué use of *et cetera* in *Listening* in "Bawdy Uses of *Et Cetera*," *American Speech* 58 (Spring 1983): 75–78.

206. Gerald Clarke, "Night Games: The *Lady from Dubuque*," *Time*, 11 February 1980, 69; Douglas Watt, "Albee on the Chill of Death and Loss," *New York Daily News*, 1 February 1980; Clive Barnes, Review of *The Lady From Dubuque*, *New York Post*, 1 February 1980, 33.

207. Ethan Mordden, "The Great American Playwright," in *The American Theatre* (New York: Oxford University Press, 1981), 240–43.

208. Jack Kroll, "Going to Hell with Albee," *Newsweek*, 11 February 1980, 102–3; Julius Novick, "Mr. Albee's Pavane," *Village Voice*, 11 February 1980, 77; Walter Kerr, "Stage: Albee's *Lady From Dubuque*," *New York Times*, 1 February 1980, C5; Robert Brustein, "Self-Parody and Self-Murder," *New Republic*, 8 March 1980, 26.

209. John Simon, "From Hunger, Not Dubuque," *New York*, 11 February 1980, 74.

210. June Schlueter, "Is It *All Over* for Edward Albee?: *The Lady from Dubuque*," in *Edward Albee: Planned Wilderness*, 112–19.

211. Mathew C. Roudané, "On Death, Dying, and the Manner of Living: Waste As Theme in Edward Albee's *The Lady from Dubuque*," in *Edward Albee: An Interview and Essays*, 65–81.

212. See Roudané's first note for a summary of reviewers' responses in Chicago and New York. For an article connecting Albee to the Theater of Cruelty, see "Towards a Theatre of Cruelty," *Times Literary Supplement*, 27 February 1964, 166.

213. Matthew C. Roudané, "An Interview with Edward Albee," *Southern Humanities Review* 16 (Winter 1983):29–44. Another revelation of Albee's attitude to art in general, and, thereby, his own work is his essay "Louise Nevelson: The Sum of the Parts," in *Louise Nevelson: Environments* (New York: Clarkson Potter, 1980), 12–13, 29–30. Of special interest are his comments about Mondrian's and Nevelson's boxes, how the spectator becomes a participant, and his praise of Nevelson as a critic of *Tiny Alice*.

214. Bigsby, *Albee*, 116–17.

215. The editors of this collection express their gratitude to the following people who

were very helpful in the making of this book: Mark Winchell of Clemson University; Jim Gillespie of the Milton S. Eisenhower Library at Johns Hopkins University; Patty Mrozowski of the Behrend College library; and Norma J. Hartner, Eric Howard Kolin, Kristin Julie Kolin, James Madison Davis III, Jonathan Tyler Davis, Simonne Davis, and Janeen L. Kolin, whose encouragement and advice were invaluable.

REVIEWS

[Review of *The Zoo Story*]

Friedrich Luft*

[*Krapp's Last Tape*] was followed by the premiere performance of an American text, an often spicy dialogue: *The Zoo Story* by Edward Albee, a thirty-year-old who has concocted, from his knowledge of Beckett, Poe and Kafka, Freud and Hollywood's cheap-but-popular technique of hitting below the belt, a shiningly sickly and, at the same time, painfully interesting, one-acter.

On a bench in Central Park an ordinary citizen, very much a philistine, is spoken to by a visionary, troubled fellow, then drawn into an evil, deep conversation. In the course of it, his wildly threatening partner rips the ground right out from under his feet, and in the end forces him to stab the threatening threatened fellow.

This is tightly wound Grand Guignol, shudder-causing drama of superintelligent style, longing for death in bluejeans, Götterdammerung from the gutter. But highly gifted, and in the dialectic of absolute evil, often possessing a shivering luster.

Kurt Buecheler plays the philistine, who is presented with mental confusion and murder; Thomas Holtzmann, Berlin's specialist for the quiet stage demonic, portrays the tempter, the poor intellectual molester.

As the applause rose for this study of fright in dialogue, the two actors brought the author onto the stage—a thin, neatly dressed, almost shy young man, a pleasure to look at. One would never have suspected such scenic deviousness of him.

*From *Die Welt*, 1 October 1959. Translated for this volume by Steven DeHart, with the advice of Irmgard Wolfe.

[Review of *The Zoo Story*]   Anonymous*

A "workshop" of Berlin's Schiller theater was opened during the festival with two thematically related pieces that deal with the lack of human contact. . . .

There was a premiere of a one-act play, *The Zoo Story* by Edward Albee, a 31-year-old American who was present for the enthusiastic applause. This two-person study, translated by Pinkas Braun, is also the desperate monologue of a person who tries in vain "to find any means of finishing with something."

This dark story has humor and wit in places, and is fascinating because of its topic. The mise-en-scene of the young director Walter Henn accentuates more the psychological aspects of the case than its philosophical attitude.

*From *Darmstadter Echo*, 2 October 1959. Translated for this volume by Steven DeHart. The dates of the German reviews of *Zoo Story* are incorrectly listed in Kimball King's *Ten Modern American Playwrights* as 29 September 1959.

Benchmanship   Henry Hewes*

Last week these columns were devoted mainly to a discussion of Samuel Beckett's rich and poetic playlet, *Krapp's Last Tape*. This play is the first half of a twin bill currently at the Provincetown Playhouse. The second play there, titled *The Zoo Story*, is equally exciting, not only because it is compelling theatre, but also because it introduces Edward Albee, a young (circa thirty) playwright of considerable potentiality.

Mr. Albee's play is quite simple in form. A dull, respectable man with that upper-middle-middle expression on his face is reading on a park bench when an obnoxious stranger approaches him with irritating personal questions and remarks. The stranger has a desperate need to make contact with someone, and as a last resort pushes his listener to violence.

The details of these events are made fascinating by the actors George Maharis and William Daniels. To the role of Jerry, the beatnik, Mr. Maharis brings a quietly hypnotic rhythm that comes across as theatrically colorful yet integrated with his own personality. And as Peter, the square, Mr. Daniels provided a genuine humor. He is at his best in the early part of the play where the tone *is* humorous, as Jerry ridicules the clichés he is able to smoke out of Peter's Madison Avenue existence. Of course, this ridicule has itself become a cliché, and if unimaginatively played would seem merely tired and predictable satire. But director Milton Katselas has

*From *Saturday Review*, 6 February 1960, 32. © 1960. Reprinted by permission.

permitted each actor an awareness of the situation and of what the dialogue means to the one who speaks it. Jerry tends to have this awareness at the precise moment he speaks. And Peter has it a second or two after he has said his line. Even an ordinary interchange (JERRY: "Well, *Time* magazine isn't for blockheads." PETER: "No, I suppose not.") becomes subtly hilarious when given this particular treatment. And it is not just funny, for as he considers each random question, Peter becomes more and more aware of inadequacies not really faced before.

Jerry, on the other hand, seems compelled by an inner, not quite understood drive, an unwillingness to stop short of scraping out the last layer of truth. And even when he is using such colorful language as "But that was the jazz of a very special hotel," it is not done for effect, but rather because that is the best way he knows to express his nostalgia without oversentimentalization. The high point of his performance is reached when he tells "The Story of Jerry and the Dog." In the parable Jerry attempts first kindness and then cruelty to a dog that tries to bite him every time he comes into his boarding house. The result is an eventual compromise in which both Jerry and the dog arrive at a state in which they neither love nor hurt because they no longer try to reach each other. This state — the basis of so many relationships in modern adult society — is what has driven Jerry into his present pilgrimage up Fifth Avenue to the zoo where he had hoped to find out more about the way people exist with animals, animals with each other, and animals with people. As he tells Peter the story of what he saw at the zoo, Jerry attempts, through cruelty, to provoke some animal feeling in Peter, and though the ending is melodramatic and violent, Jerry — like Christ — succeeds at the cost of his life in arousing the human soul out of its deep modern lethargy to an awareness of its animal self.

The Zoo Story is done so well that we can afford to point out that Mr. Katselas might have made this production even more effective if he had been able to highlight some of the author's points more distinctly and had found a more interesting way of expressing the animal stirring within Peter at the play's melodramatic end. We can also afford to wonder if Mr. Albee's suggestion that Jerry's boarding house is a West Side purgatory in which God is a queen who plucks his eyebrows and goes to the john is not one that needs the fuller development he might give it in a longer play. And doesn't his description of Jerry's deceased mother ("She embarked on an adulterous turn of our Southern states . . . and her most constant companion among others, among many others, was a Mr. Barleycorn") owe something to Tennessee Williams? No matter. Mr. Albee has written an extraordinary first play, which, next to Jack Gelber's *The Connection*, constitutes the finest new achievement in the theatre this season. Thank God for Off-Broadway, and, I guess, thank God for beatniks.

[Review of *The Zoo Story*]   Tom F. Driver*

The Zoo Story, by Edward Albee, directed by Milton Katselas, at the Provincetown Playhouse (off Broadway). This is one half of a double bill, the other half of which is a thing by Samuel Beckett called *Krapp's Last Tape*, a brilliant production of a marvelous play that I hope to write about more fully on another occasion. *The Zoo Story* is about a young executive of a book publishing firm who meets a psychotic young roustabout in Central Park. The latter forces his conversation upon the former, does most of the talking, and ends up by making his new acquaintance hold an open knife upon which the mad young fellow then runs and kills himself. It is more than a little melodramatic, and the only sense I could draw from it is the conviction that one shouldn't talk to strangers in Central Park.

*From *Christian Century*, 17 February 1960, 193–94. © 1960, The Christian Century Foundation. Reprinted by permission.

[Review of *The American Dream*]   Geri Trotta*

Albee's latest and best play, *The American Dream*, is a comedy of laughter that flays the skin and chills the bone. If Dostoevsky reveals the idiot in all of us, Albee unmasks the monstrous in our ordinary selves. He is a master at using trivial dialogue, deliberately riddled with clichés, to achieve a scathing penetration of character. Against the pedestrian façade of a comfortably tasteless apartment the middle-aged wife is adroitly redefined as a raging harpy who has emasculated her husband, is torturing her mother, and may seduce her substitute son, a physically flawless youth who is emptied of emotion and ready to do anything for money — the personification of a modern malady and all that remains (in the playwright's view) of the American dream.

If the plot awakens distant echoes of *Oedipus Rex*, it is no accident. Consider Grandma a kittenish old sphinx, and the rest is obvious: a heroic Greek tragedy ingeniously dwarfed to the scale of a side show, in which the final disaster is not stated but clearly implied. Albee's American brand of surrealism, the result of curiously incongruous action coupled with familiar idiomatic language, has a grotesque, almost macabre effect, rather like finding a live tarantula at the bottom of a box of Cracker Jack.

*From *Horizon*, September 1961, 79. © 1961, American Heritage Publishing Co. Reprinted by permission.

[*The Death of Bessie Smith*: The German Premiere]

Friedrich Luft*

. . . After the intermission, a premiere. Edward Albee, the thirty-year-old playwright from Washington, was discovered a year ago by the experimental studio of the Schiller Theater. Now the whole world is playing his *Zoo Story*. He had to go through Charlottenburg to get to New York.

This one-act play, *The Death of Bessie Smith*, is once again an evilly talented thing, a piece of shrill human deprecation, a montage of two events.

An old black female singer who has become old-fashioned wants to regain her fame. Her friend and manager wants to help her. She has an accident on her way to New York. The white hospitals will not admit her. She dies on the street.

Second event: A bitch of an attractive white nurse is driving the doctor and the black orderly of her hospital crazy with evil consistency. The person spews charming manners. She is constantly making the two men angry. She carries out an erotic cat-and-mouse game, spraying sparks and, at the same time, pouring buckets of water on her heated-up worshippers. A study of extreme female cruelty.

Only at the very end does Albee bring these two tales of woe together. The black friend brings in the singer who has bled to death in front of the hospital. It is the cold shock from the inhumanity of her death that turns the ready-to-rebel physician from his inane love and desire.

Man, Albee says with chic dramaturgical sensationalism, is an ass! Woe unto us all!

Whether he is right is not the point. It cannot be denied that he (dramaturgically, coldly) drives his evil theme right to the heart of the matter with talent and tension. Dialogues, that contain more than they appear to, flutter and provoke. A type of stylized realism in the play's method, which is evilly attractive and which Walter Henn has once again marvelously replicated.

Annaliese Römer plays the repugnant ass on the bass viol, always trampling on the hearts of others — and also on her own. She does this in admirable fashion with a repugnance that is strangely attractive. Claus Holm and Horst Bollman are her victims. Claus Hofer is the black manager and friend of the dead singer.

Following [Arthur] Miller's humanely warm panorama of the world of the employed [*A Memory of Two Mondays*], this brief, sharp, talented, cold shower. America twice, dramatically speaking. The evening was worth the trip.

*From *Die Welt*, 23 April 1960. Translated for this volume by Steven DeHart, with the advice of Irmgard Wolfe.

Albee and the Medusa-Head   Robert Brustein*

Edward Albee's new work embodies both the failings and the virtues of his previous plays. But its positive achievements are substantial, and I am finally beginning to regard this playwright's future with real expectation. Albee's technical dexterity has always been breathtaking—for sheer theatrical skill, no American, not even Williams, can match him—but like Williams, he has been inclined to falsify his native gifts, distorting experience through self-defensive reflecting mirrors. In *Who's Afraid of Virginia Woolf*, Albee is still not looking the Gorgon smack in the eye. Still, he has conjured up its outline. And if he tends to focus more on writhing snakes than on the other features of this terrifying monster, then even these quick glances are more penetrating than I have come to expect; and they are always projected in steaming, raging, phantasmagoric theatrical images.

Virginia Woolf is an ambitious play, and it evokes the shades of the most ambitious dramatists. The central conflict—a Strindbergian battle royal between George, a contemplative History professor with an unsuccessful career, and Martha, his bitterly shrewish wife, proceeds through a series of confessions, revelations, and interior journeys which recall the circuitous windings of O'Neill's late plays. Glued together by mutual hatred and mutual recriminations, the couple can connect only through enmity, each exposing the other's failures, inadequacies, vices, and secret illusions in language of savagely ironic scorn. Though the climax of the work is built on such an exposure, however, Albee seems less interested in the real history of his characters than in the way they conceal and protect their reality: the conflict is also a kind of game, with strict rules, and what they reveal about each other may not be true. This comedy of concealment reminds one of Pirandello, and even more of Jean Genet. For George and Martha—each by turns the aggressor—shift their identities like reptiles shedding skins. And as the evening grows more alcoholic, and the atmosphere more distended and surrealistic, their "total war" becomes a form of ritual play acting, performed upon the shifting sands of truth. . . .

The last episode, "Bringing Up Baby," constitutes George's revenge on Martha—not because she tried to betray him (her infidelities are apparently innumerable), but because she broke one of the rules of the game: she mentioned their "son" to strangers. Forcing Martha to recount the childhood history of this absent youth, George reads the requiem for the dead, climaxing this litany with the announcement that their son has been killed in an auto accident. But the child has never existed. He is merely the essential illusion of the childless Martha, a consoling fiction in her inconsolable reality. . .

Everyone seems to have boggled at this fictional child; and it is

*From *New Republic*, 3 November 1962, 29–30. Reprinted by permission of the journal.

certain that the play collapses at its moment of climax. But the difficulty is not that the author introduces a spurious element into an otherwise truthful play. It is, rather, that he suddenly confronts us with a moment of truth after an evening of stage illusions. Albee's theatrical inventiveness rests mainly on incongruous juxtapositions: when George aims a shotgun at his braying wife, for example, it shoots not bullets but a Japanese parasol. These shock tactics are a sure-fire comic technique, but they have the effect of alienating the spectator from the action the very moment he begins to accept it. Thus, when George launches a blistering attack on the evils of modern science, Albee undercuts it with a ludicrous non-sequitur: "I will not give up Berlin." And when Martha speaks of her need to escape reality, he has her do so in a broad Irish brogue. . . .

Truth and illusion may be confused, as one character tells us, but after three and a half hours of prestidigitation, we become reluctant to accept one of these magical tricks as the real thing. In short, Albee is a highly accomplished stage magician, but he fails to convince us there is nothing up his sleeve. His thematic content is incompatible with his theatrical content — hi-jinks and high seriousness fail to fuse.

On the other hand, the author has a fine time showing off his sleight of hand, incidentally, I suspect, conjuring his action into the outlines of a classical myth (the evidence is jumbled, and I may be crazy, but I think I can detect elements of the story of Aphrodite, Ares, and Hephaestus, mixed with pieces from the story of Aphrodite and Adonis). And he has been provided with a really superb production, deftly managed by Alan Schneider. . . .

In spite of all the excellence of play and production, however, I am left with my equivocal response. In his latest play, Edward Albee proves once again that he has wit, cunning, theatricality, toughness, formal control, poetry — in short, all the qualities of a major dramatist but one: that selfless commitment to a truthful vision of life which constitutes the universal basis of all serious art. Possibly out of fear of such commitments, Albee is still coquetting with his own talent, still resisting any real identification with his own material, so that he tends to confuse his themes, shift his attitudes, and subvert his characters. Yet, a genuine insight merely sketched in his earlier work is now beginning to find fuller expression that in a time of deadened instinct, people will use any methods, including deadly hatred, in order to find their way to others. This, or something like it, may become the solid foundation of Albee's future writing; but whatever it is, I await what is to come with eagerness. For if Albee can confront the Medusa head without the aid of parlor tricks or mirrors, he may yet turn us all to stone.

[Review of *Who's Afraid of Virginia Woolf?*]

John Gassner*

Albee's first full-length play as staged for Broadway by Alan Schneider affords so much pulsating moment-by-moment drama, so many unreeling facets of character and so many fluctuations of feeling, and one is so continuously knocked down, picked up, and knocked down again in the course of the play, that it takes a massive quantity of resistance to conclude that *Who's Afraid of Virginia Woolf?* is not drama on the grand scale. It reaches the same order of harrowing dramatic power as Elizabethan melodrama which the unfinicky Elizabethans called tragedy. The very same thing can be said indeed of a good many of O'Neill's plays; John Mason Brown may have been the first critic to refer to him as a minor Elizabethan dramatist in modern dress. For me, in fact, Albee is in the direct line of succession from O'Neill. Even if he has yet far to go if he is to achieve his predecessor's breadth of interest, variety of tone, or range of compassionate insight, Albee has the same slugging technique and the same strategy of massive assault in thrusting across the footlight area his awareness of human bedevilment. And in their writing they employ the same heavy Mahler scoring with an overplus of *ostinato* markings, although Albee's lines move faster and with more precision than O'Neill's. Interestingly enough, both O'Neill and Albee came to public notice as the authors of undeniably effective one-act plays before winning larger audiences as the authors of notably oversized full-length drama. This fact should give pause to those who see in the larger works mere repetitiveness or verbal incontinence rather than an essential dramatic pulsation and rhythm. The larger works reveal, rather, a similar fascination with the details of feeling and dramatic action, and with the momentum of recurring impulses that characterize behavior in an extensive situation of crisis and constitute its exciting vibration. . . .

That the play provides the most harrowing sex-duel on the stage since Strindberg's *The Dance of Death* at the beginning of the century is certain. Whether the play goes beyond this demonstration is another matter. If it does not, then we may be permitted to doubt that we have been sufficiently rewarded for more than three hours of concentrated attention. What insight have we won, we may well ask, that we couldn't have had an hour or so earlier? Does not the play move toward a veritable anticlimax, moreover, when cause and effect are so disproportionate; when we learn at the end that they never had a son to whom something terrible had happened? They have been tearing at each other's vitals for a deprivation that does not prevent sane human beings from behaving with decency and consideration toward each other. Can anyone doubt that the

*From *Educational Theatre Journal* 15 (March 1963):78–80. Reprinted by permission of The Johns Hopkins University Press.

final revelation of childlessness is not a convincing, let alone significant, motivation for the perversities of hatred and sado-masochism that leap at the greatly tried spectator wave upon wave? And if this is the case, may we not press a charge of superficiality and speciousness against the protracted suspense so artfully maintained by this remarkably adept young playwright? . . .

The play, which also contains a secondary exploration of character in conflict in the case of a second couple, is alive in the *struggle* rather than in the explanation. It takes place under special circumstances; when the antagonists are intoxicated. But their condition does not exonerate the characters or invalidate the reality of past tensions between the couple. It is also apparent that these characters are most alive when they are most savage, and that their savagery toward each other is combined with an emotional dependency that no amount of disappointment has succeeded in diminishing. Their personal situation and their relationship are, so to speak, *existential*.

Beyond the struggle, there is nothing but the commonplace round of occupational and social obligations of the professor-hero and his wife, the daughter of the college president. Beneath the struggle there is nothing at the core except loneliness — and so they are lonely together when they are not in the close contact of hurting each other. Beneath the intense embrace of the hurting, there is the emptiness of their being — and so they are empty together. This, then, is the drama of the "absurd" (which is not at all the same thing as "an absurd drama"), in which cause and effect *are* disproportionate. The childlessness of the couple revealed at the end is hardly a cause or an explanation of their real plight, which is their lostness, their state of being. Our reason does not have to validate it any more than it validates or can (without religious faith, as Pascal understood so well!) invalidate the infinite emptiness of the universe that overcomes the thinking reed that is Man. It is possible to work up a strong resentment of the play, to be sure, but it is not an easy one to ignore or forget. Mr. Albee has written a terrifying thing — perhaps *the* negative play to end all negative plays, yet also a curiously compassionate play (I feel plenty of compassion for the driven woman and her long-suffering husband), and exhilarating one (if for no other reason than the passionateness of the characters) and even a wryly affirmative one because of the fighting spirit of the principals whose behavior breathes the fire of protest along with the stench of corruption.

Nights with the Ripsaw
J. C. Trewin*

In the printed text of the play, *Who's Afraid of Virginia Woolf?* — and by this time the dramatist, Edward Albee, has every reason to be self-conscious about his title — the scene is given simply as "the living-room of a house on the campus of a small New England college." The programme at the Piccadilly Theatre omits even this. It merely gives labels for the three acts: "Fun and Games," "Walpurgisnacht," and "The Exorcism." Still, when the curtain rose, those who had not read the play could not have wondered long about the surroundings. William Ritman, the designer, has provided the kind of set matched to the fearful conflict within it: a large, shabby, unloved room, walled by unfriendly books, books thrust carelessly on the shelves; a room that by day would look oddly tired and forbidding, and that by night (the action of the play begins at 2 a.m.) seems to be dark with the memory of innumerable battles.

The fight that we are allowed to witness is the worst of them all. I said just now that Mr. Albee presents a "fearful conflict," and I must repeat that this is not an over-statement. We are temporarily the guests of a married couple, a history tutor in his late forties and his wife, who is six years older. They have been together for 23 years, and they are now in what Strindberg would have recognised as a state of marital bliss. That is to say, life is one long, tearing struggle. If they can draw blood, they are happy. Knowing each other through and through, each can probe straight to the other's weakness. There is all the more cause to fight while strangers are present, and they can tear, gash, and claw in public with the bottle of Bourbon or brandy near at hand. Moreover, visiting innocents will be new material for these savage verbal games.

The dramatist, on an early page of his text, describes the wife as "a large, boisterous woman, ample but not fleshy." The husband is simply: "Thin, hair going grey." Ordinary enough types, but within half an hour they have grown to be far larger than life-size, and there seems to be no way in which the monstrous incarnations of marital hate can be brought back to a normal world, genuinely humanised. Outside, it is dark. Inside, during these hours before daybreak when the pulse of life should be at its feeblest, the dreary room is possessed by evil. Two other people are drawn into it: another married couple, a biology tutor and his wife from the Middle West, who find themselves, unaware, in the flames of a private hell. Possibly they deserve this for accepting an invitation to call at two in the morning after a college party; but no doubt the hours are normal on this particular campus. Certainly it is then that George and Martha are in their strongest fighting vein.

This is, I think, as cruel a play as I remember. On the previous night

*From *The Illustrated London News*, 22 February 1964, 288. Reprinted by permission of the journal.

we had heard the Euripidean Messenger speech that reports the tearing of Pentheus to pieces on the slope of Mount Kithairon. And, during most of the Piccadilly premiere, I was seeing the New England college as another Kithairon, another world of passion unrestrained. Let me say quickly that the piece does contain a good deal of savage comedy. Though I loathed the situation and the people, I still heard myself laughing; and for two acts a listener behind me guffawed so hard that he must have advertised the play well beyond the purlieus of Denman Street. But in the third act mirth begins to wane. Finally, the glimmer of daybreak brings peace, and with it the end of the wife's dangerous fantasy about the son she could not have. The act, you will remember, is labelled "The Exorcism."

In writing of the play I am altogether unable to conceal my dislike. Yet with this there has to go a sharp admiration for Mr. Albee's theatrical drive, his damnable cleverness, his unrelenting attack. The fight endures for three-and-a-half hours. At the première the house was alert to the last, and the curtain fell upon one of the most spontaneous receptions I remember. It was a salute to Uta Hagen and Arthur Hill, the wife and husband, and to Beverlee McKinsey and Richard Easton, the subsidiary couple: it was also a salute to Mr. Albee. I have not cared much about his other work. Those short plays, *The Zoo Story*, *The American Dream*, and so on, appeared to me to be tedious and over-valued; but *Who's Afraid of Virginia Woolf?* (and we can forget the facetious title) is a quite astonishing piece of work: the Theatre of the Ripsaw and the Flail. . . .

Theater: Albee's *Tiny Alice* Opens   Howard Taubman*

The mark of a real writer is his refusal to stand still or repeat himself. In *Tiny Alice* Edward Albee has moved into the difficult, mysterious, ever tantalizing realm of faith.

In this new play, which opened last night at the Billy Rose Theater, Mr. Albee has attempted nothing less than a large, modern allegory on a theme that after almost two millenniums is essentially timeless. He is writing about the passion of a Christ-like figure, if not of Christ Himself.

Mr. Albee has not, unless I am mistaken after a first hearing, cast fresh light on this theme. But he has written with the literacy of a man who knows that the word itself can be charged with drama and with a gift for making a scene on a stage reverberate with subtle overtones.

Indeed, his command of sheer theater grows steadily, and it has been richly and imaginatively abetted by Alan Schneider's staging. Even if you find Mr. Albee's subject and treatment too enigmatic, *Tiny Alice* provides

*From the *New York Times*, 30 December 1964. © 1964 by The New York Times Co. Reprinted by permission.

the kind of exhilarating evening that stretches the mind and sensibilities. . . .

Mr. Albee knows how to make individual scenes count. He has conceived confrontations that tingle provocatively and images suffused in a muted religious light. His writing abounds in moments touched with pungency and irony. His observations on wealth, established religion, service and martyrdom emerge sharply from the dramatic context.

In the final scenes *Tiny Alice* all but drops the mask of allegory. The symbols become virtually the figures they were meant to represent. And the play itself loses the richness of texture it has had in the course of its development. One realizes that Mr. Albee is reduced to illustrating rather than illuminating his theme. If one is disappointed at the end, one does not forget the boldness and wonder of the journey Mr. Albee has dared to undertake.

Only Time Really Happens to People [A *Delicate Balance*]   Walter Kerr*

. . . Quiet is all that underlies Mr. Albee's play—not the quiet of peace arrived at or of harmony established but the stillness of mute rock or uninvaded desert. The cosmos has no core. It cannot be penetrated. Breathlessness is its ultimate condition, immobility its sole activity.

INTENDED CONTRADICTION

This last contradiction is intended. Events may seem to happen in the play, some of them decently violent. Friends come to the door driven by fears they cannot define and ask to stay the night. The daughter of the house resents their occupying her room and is willing to wave a pistol hysterically in order to gain her imagined rights. Miss Tandy and Mr. Cronyn clash at each other—she with silvered nails, he with a dog-at-heels feverishness—in an effort to arrive at decisions, decisions about love and friendship and all the pretty, empty, exasperating unrealities on which people do spend their false-face lives.

But in point of fact there are no events—nothing follows necessarily from what has gone before, no two things fit, no present posture has a tangible past. When, in the middle of a highly indeterminate speech, Mr. Cronyn blurts out that the "goddamn government is after me about some deductions" on his income tax, we are startled. What government? What

*From *New York Times*, 2 October 1966. © 1966 by The New York Times Co. Reprinted by permission.

happens in this unmoored world that could ever be taxed? We have grown away, during the course of the evening, from anything concrete enough — a meal, a yacht, a piece of office furniture — to be considered deductible. The notion of a real universe has been deducted from the outset, and we can only listen to people constructing illusory happenings out of nouns, adjectives, rhythms. Only time really happens to people. "And after enough time, there's nothing left," Miss Tandy sighs.

BIG PROBLEM

Now Mr. Albee has clearly set himself a formidable task in attempting to substantiate on the stage what he proposes as insubstantial. He must carve a great hole in the center of the stage and then make the actual actors who inhabit it seem not actual at all. His creative powers, as we know, are considerable; and there are striking times during the evening when we feel pushed to the crater's edge, one with his people. He has been extraordinarily well-served by his designer and director: William Ritman's setting slips away like a boat that has just been missed, and Alan Schneider has made of purposeless movement a kind of choral outing into the void — placid, eternally drifting, composed for composure's sake. The subject itself is much on the contemporary mind: If Harold Pinter has been here before with effective images of unspecified dread, Mr. Albee has a wrinkle to add to the cloak of anxiety that covers us. Life, he suggests, is language and nothing more.

This means that the play itself must be language and nothing more. It also requires that the language employed by the actors be detached from the normal uses and processes of speech. We normally think of speech as referring to *things*. But now there are no things, only fabricated, measured sounds which breed incestuously upon themselves for want of referents.

Thus Mr. Albee measures carefully, retracing and retracting thoughts, rearranging his word order, deleting value. When was it a cat stopped loving Mr. Cronyn? Mr. Cronyn is of many minds on the matter, struggling for verbal precision since there can be no other kind of precision. When he slapped the cat and the cat struck back, did the cat hurt him? "Yes." Then, after a pause, "No." In a world of language alone, yes and no are identical. "I dropped upstairs," Miss Tandy begins, then hesitates. "My, that doesn't make much sense, does it?" she asks herself. Gathering her wits together, she alters the idiom to "I happened upstairs" and settles for that. One must settle for something; it is all arbitrary, in any case. "She will be down or she will be up, she will stop or she will go on," Miss Tandy says of her daughter. In the absence of event, opposites are a matter of complete indifference. . . .

Some self-consciousness was no doubt inevitable once Mr. Albee decided that the play was to be sheer verbal manufacture. And the sensation of remoteness is inherent in the play's intended bones. Still, there is such a thing as poetry, a way of summoning up the intangible as though it had truly slipped through closed windows or firmly locked doors, a way of making the absent so present that we feel we can scarcely brush it off our clothes. *A Delicate Balance* fails, I think, because Mr. Albee has not got the particular kind of poetry he was after, because he has used theoretical words to describe a theoretical situation instead of using intensely practical words to show how impractical words are. The play is not so much out of a very young philosopher's notebook as *Tiny Alice* was: it is, in fact, more interesting to contend with than any of the author's last three plays. But it is still speculative rather than theatrical, an essay and an exercise when it might have been an experience.

A Weekend with the "Can Do" Family
Robert Graham Kemper*

"The motto of this family should be: We Do What We Can Do." Early in Edward Albee's surrealistic play *A Delicate Balance*, a member of his suburban family speaks that line. Whether the motto is an apt description of the family's attitude or a gross joke is systematically explored in the rest of the play. What begins as an uneventful Friday evening in the home of Agnes (Jessica Tandy) and Tobias (Hume Cronyn) becomes, by Sunday, an ethical crisis in the collective and individual lives of six people, testing the accuracy of the motto. . . .

Albee has drawn arresting, well delineated characters and he has given them arresting lines. There are some moving soliloquies that, in the hands of these competent actors, make memorable moments of theater. Here is an artistically mature Albee, channeling his gifts for language into dialogue that is a delight to hear. . . .

Ethical purists will be offended by the play. Nowhere does any of the characters ask himself what he ought to do — only what he *can* do, and the answer is exceedingly narrow. All these people are Bad Samaritans for whom the neighbor in need is not an object of compassion but a galling weight.

Albee does dramatically portray the pervasiveness of what the theologian calls sin. If a man has to ask himself what is the rightful limit of his responsibility toward another, he has already been corrupted by sin. The play also depicts the hollowness of a private ethic. Given freedom to decide what is his duty toward his fellow creatures, a man will go through

*From *Christian Century*, 23 November 1966, p. 1447. © 1966, The Christian Century Foundation. Reprinted by permission.

agony trying to find a delicate balance, but in the end he will not topple the scale. Thus Albee paints a bleak picture of what man "can do," but he also confirms the biblical view of man's freedom as a necessary but damning quality.

Still, in the last analysis, I am not sure that Albee meant this play to be taken seriously. It is too small. The play's moral struggle is fought by Lilliputians. It asks only what is one's obligation to friends and relatives. What of one's obligation to those one has never seen and does not know — to the victims of Hiroshima, Selma, Wall street, Vietnam? Could it be that this is really a play about the appalling narrowness of the average man's concern, that in *A Delicate Balance* Albee is needling provincial, unaware, middle class morality? I hope so. It would be too bad for a major American dramatist to spend his talents on problems better handled by Ann Landers.

Albee's *Seascape* Is a Major Event   Clive Barnes*

Hats off, and up in the air! A major dramatic event.

Edward Albee's play *Seascape*, which opened at the Shubert Theater last night, is fundamentally a play about life and resolution. It is that currently rare thing, a comedy rather than a farce, and it is a curiously compelling exploration into the basic tenets of life. It is asking in a light-hearted but heavy-minded fashion whether life is worth living. It decides that there is no alternative.

As Mr. Albee has matured as a playwright, his work has become leaner, sparer and simpler. He depends on strong theatrical strokes to attract the attention of the audience, but the tone of the writing is always thoughtful, even careful, even philosophic. As with any major artist he has his own distinct profile — an Albee play is recognizably an Albee play — but if he could usefully be linked with any of his contemporaries, they would be Samuel Beckett and Harold Pinter. . . .

What Mr. Albee has given us here is a play of great density, with many interesting emotional and intellectual reverberations. The trigger of the play's action is obvious enough — it is the old visitor from Mars examining human institutions and practices and comparing them with his own to the amusement and the amazement of the audience.

But the resonances go much deeper than could be offered by science-fiction pop-guns. Mr. Albee is suggesting that one of the purposes of an individual human existence is quite simply evolution — that we all play a

New York Times, 27 January 1975. © 1975 by The New York Times Co. Reprinted by permission.

part in this oddly questionable historic process. So that the purpose of life is life itself — it is a self-fulfilling destiny. We have to come out of the water and get onto the beach, we have to live and we have to die, simply because life is about life.

In a recent interview with Mel Gussow of The New York Times, Mr. Albee revealed that *Seascape* was a companion piece to his somber masterpiece about death some four years ago, *All Over.* This is an important fact for the audience to keep in mind. It is an optimistic play, a rose play rather than a black play, as Jean Anouilh would have said, but it is nevertheless serious and provocative. It is also funny, and the humor is all the funnier for having a point to it.

What marks out Mr. Albee as a comic writer is largely his compassion. Even in the bitchy dialogue of *Who's Afraid of Virginia Woolf?* there ran this deep concern for humanity — even his chilliest wit has a saving grace of warmth to it.

The tone of the beginning of the play irresistibly recalls — surely intentionally? — Beckett's *Happy Days.* There is the same discursive familiarity, the same apparent aimlessness, which is betrayed only by the occasional pellet of truth or the compellingly apt joke. With the arrival of the sea-creatures there is a sudden danger of triteness. There is a fear that after all we are just going to be told that "everyone is the same under the skin — black, white, yellow or lizard." But the danger passes as Mr. Albee, with that spare laconic language of his, probes deeper and deeper into the subterranean seascape of our pasts, presents and futures.

This is the first play that Mr. Albee has directed, and he has done so with self-evident skill and ease. The directorial difficulty is obvious enough — to make the sea-creatures both strange enough to cast contrasting light upon our own humanity yet credible enough to speak English, and also to draw the humor out of the similarities between the two couples with subtlety rather than obviousness. This he achieves by virtually choreographing the sea-creatures (he is much helped by the splendid costumes of Fred Voelpel) and giving them a special diction rather than a special language or even a special accent. It works well, as does the handsome sand-duned set by James Tilton. . . .

Who Died?   Brendan Gill*

Edward Albee has been characteristically precise, ironic, prankish, and gallant in naming his new play, *All Over.* Precise because the play measures the effect of the slow dying of an elderly man of apparent great

*From the *New Yorker*, 3 April 1971. © 1971, The New Yorker Magazine, Inc. Reprinted by permission.

international importance on a group of people gathered in a mood of grisly self-revelation to await his end, and the two words of the title, spoken by an attending physician, serve to announce with succinct relish that welcome event; ironic because the man's death, far from putting a stop to any of the lacerative relationships we have watched unfolding onstage, marks the beginning of a series of new relationships, some of which promise to be even more painful than the earlier ones; prankish because the words of the title are the last to be uttered in the play and exist, Pirandello-fashion, both inside and outside its proper structure, simultaneously furthering the action of the play and terminating our evening at the Martin Beck; and gallant because Mr. Albee, conscious of himself as a prominent figure in our contemporary cultural landscape (to the point, indeed, of inviting the press to his Fifth Avenue apartment so that it could record for all time a preliminary running through of this play), cannot fail to have anticipated the possibility that people who dislike *All Over* will seize upon the title as an accurate summary judgment of his career.

To speak of the last first, I eagerly affirm my confidence in Mr. Albee's talent; disappointing as I find *All Over*, I don't regard it as being any more or less significant than the other failures — and, for that matter, the successes — of his bold, chance-taking professional life. The play is resourcefully plotted and is written with skill and care, in a heightened language that echoes James and sometimes, in its elegant syntactical idiosyncrasy, Ivy Compton-Burnett, and several of the characters are shown to have wry, wary, and unusual views on how one best gets through life. So far so good. But Mr. Albee has withheld practically all the means by which we might have been encouraged to care about his assortment of troubled souls. Our irritation begins when we learn from the program that nobody in the play is to have either a first or a last name — keeping vigil outside the bedroom of the dying man are The Wife, The Mistress, The Best Friend, and so on. Deprived of the minuscule individual distinction bestowed by a Jane, or even a Jones, the figures threaten to become tendentious, and even allegorical. Moreover, we discover almost nothing about the permanently invisible central character of the play except that he felt that "to be" was, by its nature, too lively an auxiliary verb to be coupled with the participle "dead." This hint of a speculative turn of mind doesn't suffice to raise our interest in him to fever pitch, nor does it help much that, though he is famous enough for a crowd of reporters to be waiting in the street below for news of his death, we never hear what his fame sprang from, or what it was in his supposedly remarkable nature that led his children to grow up so cowed and unloving. What did his mistress see in him? What did his wife see? At the heart of the play, Mr. Albee has sedulously carved a huge hollow, and he has then seen to it that the hollow does not reverberate. It is a curious decision for him to have made, and for him to have made it with such deliberation and finesse is still more curious; it is as if The Playwright had coolly ordered his play to die of starvation in the midst of plenty, as his undeciperable hero dies unspoken to among so many.

The cast of *All Over* is exemplary. Jessica Tandy, Colleen Dewhurst, Madeleine Sherwood, Neil Fitzgerald, George Voskovec, James Ray, and Betty Field carry their often heavy burdens of silence and inactivity without a trace of strain, and Miss Tandy makes a fine thing out of her final cry—"I am unhappy! I am unhappy! I am unhappy!" The play has been directed—and perhaps one should say choreographed and, in its occasional contrapuntal moments, conducted—by Sir John Gielgud, and the handsome set is by Rouben Ter-Arutunian.

Going to Hell   Jack Kroll*

Edward Albee's *The Lady From Dubuque* frightened me. There was nothing onstage beyond the forced gestures and stilted language that were so dispiriting in Albee's work of the '70s. The air of the theater seemed scorched by a negative charge, the electrocution of creative force. As a young playwright, Albee brought a savage eloquence to the sense of alienation that seemed to find its natural voice in the theater of Beckett, Genet, Ionesco and Pinter. Albee was angrier than the so-called Angry Young Men of the British theater, and his anger had a metaphysical force that carried the day with a vaunting theatricality that culminated in *Who's Afraid of Virginia Woolf?* Why was he angry? The feeling transcended cause, just as Leontes in *The Winter's Tale* is jealous because jealousy expresses his deepest nature. The young Albee *was* his anger, his vituperation that expressed his deep dissatisfaction with the universe and with himself.

Behind metaphysical rage and despair lies a kind of prayer—the despairing consciousness doesn't want to be alone with its self-incinerating knowledge. In *Tiny Alice*, Albee tried to synthesize the anguish and the prayer: the result was deeply fractured but still had a shaking power; theatrically, Albee still could pull the trigger. *The Lady From Dubuque* is a popgun of a play. Outwardly, it has the form of *Virginia Woolf*, the internecine wolf pack ravaging between husbands and wives, friends and colleagues. In a starkly chic living room with gray walls and black furniture, three couples belt back the booze and belt each other all over the place with insults. . . .

It's "your nice, average, desperate evening," as someone says, but the perverse exultation that Albee generated in *Virginia Woolf* is replaced here

*From *Newsweek*, 11 February 1980. © 1980, Newsweek, Inc. All rights reserved. Reprinted by permission.

by an almost abstract blankness: the insults, the drinking, the tears of poor Lucinda, the violent loutishness of Fred, the philosophic geniality of Carol, are all stupefyingly boring and empty. So is Sam's identity problem, which he turns into a cheerless game of Twenty Questions, and any pity we feel for the horrid but expiring Jo comes from the powerful acting of Frances Conroy, who creates an unsettling choreography of ultimate pain that seems to come from her body and spirit at the same time.

The Lady From Dubuque is Albee's dea ex machina (Irene Worth), who arrives in her wide-brimmed black hat and long fur boa, accompanied by a dapper black assistant and karate expert named Oscar (Earle Hyman). She claims to be Jo's mother, but Sam insists vehemently that she's not, which gets him tied up and slapped around for his trouble by his vengeful guests. The Lady From Dubuque is the famous phrase of Harold Ross, the original editor of The New Yorker who defined his sophisticated magazine by saying that it wasn't for her. Albee seems to intend it as an ironic title for a contemporary God figure, and as that it makes a thin eschatological joke. Irene Worth's high style and grandiose irony only heighten the emptiness of the character as an embodiment of cosmic resolution.

There's an appalling amount of chatter about identity, death, finality and the end of the world, which may mean that Albee's living room is really a Hi-Tech Hell for the posthumous spirits of a burnt-out civilization. Director Alan Schneider keeps the play running briskly, but it's the briskness of one of those self-destructing machines that were chic in the art world twenty years ago. The entire enterprise is a hollow echo of the playwright who was once able to express the terror of spiritual death in a universe poisoned by the bad faith of mankind.

[Review of *Counting the Ways*]   Thomas P. Adler*

The first new play to receive its world premiere in the Olivier, largest of the three theatres comprising the National complex on London's South Bank, was not, as one might have anticipated, by Pinter or Stoppard, but by Edward Albee. And *Counting the Ways* is hardly even a play in any traditional understanding of the term. But then, Albee's works have come more and more of late to resemble musical compositions, and this is no exception; as he says of it: "What I intended was something like a set of piano pieces by Satie."

If in *Seascape*, his most recent full-length play, there was still a conflict eventuating in one of Albee's typical highly charged climaxes, here

*From *Educational Theatre Journal* (October 1977):407–8. Reprinted by permission of The John Hopkins University Press.

one can just barely discern the outlines of a conflict, and certainly nothing resembling a resolution. The movement (not progression, mind you) of this two-character play is circular: at the opening, She demands, "Do you love me?" — the same question He puts at the end.

The work's subtitle, "A Vaudeville," indicates what the audience should expect: a series of skits, or turns, twenty or so during the seventy-minute evening, each punctuated by a blackout and the sound of a whipcrack. (Inexplicably, a companion piece entitled *Listening* that Albee intended to round out the evening is omitted from this production.) Several of these brief scenes, which more than one London critic aptly compared to animated *New Yorker* or Thurber cartoons, are duets, some — including a memorable one about the time She received twin gardenia corsages for a dance — are monologues, while at least one is wordless.

Miraculously, this admittedly slight play did not get lost on the vast Olivier stage, mainly because it was so engagingly performed by Michael Gough and Beryl Reid. Given the chance to extemporize, when the legend "Identify Yourselves" flashes on, Reid regales us with a marvelously comic yarn about dispatching unwanted late-night visitors by apologizing: "I'm in bed with someone I don't know very well."

In the parts Albee has written, He and She, who resemble a sketchier but slightly more hopeful Tobias and Agnes from *A Delicate Balance*, pursue the author's recurrent concerns in an appropriately wistful mood: the death of sexual ardor (they have exchanged their double bed for twins); the waning of culture and civilization; the advancing existential void. But mostly, it is about the difficulty — the impossibility — of "counting the ways," of telling how we love, or even that we love, now that the words we have for expressing things of the heart have been so debased that they appear no more honest than the shop-worn formulas on greeting cards. Yet Albee's own poetic dialogue runs the same risk, and cannot always avoid seeming too studied, too precious.

All of which Albee encapsulates in two successive scenes here: In the first, He plays "She loves me, she loves me not," pulling the petals off a rose, finally popping the bud into his mouth when the answer appears to be coming out wrong; in the next, She turns the game around, putting the petals back on the rose, frantically saying, "Me loves he, not me loves he." Absurd, yes. But no more so than questing after verbal assurances as if they could substitute for, let alone adequately demonstrate, an emotional truth. And even if we could attain such certitude, might it not lead to a stultifying complacency?

A major dramatic work like *Who's Afraid of Virginia Woolf?* or *A Delicate Balance*? Hardly. Destined to be a commercial or critical success? Never. And yet, accepted on its own terms, this entertaining "diversion" — for that seems an apt classification — can delight with its considerable charm and wit and occasional beauties of language. For this one viewer, at least, it held the stage better than Peter Hall's sumptuously fitted-out yet essentially characterless mounting of *Tamburlaine I and II* with which it was alternating at the Olivier.

ALBEE AND WORLD THEATER

[Albee as Absurdist]

Martin Esslin*

Edward Albee (born in 1928) comes into the category of the Theatre of the Absurd precisely because his work attacks the very foundations of American optimism. His first play, *The Zoo Story* (1958), which shared the bill at the Provincetown Playhouse with Beckett's *Krapp's Last Tape*, already showed the forcefulness and bitter irony of his approach. In the realism of its dialogue and in its subject matter — an outsider's inability to establish genuine contact with a dog, let alone any human being — *The Zoo Story* is closely akin to the world of Harold Pinter. But the effect of this brilliant one-act duologue between Jerry, the outcast, and Peter, the conformist bourgeois, is marred by its melodramatic climax; when Jerry provokes Peter into drawing a knife and then impales himself on it, the plight of the schizophrenic outcast is turned into an act of sentimentality, especially as the victim expires in touching solicitude and fellow-feeling for his involuntary murderer.

But after an excursion into grimly realistic social criticism . . . Albee produced a play that clearly takes up the style and subject-matter of the Theatre of the Absurd and translates it into a genuine American idiom. *The American Dream* (1959–60; first performed at the York Playhouse, New York, on 24 January 1961) fairly and squarely attacks the ideals of progress, optimism, and faith in the national mission, and pours scorn on the sentimental ideals of family life, togetherness, and physical fitness; the euphemistic language and unwillingness to face the ultimate facts of the human condition that in America, even more than in Europe, represent the essence of bourgeois assumptions and attitudes. *The American Dream* shows an American family — Mommy, Daddy, Grandma — in search of a replacement for the adopted child that went wrong and died. The missing member of the family arrives in the shape of a gorgeous young man, the embodiment of the American dream, who admits that he consists only of muscles and a healthy exterior, but is dead inside, drained of genuine

*From *The Theatre of the Absurd*, rev. ed. © 1961, 1968, 1969 by Martin Esslin. Reprinted by permission of Doubleday & Company, Inc.

feeling and the capacity for experience. He will do anything for money —
so he will even consent to become a member of the family. The language of
The American Dream resembles that of Ionesco in its masterly combina-
tion of clichés. But these clichés, in their euphemistic, baby-talk tone, are
as characteristically American as Ionesco's are French. The most disagree-
able verities are hidden behind the corn-fed cheeriness of advertising
jingles and family-magazine unctuousness. There are very revealing contrasts in the way these writers of different nationalities use the clichés of
their own countries — the mechanical hardness of Ionesco's French platitudes; the flat, repetitive obtuseness of Pinter's English nonsense dialogue;
and the oily glibness and sentimentality of the American cliché in Albee's
promising and brilliant first example of an American contribution to the
Theatre of the Absurd.

With his first full-length play *Who's Afraid of Virginia Woolf?* (first
performed in New York on 14 October 1962) Albee achieved his break-
through into the first rank of contemporary American playwrights. On the
surface this is a savage marital battle in the tradition of Strindberg and the
later O'Neill. George, the unsuccessful academic, his ambitious wife, and
the young couple they are entertaining, are realistic characters; their
world, that of drink-sodden and frustrated university teachers, is wholly
real. But a closer inspection reveals elements which clearly still relate the
play to Albee's earlier work and the Theatre of the Absurd. George and
Martha (there are echoes there of George and Martha Washington) have
an imaginary child which they treat as real, until in the cold dawn of that
wild night they decide to 'kill' it by abandoning their joint fantasy. Here
the connexion to *The American Dream* with its horrid dream-child of the
ideal all-American boy becomes clear; thus there are elements of dream
and allegory in the play (is the dream-child which cannot become real
among people torn by ambition and lust something like the American
ideal itself?); and there is also a Genet-like ritualistic element in its
structure as a sequence of three rites: act I — 'Fun and Games'; act II —
'*Walpurgisnacht*'; act III — 'Exorcism'.

With *Tiny Alice* (1963) Albee broke new ground in a play which
clearly tried to evolve a complex image of man's search for truth and
certainty in a constantly shifting world, without ever wanting to construct
a complete allegory or to offer any solutions to the questions he raised.
Hence the indignant reaction of some critics seems to have been based on a
profound misunderstanding. The play shows its hero buffeted between the
church and the world of cynical wisdom and forced by the church to
abandon his vocation for the priesthood to marry a rich woman who made
a vast donation dependent on his decision. Yet immediately the marriage
is concluded the lady and her staff depart, leaving the hero to a lonely
death. The central image of the play is the mysterious model of the great
mansion in which the action takes place, that occupies the centre of the
stage. Inside this model every room corresponds to one in the real house,

and tiny figures can be observed repeating the movements of the people who occupy it. Everything that happens in the macrocosm is exactly repeated in the microcosm of the model. And no doubt inside the model there is another smaller model, which duplicates everything that happens on an even tinier scale, and so on *ad infinitum*, upwards and downwards on the scale of being. It is futile to search for the philosophical meaning of such an image. What it communicates is a mood, a sense of the mystery, the impenetrable complexity of the universe. And that is precisely what a dramatic poet is after.

Albee and the Absurd:
The American Dream and
The Zoo Story

Brian Way*

As the American dramatist is often torn between a desire for the apparent security of realism and the temptation to experiment, so in Edward Albee's work, we see a tension between realism and the theatre of the absurd. *The Death of Bessie Smith* is a purely realistic play, and *Who's Afraid of Virginia Woolf?* is, for all its showiness, no more than a cross between sick drawing-room comedy and naturalistic tragedy. *The Zoo Story, The Sandbox* and *The American Dream* are, on the face of it, absurd plays, and yet, if one compares them with the work of Beckett, Ionesco or Pinter, they all retreat from the full implications of the absurd when a certain point is reached. Albee still believes in the validity of reason – that things can be proved, or that events can be shown to have definite meanings – and, unlike Beckett and the others, is scarcely touched by the sense of living in an absurd universe. Interesting and important as his plays are, his compromise seems ultimately a failure of nerve – a concession to those complementary impulses towards cruelty and self-pity which are never far below the surface of his work.

Albee has been attracted to the theatre of the absurd mainly, I think, because of the kind of social criticism he is engaged in. Both *The Zoo Story* and *The American Dream* are savage attacks on the American Way of Life. . . .

The American Way of Life, in the sense in which I am using the phrase, is a structure of images; and the images, through commercial and political exploitation, have lost much of their meaning. When the Eisenhower family at prayer becomes a televised political stunt, or the family meal an opportunity for advertising frozen foods, the image of the

*From *American Theatre*, Stratford-Upon-Avon Studies 10 (London: Edward Arnold, 1967), 189–208. Reprinted by permission of the publisher.

family is shockingly devalued. The deception practised is more complex than a simple lie: it involves a denial of our normal assumptions about evidence — about the relation between the observed world and its inner reality. This is why the techniques of the theatre of the absurd, which is itself preoccupied with the devaluation of language and of images, and with the deceptive nature of appearances, are so ideally suited to the kind of social criticism Albee intends. It is for this reason, too, that he has felt able to use the techniques of the theatre of the absurd, while stopping short of an acceptance of the metaphysic of the absurd upon which the techniques are based. It is possible, clearly, to see the absurd character of certain social situations without believing that the whole of life is absurd. In Albee's case, however, this has meant a restriction of scope, and his plays do not have the poetic quality or imaginative range of *Waiting for Godot*, for instance, or *The Caretaker*, or *Rhinoceros*. . . .

Albee has used these images of non-reason in his attack on the American Way of Life without, as I have said, accepting the underlying vision which generated them. His work belongs to the second level of the theatre of the absurd: it shows a brilliantly inventive sense of what can be done with the techniques, but stops short of the metaphysic which makes the techniques completely meaningful. Nevertheless, *The American Dream* and *The Zoo Story* are the most exciting productions of the American theatre in the last fifteen years, and I propose to analyse them in detail in such a way as to bring out particularly what they have in common with other absurd plays and where they diverge from them.

In *The American Dream* (1961), Albee is closer to Ionesco than to any other dramatist. Like Ionesco, he sees the absurd localized most sharply in conventions of social behaviour. For both dramatists, the normal currency of social intercourse — of hospitality, or courtesy, or desultory chat — has lost its meaning, and this "devaluation of language," to use Martin Esslin's invaluable phrase, is an index for them of the vacuity of the social life represented. The inane civilities exchanged by the Smiths and the Martins in *The Bald Prima Donna* enact the complete absence of human contact which is the reality beneath the appearance of communication. We see similar effects in *The American Dream* in the opening exchanges:

DADDY: Uh . . . Mrs. Barker, is it? Won't you sit down?

MRS. BARKER: I don't mind if I do.

MOMMY: Would you like a cigarette, and a drink, and would you like to cross your legs?

MRS. BARKER: You forget yourself, Mommy; I'm a professional woman. But I will cross my legs.

DADDY: Yes, make yourself comfortable.

MRS. BARKER: I don't mind if I do.   (p. 28)

Ionesco and Albee use this method of exposing the essential meaning-lessness of most middle-class language and gesture as a basis for much wider effects than the mere deflation of certain speech-habits. In Ionesco, particularly, it becomes a major principle of dramatic construction. He subjects conventional patterns of behaviour, the clichés of which much everyday speech is entirely composed, and the most complacent and unthinking of our normal assumptions and attitudes, to a disturbing shift of perspective: he places them in grotesque situations where they are ludicrously inappropriate, and their meaninglessness is stripped bare. *Amédée* (1954) is probably his most elaborate exercise in this technique. . . .

The dialogue is composed entirely of clichés, and is dominated by mundane bourgeois attitudes — chiefly the anxiety to preserve appearances before neighbours, and the desperate determination to act as if everything were normal. (Ionesco's final stage direction, of course, underlines this.) As so often in absurd drama, the language and the action contradict each other. The grotesque horror of the situation is played off against the ludicrous pretense at maintaining a sense of the ordinary suggested by the language. When middle-class clichés and stock attitudes are shown to be so evidently meaningless in this situation, one is directed to the conclusion that they are in fact meaningless in all situations, and that only the blindness of habit conceals this fact from us.

Albee develops the situation in *The American Dream* along similar lines. He sees the American Way of Life as one in which normal human feelings and relationships have been deprived of meaning. The gestures of love, sexual attraction, parental affection, family feeling and hospitality remain, but the actual feelings which would give the gestures meaning have gone. To show this in sharp dramatic terms, Albee constructs a situation of gestures which are normally supposed to have meaning but, as transposed by him, are seen to have none. . . .

The characters are isolated from each other in little worlds of selfishness, impotence, and lovelessness, and all warmth of human contact is lost. It would be inaccurate to say that the gestures of love and connection ("You're my sweet Daddy" — "I love my Mommy") are deflated; their meaninglessness is exposed by tagging them on as after-thoughts to phases of the action where they are — as here — ludicrously inapplicable.

This method of scene-construction determines not only the local effects of *The American Dream*, but the major patterns of the play. Albee is disturbed and agonized by the extent of the dislocation of people's relationships and the imprisoning isolation of which these scenes are images. The play's central image of this failure of human feeling and contact is sterility — the inability to beget or bear a child — and as its title suggests, Albee tries to give the image the widest possible social reference.

He implies that the sterility which the audience sees in his characters is typical of the society as a whole, and is created and perpetuated by the society. For him, the American Way of Life systematically eliminates, in the name of parental care, and social and moral concern, every trace of natural human feeling and every potentiality for warm human contact from those who have to live by it, and especially from the young.

When Mommy, Daddy and Grandma, and the quality of their lives, have been firmly established, Mrs. Barker, a representative of the Bye-Bye Adoption Service, calls on them. She forgets why she has called (a common motif in absurd plays, underlining the arbitrariness and irrelevance of all action in an absurd world, though little more than a gimmick here). Grandma, to help her, gives her a "hint" — the story of "a man very much like Daddy, and a woman very much like Mommy", and "a dear lady" very much like Mrs. Barker. It is a story of individual sterility:

> The woman who was very much like Mommy, said that she and the man who was very much like Daddy had never been blessed with anything very much like a bumble of joy . . .
> . . . she said that they wanted a bumble of their own, but that the man, who was very much like Daddy, couldn't have a bumble; and the man, who was very much like Daddy, said that yes, they had wanted a bumble of their own, but that the woman, who was very much like Mommy, couldn't have one and that now they wanted to buy something very much like a bumble.   (p. 40)

It is also a story of that collective sterility which eliminates natural impulses in others. Mommy and Daddy buy "a bumble of joy," and its upbringing is a series of mutilations at their hands:

> GRANDMA:. . . *then*, it began to develop an interest in its you-know-what.
>
> MRS. BARKER: In its you-know-what! Well! I hope they cut its hands off at the wrists!
>
> GRANDMA: Well, yes, they did that eventually. But first, they cut off its you-know-what.
>
> MRS. BARKER: A much better idea!
>
> GRANDMA: That's what they thought. But after they cut off its you-know-what, it *still* put its hands under the covers, *looking* for its you-know-what. So, finally, they had to cut off its hands at the wrists.
>   (pp. 40–1)

The child's eyes are gouged out, it is castrated, its hands are cut off, its tongue is cut out, and finally it dies. In this brilliant sequence of dramatic writing, Albee has given us a fable of his society, where all the capabilities for connection — eyes to see, sexual organs with which to love, hands to touch, and tongue to speak — are destroyed, and the victim of the socializing processes of the American Way of Life, humanly speaking, dies. And it is all done in the name of affection and care. Once again, the gestures of human contact survive grotesquely in the coyness with which the sexual act and the begetting and rearing of children are described ("being blessed with a bumble of joy," "its you-know-what"), and the gestures are seen to be hideously and mockingly at odds with the reality.

Towards the end of the play, the victim himself appears — the "twin" of "the bumble of joy." He is a young man with all the external marks of youth and vitality, handsome, muscular and self-confident. Grandma recognizes in him immediately the American Dream. But just as the gestures of parental love have been only a sham, his outwardly vigorous youthful appearance is only a shell. His life is a terrible emptiness, a series of deprivations identical with the mutilations practised on his "twin" brother:

> I don't know what became of my brother . . . to the rest of myself . . . except that, from time to time, in the years that have passed, I have suffered losses . . . that I can't explain. A fall from grace . . . a departure of innocence . . . loss . . . loss . . . Once . . . it was as if all at once my heart . . . became numb . . . almost as though I . . . almost as though . . . just like that . . . it had been wrenched from my body . . . and from that time I have been unable to love . . .
>
> And there is more . . . there are more losses, but it all comes down to this: I no longer have the capacity to feel anything. I have no emotions. I have been drained, torn asunder . . . disembowelled. I have, now, only my person . . . my body, my face. I use what I have . . . I let people love me . . . I accept the syntax around me, for while I cannot relate . . . I know I must be related *to* . . .   (pp. 50-1)

This moving speech is one of those moments of total illumination in absurd drama (Aston's account of his experiences in the psychiatric ward in *The Caretaker* is the finest example) where a character, for a moment, sees the entire hopelessness and confusion of his existence before lapsing once more into the "syntax around" him. The Young Man has to accept that syntax — the meaningless gestures of human affection and contact — when he is adopted, or re-adopted, by Mommy and Daddy. While they celebrate with Sauterne, Grandma observes sardonically from the wings: "Well, I guess that just about wraps it up. I mean, for better or worse, this is a comedy . . ." The bad Sauterne is drunk, and sterility, impotence, lovelessness and disconnection are masked with the gestures of celebration, conviviality and family-love, suggesting as they do all that is lacking — the physical warmth of sex and parenthood, and the meaningfulness of people being together. Only the gestures remain, these gestures which have been simultaneously canonized and deprived of meaning by the publicists of the American Way of Life: the politicians, the admen, the columnists and the TV commentators.

It is significant that the only character in *The American Dream* with any vitality or attractiveness is Grandma — and she is "rural," from an older way of life. The way in which she is juxtaposed against the Young Man who is the American Dream seems to symbolize a society in which the natural order of life has been reversed, in which the younger one is the less chance one has of being alive.

These patterns and images occur elsewhere in Albee's work. His sense of human isolation and despair is the central preoccupation of *The Death of Bessie Smith* (a bad play, it seems to me), and in *The Sandbox*, which parallels the situation of *The American Dream* most interestingly, though on too cramped a stage. The image of sterility is very prominent in *Who's Afraid of Virginia Woolf?*, but is used there much less effectively than in *The American Dream*. Apart from its spectacular ability to amuse and shock, *Virginia Woolf* has a certain emptiness — no incident or image in it has reference to anything wider than the neuroses of its characters.

His first play, *The Zoo Story* (1959), however, contains some very fine dramatic writing. Again it is an exploration of the farce and the agony of human isolation. . . .

In its finest scene, the long speech in which Jerry describes his attempt to form a relationship with his landlady's dog, *The Zoo Story* offers a superb example of what I call pseudo-crisis — the second pattern of absurd writing that is central to Albee's work. In classic drama, crisis is one of the most important means by which the action is significantly advanced. In *Othello*, for instance, when Iago tells Othello that he has seen Desdemona's handkerchief in Cassio's hands, a whole complex of tensions is brought to a head, and after this crisis, the catastrophe is measurably nearer, and Othello is demonstrably a stage further on his course of violence and madness. In the absurd play, on the other hand, what I call a pseudo-crisis occurs when a similar complex of tensions is brought to a head without resolving anything, without contributing to any development or progression, serving in fact to demonstrate that nothing as meaningful as progression or development can occur, emphasizing that complexity and tension are permanent and unresolvable elements of a world of confusion. Lucky's speech in *Waiting for Godot* is perhaps the most elaborate and extreme occurrence. Harold Pinter's work, too, is full of pseudo-crisis, the funniest instance, perhaps, being Davies's account of his visit to the monastery at Luton in search of boots (*The Caretaker*). . . .

The dramatic structure of this part of Jerry's speech reflects very closely the rhythms of pseudo-crisis — the excitement, the tensions, rising to the shouted climax ("WITH GOD WHO IS . . .") and then slipping away into the lax despairing tempo of its inconclusive end ("with . . . some day, with people"). The hopelessness of this is quickly recognized, and Jerry reverts to his attempt with the dog, but this, too, has failed and proved nothing. In this final downward curve of the pseudo-crisis everything is conditional and hypothetical ("It would be a A START! Where better to make a beginning ... . to understand, and just possibly be understood . . .").

In this early play, there is an attempt, too, to relate Jerry's agony to the wider social pattern — to see it as a product of the American Way of Life:

> I am a *permanent transient,* and my home is in the sickening rooming-houses on the West Side of New York City, which is the greatest city in the world. Amen.   (p. 133)

In spite of the bitter force of this, however, it is clear that the impulse of social criticism has only been very partially translated into dramatic terms. Jerry's outburst here tells the audience how to react; it is almost a piece of editorializing, and doesn't have the persuasiveness of art, the sense that ideas have become vision and are being enacted.

At such moments in *The Zoo Story,* and most of all, of course, at the moment of Jerry's melodramatic and sentimental death, we are left with a sense of dissatisfaction whose root causes are to be found in that compromise with the experimental theatre that seems to me so characteristic of American dramatists. The action and the dialogue are dislocated, arbitrary and absurd (pre-eminently in Jerry's story of the dog) up to the moment of Jerry's death, and then all the traditional assumptions of naturalism flood back into the play. It is postulated, quite as firmly as in any Ibsen social drama, that a catastrophe is also a resolution of the situation of the play, and that events, however obscure, ultimately have a definite and unambiguous meaning. Jerry spent his dying breath telling us what the play means as explicitly as does Lona Hessel at the end of *Pillars of Society.* This sudden reversion to a faith in the validity of rational explanations makes previous events in the play seem arbitrary in a wholly unjustified way: they can no longer be seen as appropriate symbols of life in an absurd universe. The slightest hint that events in an absurd play are amenable to everyday explanation is completely destructive of their dramatic effectiveness. If it were possible to say of Vladimir and Estragon, or of Davies, that they are crazy bums who should be locked up, *Waiting for Godot* and *The Caretaker* would be ruined. In spite of some striking effects, it is possible to entertain this suspicion about Jerry, and it is largely because of this misguided attempt to exploit the advantages both of the theatre of the absurd and of realism, that *The Zoo Story* misses the greatness which at times seems so nearly within its grasp.

The American Dream does not show so straightforward an evasion of the absurd as *The Zoo Story,* but it lacks even more completely the metaphysical dimension. One can perhaps best begin accounting for its limitations by noting a distinction which Martin Esslin makes most perceptively: first there is —

> . . . the experience that Ionesco expresses in plays like *The Bald Prima Donna* or *The Chairs,* Adamov in *La Parodie,* or N. F. Simpson in *A Resounding Tinkle.* It represents the satirical, parodistic aspect of the Theatre of the Absurd, its social criticism, its pillorying of an

inauthentic, petty society. This may be the most easily accessible, and therefore most widely recognized, message of the Theatre of the Absurd, but it is far from being its most essential or most significant feature.

Behind the satirical exposures of the absurdity of inauthentic ways of life, the Theatre of the Absurd is facing up to a deeper layer of absurdity — the absurdity of the human condition itself in a world where the decline of religious belief has deprived man of certainties.   (pp. 291–2)

The American Dream is effective only within the limits of the first category. It is too exclusively and merely a satire of American middle-class aspirations and self-deceptions. It is, above all, a play about Other People, not about ourselves: when we laugh at Mommy and Daddy, we are laughing at emotional and sexual failures which we do not recognize as our own and in which we refuse to be implicated, whereas when we laugh at Davies, or at Vladimir and Estragon, we are laughing at our own illusions and recognizing our own acts of hubris, self-deception and failure. Since *The American Dream* doesn't implicate us, it never becomes tragic. Harold Pinter has said of his own play:

> As far as I am concerned *The Caretaker* is funny up to a point. Beyond that point it ceases to be funny, and it was because of that point that I wrote it.[1]

Albee never reached this point except perhaps for the brief moment I have noted where the Young Man's sense of loss is met with Grandma's compassion. But we do not otherwise have to regard the characters — certainly not Mommy and Daddy — as tragic or even terrifying: they enact for us a certain attitude to America in 1960; they do not go beyond it to tell us anything about the human condition.

In one important sense, *The American Dream* does not belong even to the "satirical, parodistic" category of absurd plays. It is, like *The Zoo Story*, a play which reaches a definite conclusion and which implicitly claims that its events have an unambiguous meaning. Grandma's "hint" to Mrs. Barker is a fable of almost diagrammatic directness and simplicity; by contrast, the Fireman's fables in *The Bald Prima Donna* are absurd parodies, satirizing the assumption that a tale has a "moral," and further, undermining our confidence in the kind of popular wisdom represented by the morals of Aesop's fables.

Above all, at the end of *The American Dream*, Grandma can tell the audience:

> Well, I guess that just about wraps it up. I mean, for better or worse, this is a comedy, and I don't think we'd better go any further. No, definitely not. So let's leave things as they are right now . . . while everybody's happy . . . while everybody's got what he wants . . . or everybody's got what he thinks he wants. Good night, dears.

Her remark, "Well, I guess that just about wraps it up," is ironical only in the most external sense — in the sense that Mommy and Daddy and the Young Man and Mrs. Baker, who have all just drunk "To satisfaction," are in for some unpleasant surprises. As far as Grandma and the audience are concerned the situation really is wrapped up, and the play has proved its point as self-consciously as any theorem. Again, *The Bald Prima Donna* is a significant contrast, ending not with a proof but returning in a circle to the point at which it began.

It is only when one compares *The American Dream* with the greatest absurd plays that the real damage done by this compromise between reason and the absurd can be fully reckoned. In the first place, many of the local effects seem to be, in retrospect, merely tricks. The way in which it handles argument will illustrate what I mean. The metaphysic of the absurd, as I have said, involves a loss of faith in reason and in the validity of rational explorations of experience, and one of the most characteristic forms of writing of the absurd theatre, developed to represent this on the stage, is the systematic pursuit of the irrelevant. Absurd plays are full of arguments which lead nowhere, or which parody the processes of logic, or which are conducted from ludicrous premises. At the beginning of *The American Dream* Mommy's account of her argument in the department store as to whether her hat was beige or wheat-coloured is a clear instance of this. But it does not symbolize anything deeper: far from being an index of a world in which everything is too uncertain to be settled by argument, it takes its place in a play which, from its determination to prove a point, is naïvely confident in the power of argument. It therefore seems, in retrospect, no more than a trick to get the play started. By comparison, the argument in *Rhinoceros,* as to whether the animals which charged down the street had one horn or two, is funnier and also infinitely more disturbing: it represents the last feeble efforts of ordinary men to cling to their reassuring certitudes as their world founders into chaos, and, as they themselves, through turning into rhinoceroses, are about to lose their very identities. Albee's work lacks this imaginative dimension, to say nothing of the compassion, horror and despair, implicit in the periodic speculations of Vladimir and Estragon on the nature of Godot. . . .

Notes

1. Letter to *Sunday Times* (14 August, 1960); quoted Esslin, p. 218.

The Playwright in the Making   Gilbert Debusscher[*]

. . . It took Albee another five years to embark on a playwrighting career with *The Zoo Story*.

It is hard to imagine a stranger odyssey than that which brought this play full circle from its initial polite rejection by Off-Broadway producers (under the pretext that it was too short and that "audiences don't like short plays") to its ultimate smashing success in Greenwich Village where it has been continuously performed since January 14, 1960. In his Preface, written in July 1960 for the printed play, Albee describes its long journey:

> . . . a young composer friend of mine, William Flanagan by name, looked at the play, liked it, and sent it to several friends of his, among them David Diamond, another American composer, resident in Italy; Diamond liked the play and sent it on to a friend of *his*, a Swiss actor, Pinkas Braun; Braun liked the play, made a tape recording of it, playing both its roles, which he sent on to Mrs. Stefani Hunzinger, who heads the drama department of the S. Fischer Verlag, a large publishing house in Frankfurt; she, in turn . . . well, through her it got to Berlin, and to production. From New York to Florence to Zurich to Frankfurt to Berlin.

Albee went to Berlin to attend his first success. *The Zoo Story* was favorably received by the audiences of the Berlin Festival, which surprised the author himself:

> One concentrates, but one cannot see the stage action clearly; one can hear but barely; one tries to follow the play, but one can make no sense of it. And, if one is called to the stage afterwards to take a bow, one wonders why, for one can make no connection between the work just presented and one's self. Naturally, this feeling was complicated in the case of *The Zoo Story*, as the play was being presented in German, a language of which I knew not a word, and in Berlin, too, an awesome city. But it has held true since. The high points of a person's life can be appreciated so often only in retrospect.

After its success at the Schiller Theater Werkstatt, *he Zoo Story* returned to New York. The Provincetown Playhouse, a Greenwich Village theater whose name remains linked with the career of O'Neill, presented it to the American public on January 14, 1960, as part of a double bill also featuring *Krapp's Last Tape* by Samuel Beckett. The audience was subjected to an uninterrupted crescendo, a one-act play blending on the one hand the revolt of the flamboyant bohemian against a placid bourgeoisie, and on the other the solitude of the vagabond, the emotional

*From *Edward Albee: Tradition and Renewal*, trans. Anne Williams (Brussels: Center for American Studies, 1969), 9–21. Reprinted by permission of the author.

isolation of the social exile, the envious obsession with bourgeois comfort, the basic need for communication even at the price of death. . . .

The primary theme which emerges from this play is the virulent criticism of bourgeois complacency, of the hypocrisy of a good conscience, the emptiness of the false values of American life supported by advertising and pseudo-intellectual magazines. In the person of Peter, the middle class is heckled, ridiculed, degraded, denounced and finally driven to crime. Peter lets himself be swept along in a conversation he has not desired, ridiculed with jokes he does not understand, led to reveal what he hides even from himself, enraged by Jerry's childish absurdities, and finally forced to kill without suspecting for a moment that he has been lured into a trap. This trap, which his middle-class blinkers prevent him from seeing, is his true identity. The real pain which he experiences at the sight of his involuntary crime exorcises him of his former myths. In his final flight he carries with him the ghastly images which Jerry has evoked; he will never be able to rid himself either of them or of his remorse. His life is irrevocably changed, and thus his final cry is charged with a significant ambiguity: we sense that he laments less for Jerry, the voluntary victim, the disguised suicide, than for himself, for his lost peace, for the discovery of his own inanity, for the exposure of the delusion that is his life.

Can we say in corollary, as Robert Brustein implies in reproach, that Edward Albee glorifies the bohemian and presents him as authentic man fully realized? It is highly questionable. Jerry's ironic attitude and his constant superiority are played, not against an antagonist worth conquering, but against a man reduced to a vegetal state. If he seems more engaging, it is because he has suffered more than Peter, because "nothing of man is alien to him." Rather than a victory, his death appears to be an escape from an unbearable world and a hellish life, a capitulation to the interior contradictions which tear him apart. His last words do not express the jubilation of a victor but the humble thanks of a wounded animal put out of his misery at last.

For him, death is the end of a long calvary, the confirmation of his human and social inadequacies. What gives it validity in our eyes is its power to enlighten another man, to reveal him to himself, to save him from the unreal life in which he had stagnated for so long. But Jerry is far from being the idealistic planner, the Gregers Werle of *The Wild Duck*, for at the moment of death he says: "Well, here we are. You see? Here we are. But . . . I don't know . . . could I have planned all this? No . . . no, I couldn't have. But I think I did." Albee reverses the Ibsen roles: it is Jerry who pays for opening Peter's eyes, while for Peter perhaps, it is the start of a new life, the life of a man instead of an ostrich. In the didactic Jerry-Peter relationship, we see the prefiguration of that which links Martha and George, the older couple, with young Honey and Nick in *Who's Afraid of Virginia Woolf?* There too the elders have exposed by their pathetic example the deceptions on which Nick and Honey's life is based. When the night is over, the young couple have been exorcised. Like Peter, they cannot escape the sordid reality which has just confronted them. In fact, it is because they recognize themselves in the picture of a younger George and Martha which has unfolded that they remain all night listening to them: they are fascinated and horrified by their own image.

Jerry pays with his life for his attempt to communicate, to enter into contact with another man. This is the second dominating theme of the play. The impossibility of communicating with "the other" is remarkably expressed by the slowness, awkwardness and difficulty of the dialogue, which often tends toward monologue with Peter a reluctant and monosyllabic partner. The tendency to return to empty commonplaces may be the first trace of Ionesco's influence in this play, but it is also an expression of the difficulty of dealing with essential things. The necessity of speaking, of trusting, of drawing near, is so strong in Jerry, however, that he overcomes the terseness of his interlocutor, social and ideological fetters, and finally physical distance. The final communication, the only real one, is achieved at the price of life itself. Albee suggests here that the essence of the life of Jerry and his kind is solitude, separation and captivity inside one's own skin. An important network of images repeats, modulates and reinforces this theme in the course of the play, and extends it to the human condition in general. First, there is the image of the title, where the world appears as a gigantic zoo in which we all live separated from one another by the bars of our individual cages. The image is repeated in the description of Jerry's pitiable home, with the invert who admires himself in the mirror behind the partition, the Puerto Rican family with their incomprehensible language, and the woman who locks herself in to weep. The theme finally culminates in the long parable of Jerry and the dog, which retraces his vain and pathetic efforts not merely to conciliate but to communicate even with his landlady's Cerberus. All the efforts at rapprochement between human beings are doomed to fail; even sexual experience brings us together only for a ridiculously short moment. Physical contact is only a palliative and not a lasting remedy for the solitude to which we are all condemned.

Albee's sexual preoccupations form the underlying theme of all his works. In *The Zoo Story*, Peter is a man who has been made sterile by his environment; in the eyes of Jerry, his inability to produce sons labels him impotent. Jerry's sexual past is much more oppressive: his family was disrupted when he was at a particularly delicate stage of development; the departure and death of his mother retarded his physical growth and his puberty. All this fills him with shame, and had earlier made him easy prey for the Greek park superintendent's son one year his senior. After this homosexual episode, he became incapable of love. His subsequent heterosexual adventures were purely physical: "And now; oh, do I love the little ladies; really, I love them. For about an hour." The two picture frames in his room remain empty, a symbol of his emotional life, because his affairs are too brief, and because most of his partners "wouldn't be caught in the same room with a camera." This concern with deficient or exacerbated sexuality, with impotence, mutilation or inversion, is also present in all of the later plays, and in *The Ballad of the Sad Cafe* attains grotesque and horrible dimensions.

These three themes — criticism of the bourgeoisie, impossibility of communication, sexual obsession — are combined in what may at first appear to be a purely naturalistic play. But a closer examination reveals the author's much more ambitious intentions. Peter is not a living person; he is an agglomeration of exaggerated traits, a collage of burlesqued and farcical bourgeois characteristics — the incarnation or the caricature of an idea. In him, Albee personifies all the men of his class. He is a bourgeois Everyman, closer to the allegory than the realistic portrayal. But the play is predominantly the story of Jerry, whose portrait is more convincing and more complete. A child crippled by his mother's rejection and abandonment, and an adolescent full of complexes, exposed too early to sexual experience, who grows up without becoming an adult, he is the perpetual wanderer, who commits himself neither emotionally, physically nor geographically. If Peter lacks human substance, Jerry, on the contrary, overflows with authentic detail, true and precise observations. There appears little doubt that in him Albee presents a scarcely disguised self-portrait. But even here the author wanted to surpass pure naturalism. Around this thirty-year-old bohemian whose sacrifice can save Everyman from his limbo is organized a web of symbols which reveal "the face in the carpet," the prototype of Jerry, Jesus-Christ. . . .

[However,] it seems to me that even if the play can be read and the characters understood without symbolic implications, Albee's obvious desire is to universalize their significance and give them a transcendent value. Clearly, then, his design seems to have been to write a sort of modern morality play in the manner of Beckett in *Waiting for Godot*. To do this he used two diametrically opposed methods: he stripped one character of all humanity, removing any possibility that he might inspire emotional identification; at the same time he laid on the other a symbolic burden too heavy for him. But Jerry as Christ-vagabond is not convincing because he dies above all to escape himself and his own isolation, and only secondarily to reveal Peter to himself. To the extent that Jerry is a convincingly naturalistic character, he resists being reduced to a prototype, and the character's content is too specific to support the overwhelming symbolic weight. Finally we should note that if the Christian symbolism is dominant, it is not exclusive: if we have the Crucifixion, descent into hell, resurrection and redemption, we also have Cerberus, Hades and Theseus — and who is to say that the descent into hell is not rather that of Orpheus (the redemption, in fact, remaining unexpressed if not highly doubtful)? This ambitious search for signs seems to have led Miss Zimbardo[1] to codify or organize what are only allusions — certainly present but hardly so systematic as she would make them. Spectators and readers will note these implications and coincidences without the necessity of setting up a coherent system which adds but little to the play.

Moreover it is significant that it was as a naturalistic play that *The Zoo Story* was presented, criticized and praised. From its New York premiere the critics have acclaimed Albee as "a new personality" in the American theater. It seems to me now that that description was premature. *The Zoo Story* stages well, its carefully built up suspense holds the audience, its imaginative flow is faultless. But I would disagree that it is therefore an original work. In fact, the three principal themes which I have discussed above are standard currency in the American theater. Henry Popkin, the critic for the *Sewanee Review*, has pointed out that the type of the obtuse and complacent bourgeois is a frequent character among Off-Broadway authors, citing the television director in Molly Kazan's *The Alligators* and the producer in Jack Gelber's *The Connection*.[2] The impossibility of communicating and the resulting solitude are almost universal themes of contemporary literature. The emphasis placed on sexuality, preferably perverted, is equally common.

The three elements thus united are also integral to the work of Tennessee Williams. Jerry's physical appearance is almost identical, feature for feature, with Val Xavier's in *Orpheus Descending* or Chance Wayne's in *Sweet Bird of Youth* or Kilroy's in *Camino Real*. All of these wanderer-gigolos have passed the age of their splendor and are marked by weariness. It is significant in this regard that all three die at the end of their respective plays (Wayne is castrated, which in Williams amounts to death). The identity is even found at the linguistic level: Jerry acknowledges that he is "an eternal transient;" Val classifies himself among the "fugitive kind." The withered Adonises of Williams have also known "the gothic horror" of hell. Those especially of his short stories in *One Arm* and *Hard Candy*, or his first one-act plays, have a profound kinship with Jerry: although they are beautiful and pure, life has too soon frustrated, disfigured and degraded them. Like Jerry, they live in rooming houses with libidinous tenants (*The Mattress by the Tomato Patch*), homosexual neighbors (*The Angel in the Alcove*), and weeping women (*Portrait of a Madonna* and *The Dark Room*). Williams, like Albee later, wants his character to be greater than he has made him: Val is Orpheus, Kilroy an American Dream prototype. Williams' recent creations are even more characteristic of this tendency, beginning with Sebastian Venable, the doomed poet of *Suddenly Last Summer*, who is surrounded with a Christian symbolism comparable with Jerry's.

In noting the parallels between the two plays, it is interesting to remember that *Suddenly Last Summer* was the great success of the 1957–1958 Off-Broadway season, which corresponded exactly to the period in which Albee wrote *The Zoo Story*. Both authors use the technique of the dominant metaphor, the central image which pervades the play—for one, the omnipresent cage, for the other, the devouring destruction. The structure and rhythm of *The Zoo Story* seem to me to owe much to the last scene of *Suddenly Last Summer*: the cleverly interrupted monologue moves forward first by jerky and monosyllabic staccatos, then through the largo of long confessional passages, toward an unbearable tension which is resolved in a violent and sensational climax. Sebastian throws himself desperately on the hill toward "the sun, that was like a great white bone of a giant beast that had caught on fire in the sky." He is pursued by starving young people, companions of his past perversions, from whom he tries to escape. Death takes on the aspect of a mystical ecstasy, a physical reunion with the god to whom he has given himself, symbolized here by a gigantic phallus. In this final scene Eros-Theos and Thanatos are assembled and blended. It is the same in *The Zoo Story*, particularly if one recognizes in the knife of the final sacrifice the phallic value which the stage-directions try to impose: before the act, Peter "holds the knife with a firm arm," then Jerry throws himself on the arm while "for just a moment, complete silence, Jerry impaled on the knife at the end of Peter's still firm arm. Then Peter screams, pulls away." The mystical ecstasy and the deaths of Sebastian and Peter are thus, in varying degrees, tinged with eroticism.

Albee lacks the repetitive and singing language of the South, the strange poetry, the colorful exoticism of Williams. He distinguishes himself from his predecessor by his tight dialogue, his biting irony verging on sarcasm, his scurrilous vocabulary and his explicit scatological images. In the version of the play which I saw performed in New York, the hallucinatory effect of the description of the dog in "The Story of Jerry and the Dog" made this passage a masterpiece of obscenity, but it was toned down for the printed text. Albee's masters are discernible here, Jean Genet directly, and beyond him Baudelaire.

What remains then that can be called truly original in this first play? Certainly the initial situation, and above all the tardily revealed explanation of the title. It is not to some anecdote exterior to the structure that one owes the final revelation—that this "zoo story" has been precisely that of two beasts who have fought throughout the play with weapons of irony and sarcasm—but to the denouement itself. It must be noted, of course, that a similar process takes place at the end of *Suddenly Last Summer*, where Cukrowicz' retort invites a rereading of the play in a new light. The device of successive and contradictory illumination of the plot will appear again in *Who's Afraid of Virginia Woolf?* where the son of George and Martha is presented under two different aspects in the first and third acts.

Albee's first play falls far short of the shattering originality acclaimed by the enthusiastic critics of the premiere. Nevertheless, it recaptures to its advantage the best of the American theatrical tradition, and bears comparison with the work of Beckett on the same program. Noteworthy for its naturalistic approach to the human being and for its sense of realistic and expressive detail, the play is sustained by a sincerity of tone which sometimes borders on exhibitionism. Albee's overflowing imagination, his gift for repartee, his sense of dialogue are already evident, and these qualities were all recognized by the New York critics four months after its success at the Berlin Festival. And thus the triumph — sudden, unexpected, brutal, and short.

Notes

1. Rose A. Zimbardo, "Symbolism and Naturalism in Edward Albee's *Zoo Story*," *Twentieth Century Literature*, 8 (1962): 10–17.

2. Henry Popkin, "Theatre Chronicle," *Sewanee Review*, 69 (1961):333–345.

Confronting Reality: *Who's Afraid of Virginia Woolf?*

C. W. E. Bigsby*

Richard Schechner, the editor of the *Tulane Drama Review*, greeted Albee's next play, *Who's Afraid of Virginia Woolf?*, as a "persistent escape into morbid fantasy." Like W. D. Maxwell he found it a filthy play and indicted it for its "morbidity and sexual perversity which are there only to titillate an impotent and homosexual theatre and audience." More perversely he saw in the play "an ineluctable urge to escape reality and its concomitant responsibilities by crawling back into the womb, or bathroom, or both."[1] The vigour of this revulsion was shared, however, by other critics who similarly misapprehended Albee's intention in a play which far from endorsing illusion remorselessly peels off protective fantasies in order to reach "the bone . . . the marrow" (v.w. p. 213). Indeed as Alan Schneider, the play's Broadway director, has pointed out, ". . . is Albee not rather dedicated to smashing that rosy view, shocking us with the truth of our present-day behaviour and thought, striving to purge us into *an actual confrontation with reality?*"[2] (my italics).

Who's Afraid of Virginia Woolf? is indeed concerned with the purgation and ultimate destruction of illusion and was in fact at one time to have been called *The Exorcism*. If the play's present title seems at first to be little more than an incomprehensible private joke, however, it is clear that Albee's concern with confrontation does establish something more than a tenuous link between his work and that of Virginia Woolf. For while Mrs. Ramsay, in *To The Lighthouse* (1927), had felt that "To pursue truth with . . . lack of consideration for other people's feelings, to rend the

*From *Confrontation and Commitment: A Study of Contemporary American Drama, 1959–1966* (Columbia: University of Missouri Press, 1968), 79–87. Reprinted by permission of the publisher.

thin veils of civilisation so wantonly, so brutally, was to her . . . an outrage of human decency"[3] on a more fundamental level she had acknowledged the inadequacy of such a reaction for with her mind "she had always seized the fact that there is no reason, order, justice: for suffering, death, the poor. There was no treachery too base for the world to commit; she knew that. No happiness lasted; she knew that."[4] This was the very perception which had been granted to Miller's Quentin, while, like Miller, Virginia Woolf urges confrontation as a genuine response to this perception. Mr. Ramsay accepts that "life is difficult; facts uncompromising; and the passage to that fabled land where our brightest hopes are extinguished, our frail barks founder in darkness . . . one that needs, above all, courage, truth, and the power to endure."[5] . . .

In retreat from reality Albee's characters resort to Faustian distractions, passing through the varying degrees of sensuality from drunkenness to sexuality in a play whose second act is aptly entitled Walpurgisnacht. The retreat into illusion which seems to provide an alternative to a harsh existence is not, however, an attractive alternative. For Albee points out that far from facilitating human contact, illusions rather alienate individuals from one another and serve to emphasise their separation. Out of contact with reality they are like the mad — undeveloped. Indeed this immaturity is emphasised by the child-language which recurs throughout the play.

In a story parable which George recounts, a boy accidentally kills his parents. When he loses his mind as a result he is locked up. Finding him unable to face reality "they jammed a needle in his arm" (v.w. p. 96). This is an image of contemporary life as Albee sees it. For if the needle is replaced by liquor the escape of the child becomes valid for the man, ". . . we cry, and we take our tears, and we put 'em in the ice box, in the goddamn ice trays until they're all frozen and then . . . we put them . . . in our . . . drinks" (v.w. p. 186). Where the young boy retreats into the protection of an asylum man retreats into the closed world of illusion. "Do you know what it is with insane people?" George asks, "Do you? . . . the quiet ones? . . . They don't change . . . they don't grow old . . . the under-use of everything leaves them . . . quite whole" (v.w. p. 97). So the characters in the play itself seem to have arrested their development. In essence they are children. Honey is referred to in Dr. Seuss terms and curls up on the floor like a young child while George and Martha play sad games like "Vicious children" with a "manic" manner.

The play is divided into three acts, "Fun and Games," "Walpurgisnacht," and "The Exorcism" — a progression which, like that of The Zoo Story, leads from humiliation to humility. In the first act Albee begins to probe into the pragmatic values which direct the lives of his four characters and initiates the conflict between Martha and George in which they employ as weapons those fantasies which were to have acted as an asylum. George accuses Martha of having "moved bag and baggage into your own fantasy world." She has, he claims "started playing variation" on these "distortions" (v.w. p. 155). Martha, searching for a weapon with which to hurt her husband, breaks their own code and mentions their son. So the substance of their illusion is used to injure rather than to unify and Martha tells Nick and Honey that "George's biggest problem . . . about our son, about our great big son, is that deep down in the private-most-pit of his gut, he's not completely sure it's his own kid" (v.w. p. 71). The act ends therefore, with George's humiliation.

The second act continues the savage games as George mercilessly lays bare the true nature of his guests' relationship, just as Jerry had penetrated Peter's illusions in Albee's earlier play. With the truth revealed Honey rushes from the room to be sick while Nick retreats into the distraction of drink and sexuality which gives the act its name. This is a retreat familiar enough to George whose whole life since coming to New Carthage has consisted in a similar distraction. He confesses that, "I'm numbed enough . . . and I don't mean by liquor, though maybe that's been part of the process – a gradual, over-the-years going to sleep of the brain cells" (v.w. p. 155). The final physical humiliation which Martha inflicts on him at the end of the act, however, spurs him to wake from this coma. He hurls away the book, which is the symbol of his escapism, as it had been in *The Zoo Story*, and determines to force a direct confrontation with reality.

The third act is thus concerned with the ritualistic exorcism of all illusion. While Martha confesses that she has passed her life "in crummy, totally pointless infidelities" (v.w. p. 189) she pleads with George not to continue "Truth or illusion, George. Doesn't it matter to you . . . at all?" (v.w. p. 204). His answer consists in his conscious murder of their fantasy child – a rite watched with growing apprehension by Honey whose own fear of physical reality had resulted in her present sterility, "NO! . . . I DON'T WANT ANY . . . GO 'WAY . . . I . . . don't . . . want . . . any . . . children. I'm afraid! I don't want to be hurt" (v.w. p. 176). George chants the Latin of the burial service as Martha repeats the detailed mythology which they have invented to give substance to their illusion. This act completes the progression from humiliation to humility for all of the characters. Thus the ending, although not definitive, does hold out the hope of "a real companionship, founded on truth and purged of all falsehood."

In essence the violent games which George and Martha play are the means whereby they finally attain to this simple acceptance – just as Bellow's protagonists win through to affirmation as a result of humiliation. At first the games clearly act as a substitute for sexual excitement. The mounting fury of their bitterness and invective reaches a shouting crescendo and then relaxes abruptly into tenderness. When George pulls a fake gun on Martha at the climax to one of their fights the symbolism becomes overt and is re-enforced by the conversation between them which follows:

GEORGE: You liked that, did you?

MARTHA: Yeah . . . that was pretty good. (*Softer*) C'mon . . . give me a kiss. (v.w. p. 58)

Martha then tries to put George's hand on her breast but he breaks away and aborts the action. Nevertheless their continuing violence does serve to "get down to the bone . . . the marrow." If George is not altogether conscious that their games constitute a gradual disintegration of illusion, however, his final act of sacrifice is made with a full understanding of its implications. Indeed there is evidence that, aware of the danger of illusion, he had previously attempted to destroy the fantasy child:

MARTHA: And George tried.

GEORGE: How did I try, Martha? How did I try?

MARTHA: How did you . . . what? . . . No! No . . . he grew . . . our son grew . . . up; (v.w. p. 224)

While there is no concrete assurance that a confrontation of reality will permanently restore their fractured relationship the closing tableau is of Martha leaning back on George's arm as he puts his hand on her shoulder. The language of this closing section is drastically simplified and the whole scene provides an audible and visual confirmation of the simple and uncomplicated state to which their relationship has returned,

MARTHA: . . . You had to?

GEORGE: Yes.

MARTHA: I don't know.

GEORGE: It was . . . time.

MARTHA: Was it?

GEORGE: Yes.   (v.w. p. 240)

While before they had disavowed their own failure in attacking others they now admit to their joint responsibility for sterility. Together they accept their inability to have children, "*We* couldn't" — a confession to which Albee adds his own comment in a stage direction, "*a hint of communion in this*" (v.w. p. 238). Accepting the Faustian imagery which Albee introduces their final redemption is in essence that which Faust had grasped, "Those who their lives deplore / Truth yet shall heal."[6]

If George and Martha are capable of creating a complex mythology rather than face their true situation then so too is the society which they represent. It is Albee's contention that there is as great a need for society to abandon its complete faith in these abstractions — the American Dream, religion and science — as there had been for George and Martha to abandon theirs.

To both Miller and Albee abstractions such as the American Dream are less visions of the future than alternatives to the present. Since this serves to take individuals out of their direct relationship with actuality, which is a factor of the present, it serves also to take them out of any genuine relationship with each other. Alienation thus becomes less an aspect of the human situation than a consequence of an inauthentic response to that situation. The watch-word of this "success-society" thus becomes "non-involvement." Honey does not "want to know anything" (v.w. p. 178) while her husband preserves his "scientific detachment in the face of . . . life" (v.w. p. 100). Attempts at establishing contact are scornfully rejected:

> GEORGE: (*After a silence*) I've tried to . . . tried to reach you . . . to . . .
>
> NICK: (*Contemptuously*) . . . make contact?
>
> GEORGE: Yes.
>
> NICK: (*Still*) . . . communicate?
>
> GEORGE: Yes. Exactly.
>
> NICK: Aw . . . that *is* touching . . . that is . . . downright moving . . . that's what it is. (*With sudden vehemence*) UP YOURS!   (v.w. p. 116)

In the face of this failure in society both Miller and Albee advance the same solution. As an alternative to euphemism and self-delusion Miller urges the necessity to "take one's life in one's arms" while Albee insists on the need to face "Virginia Woolf" however harrowing that prospect may be.

Who's Afraid of Virginia Woolf? and After the Fall are in essence both modern secular morality plays. The gospel which they teach, as we have seen, is the primacy of human contact based on an acceptance of reality. If Albee sees this as essentially a Christian objective in The Zoo Story and, indeed, Who's Afraid of Virginia Woolf?, in which a son is sacrificed for redemption, then Miller recognises it as an empirical truth intuitively felt by Holga and painfully and laboriously learnt by Quentin. The religious overtones which abound in all three plays serve to create a myth for this secular religion which is not so far removed from the liberal humanism of Tillich. Where Gelber's Jaybird had congratulated himself on creating "no heroes, no martyrs, no Christs"[7] Albee creates all three. For deprived of God man is of necessity his own salvation. Following his "sanctification" of Jerry, in The Zoo Story, it is not too fanciful, I believe, to note the consistency with which George, the man who is finally responsible for the destruction of illusion, is associated with Christ. The first line of the play, which heralds George's entrance, is "Jesus" while the act ends with the same apparent identification. Martha leaves George alone on stage with the same contemptuous expletive, "Jesus." This identification is repeated in the third act when Nick throws the door open and "with great rue" shouts out "Christ" (v.w. p. 195). Once again this heralds George's entrance. It is clear, however, that this play lacks the precise parallels which had brought The Zoo Story to the verge of allegory.

Reduced to its simplest terms New Carthage is a kind of Vanity Fair in which the Worldly Wise distract the pilgrim from his true path. Modern Christian, however, is not urged to forego the pleasures of the American Dream in order to obtain the fruits of his virtue in a later world but rather to enjoy the real consolation of fellow humanity in the alienated world of the present. Failure to accept the need to confront reality is not only to deprive man of dignity but also to leave him adrift in incomprehension, in flight from the world as it really is. This is the modern hell of Albee's morality plays. The salvation of human contact is aborted by the refusal to abandon illusion. All that remains is a frustrating parody of contact in which love begets revulsion, humour begets anger and the aspirations of the two seeking contact are disastrously out of phase. "George who is good to me, and whom I revile; who understands me, and whom I push off; who can make me laugh, and I choke it back in my throat . . . who tolerates, which is intolerable; who is kind, which is cruel; who understands, which is beyond comprehension . . ." (v.w. pp. 190–1).

Strindberg's tortured life gave to his concern with the battle of the sexes almost a manic dynamism which has only really been matched by O'Neill, whose own experience drew him to the Scandinavian's work. It would be an error, however, to see Albee as an extention of this revolt against the natural order. For to him human relationships are out of phase not because of the workings of an ineluctable destiny or because of the arbitrariness of sexual attraction (although, in *The Ballad of the Sad Café* (1963) he shows he is not blind to this) but because of the demonstrable failure of the individual to establish a genuine relationship between himself and his situation. To Albee, as to Miller, the failure of the man/ woman relationship epitomises a more general failure. For it is in this relationship that fruitful contact should be most easily attained. Where O'Neill had been concerned with establishing a compromise between the individual and his situation, and where Beckett presents a vision of that individual overwhelmed by his situation, Albee discovers genuine hope. For he sees in confrontation the first step towards a genuine affirmation, which lies not through "pipe-dreams" or "flight" but through a positive acceptance of human limitations.

Albee's success on Broadway with *Who's Afraid of Virginia Woolf?* presented many critics with a paradox. For while he had formerly been hailed as the leader of the off-Broadway avant-garde his success on Broadway seemed near to sacrilege. Indeed Diana Trilling saw it as proof of his basic conservatism and triviality, although where this leaves Shakespeare is not clear. Yet Albee's play was in truth something of a landmark in American drama. It is the first full-length play to accept the absurdist vision and yet to formulate a response which transcends at once both despair and casual resolution. To the abstract speculation of Pirandello and Genet — who doubt the very existence of an objective reality — he adds a moral dimension while re-instituting the "humanist heresies" for which

Tynan had called. If he abandons the style of the absurdists as demonstrably unsuited to his theme then he still retains the analogical structure of *The Zoo Story*. For while he clearly has roots in Strindberg it is equally clear that structurally his plays have more in common with Brecht and Beckett and even the later O'Neill. Like *The Good Woman of Sezuan* (first produced 1943) and *Waiting for Godot* his plays are structured on the metaphor. Albert Camus prefaces his novel, *The Plague* (1947), with a quotation from Defoe which is in essence a justification of the analogical form, "It is as reasonable to represent one kind of imprisonment by another, as it is to represent anything that really exists by that which exists not!"[8] This is a justification which not only Albee but also Durrenmatt and Frisch would endorse, for the extended metaphor is equally the basis for their work. Indeed it is, perhaps, from these writers also that Albee derives his masterful blending of comedy and anguish.

John Gassner has called *Who's Afraid of Virginia Woolf?* "essentially naturalistic,"[9] and certainly the play has a naturalistic "texture," that is to say we are not in Willy Loman's insubstantial house. The walls are solid; the setting is "real." Yet naturalism implies a concern with surface exactitude which has nothing to do with Albee's method. He himself has described the play's setting as "womb-like" and while avoiding the simplicities of symbolism (simplicities to which he submits in his next play, *Tiny Alice*) he is not so much concerned with maintaining a precision of appearance as with seizing an essential reality. Like Brown after him he is concerned with presenting an analogue of the human situation. He himself has called his play realistic, defining the term to mean that drama which faces "man's condition as it is." In defining realism in these terms he is clearly also defining what he sees as the role of the dramatist in a society in which the audience is "so preconditioned by pap as to have cut off half of its responses." In refusing to pander to a supposed need for "self-congratulation and reassurance"[10] Albee was not only maintaining his artistic integrity but he was demonstrating that in *Who's Afraid of Virginia Woolf?* — originally written for off-Broadway production — he had produced a play which could seemingly resolve the paradox of the avant-garde. For where *The Zoo Story* played to only moderate audiences in *The Provincetown Playhouse*, *Who's Afraid of Virginia Woolf?* proclaimed the same message from the stage of the *Billy Rose Theatre* on Broadway and, but for the squeamishness of W. D. Maxwell would have received the Pulitzer Prize it so obviously deserved.

Notes

1. Richard Schechner, "TDR Comment," *Tulane Drama Review*, VII, iii (Spring, 1963), pp. 8–10.

2. Alan Schneider, "Why so Afraid?" *Tulane Drama Review*, VII, iii (Spring, 1963), p. 11.

3. Virginia Woolf, *To The Lighthouse* (London, 1960), p. 54.

4. *Ibid.*, p. 102.

5. *Ibid.*, p. 13.

6. Johann Wolfgang Goethe, *Faust — Part Two*, trans., Philip Wayne (Harmondsworth, 1959), p. 277.

7. *The Connection*, p. 62.

8. Albert Camus, *The Plague*, trans., Stuart Gilbert (Harmondsworth, 1962), p. 3.

9. *Directions in Modern Theatre and Drama*, p. 358.

10. "Which Theatre is the Absurd One?" pp. 334–5.

Who's Afraid of Virginia Woolf? and the Tradition
Emil Roy*

Since the appearance of Edward Albee's *The Zoo Story* in 1959, he has been hailed variously as the new Eugene O'Neill, as the king of off-Broadway, and as the likely one to be America's first dramatic artist. With the Broadway production of *Who's Afraid of Virginia Woolf?* in 1962, Albee has apparently fulfilled a measure of the promise glimpsed in him. Yet *Virginia Woolf*, like most great American plays, is not a seminal work which makes a radical departure in theatrical conventions. Strindberg's expressionism, Ibsen's realistic drawing rooms, Chekhov's juxtaposition of poignant images of despair, Pirandello's brilliantly unresolved paradoxes and Shaw's disquisitions were all established in the theater by plays of this sort. Rather, *Virginia Woolf* is another of the great culminating compositions which integrate a tradition and, to an extent, exhaust its vitality. "I have been influenced by everyone," Albee has said. Like O'Neill's *The Emperor Jones*, Elmer Rice's *The Adding Machine*, Thornton Wilder's *The Skin of Our Teeth* and Arthur Miller's *Death of a Salesman*, Albee's best play to date manages to be fully contemporary without signalling a new point of departure for either the author or the American theater. While the Rice play is pure expressionism, both *Emperor Jones* and *Death of a Salesman* merge this convention with naturalism. Wilder, for his part, blends the multi-layered allegory of Joyce's *Finnegans Wake* with the farce of *Hellzapoppin'*. That Albee should fuse the conventions of naturalism, existentialism, and the Theatre of the Absurd (Martin Esslin's term) in a uniquely original way is in itself a traditional accomplishment. This merger of divergent conventions into a brilliant, coherent work of art seems to be a peculiar distinction of American drama at its best. Judging by the development of Albee's predecessors, however, we may expect a period either of restless, frustrating experimentation or of a slow harden-

*From *Bucknell Review* 13 (March 1965):27–36. Reprinted by permission.

ing into self-imitation ending in an embrace of the values he now so bitterly castigates.

In his published comment Albee has called for a theater of involvement, of drawing the moment and thought together with the audience; he has confessed his guidance in this effort by Genêt, Beckett and Williams "not necessarily in that order." Albee also has links with the theater of the French Existentialists, which includes Giraudoux, Anouilh, Sartre and Camus, with whom he shares a sense of the irrationality of the human condition. Like them he presents his perceptions in the form of highly lucid and logical progression, although two of his previous plays (*The Sandbox* and *The American Dream*) had openly abandoned this form. Like Sartre, Albee appears to assume that human personality can be reduced to pure potentiality and the freedom to choose at any moment. George's willingness to continue his apparently futile quest for an ideal intimacy, both his and Martha's improvised reconstructions of the past, and George's final destruction of their "child" are all existential. More specifically, *Virginia Woolf* resembles Sartre's *No Exit* in mode and theme. In both plays, two men and two women are arbitrarily isolated although only three take major roles; each acts as torturer of the others; and all of them strip illusion from the reality which Garcin finally glimpses and sums up: "Hell is — other people!"

Although Martin Esslin[1] has placed Albee's earlier work within the Theatre of the Absurd (including Ionesco, Genêt and Beckett) because it attacks the foundations of American optimism, Albee has used the dramaturgy of the Absurd mainly to deepen the complexity of *Virginia Woolf*. To inhibit the audience's sympathetic identification with the characters on the stage and replace it with a detached, critical attitude, the Theatre of the Absurd presents characters whose motives and actions seem incomprehensible, and whose representation involves all sorts of verbal and staged nonsense. Unlike the Existentialists, as Esslin points out, the dramatists of the Absurd try to achieve a kind of unity between the assumptions which they share with Sarte and Camus and the form in which these are expressed. The toy shotgun with its parasol, the title song of ridicule, George's mock flower-selling, and word-plays such as George and Nick's argument about the painting reflect a prominent idea in the Theatre of the Absurd: that reality and illusion are both present but mixed, and that man has only illusions upon which to reconstruct his sense of reality.

However, the single setting of *Virginia Woolf*; the drinking, vomiting and sexual obsessions; the allusions to disease, insanity, and animalism; and the highly colloquial, profane and specific language all place Albee in the naturalistic mainstream of Williams and O'Neill. Certainly the eavesdropping scene, the paired couples' betrayal of one another and George's flower-selling parody closely resemble similar devices in *A Streetcar Named Desire*. And Albee has certainly followed Williams in his dissection of the apparent collapse of the arts, learning and the church as viable moral guides. His muscular and beautiful but spiritually empty young men are the ironic symbols of the sterility which Williams' failed poets, neurasthenic spinsters and alcoholic playboys seek to escape. It is not surprising that Albee and Williams, like so many other great realists (Ibsen, O'Casey and O'Neill among them) should have served an apprenticeship to poetry. John Simon has observed that in *Virginia Woolf* Albee uses

> the same device as the lyric poet — high flown imagery, refrains, incremental repetition, incantatory rhythm — in the service of detestation instead of love, achieving a poetry of desperate embattledness.[2]

This partly involves a rejection of the rigid limitations of prose realism, an attempt at refinement and subtlety which often results in a self-contained, obtrusive framework of symbolism. Works such as O'Neill's *Lazarus Laughed* and Williams' *The Rose Tattoo* are notable offenders in this regard. Too often the symbols come to stand for an experience which cannot be realized by character conflict or plot development, and hence must be represented by inert objects. Albee has been consistently more successful with his symbolism than Williams, as in his accomplished use of classical and Christian myths in *Zoo Story*, the black-white antitheses in *The Death of Bessie Smith*, and the family figures in *The Sandbox* and *The American Dream*.

However, it is through his links with the O'Neill of *The Iceman Cometh* and *Long Day's Journey into Night* that Albee is tied to dramatic naturalism. These two plays "enormously involved and enveloped" him, Albee has said. Although *Virginia Woolf* differs greatly from *Iceman* in setting, action and cast, they both involved a preoccupation with alienated parents and lost children, alcoholic pipe dreams, attempted exorcism of a ghostly past, the use of symmetrical pairings to characterize and a marked likeness in protagonists. Both Larry and George possess a historical perspective so objective that they are virtually immobilized: no effective action seems tenable for either. Moreover, the offstage parental figures are as grotesque and compulsive as any of the characters in either play.

Even closer parallels can be drawn between *Virginia Woolf* and *Long Day's Journey*, which John Chapman wished to re-title *Long Night's Journey into Day*. Once again we have the constricted New England setting, the theme of frustration and the inter-familial flagellations swirling around the supposed failures of the male parent. While the characters in both plays occasionally achieve enlightened tenderness, the bitterness which rapidly follows it is pathetic in its inevitability. Martha's alcoholism can be equated with Mary's dope addiction, leading them both into despairing dreams of lost innocence. The elder Tyrone is humiliated, angered and boastful by turns, but the end of the play brings him no insight into his peculiar mixture of pride and vanity. George's position is even more hopeless, a tragedy sharpened by the closeness of his role to caricature. But he is ultimately enlightened, resolving in a small way to help rescue his society.

In both Albee and O'Neill the painful striving of isolated individuals for communion leads mainly to even more terrifying solitude. As in much American drama the crucial distinction between characters involves degrees of awareness. O'Neill's determinism is leavened into Albee's existentialism without much more optimism. And in *Virginia Woolf*, as in so much O'Neill, the "weak" characters finally determine the course of the "stronger" ones. Moreover, Albee's command of American speech rhythms is among the best ever displayed in the theater, in contrast to O'Neill's often faulty efforts.

Paradoxically, the more firmly a writer grasps the convention of realism, the more closely his work draws toward allegory and symbolism. This is not to say that Albee has abandoned any of the machinery of contemporary realism: the well-made secrets and letters, the careful exposition, the eternal triangle and the attacks on the oppressive bourgeois family. But these devices existed long before Scribe and Ibsen, and they serve Albee's means rather than his ends. In the mode of O'Neill's last plays, *The Zoo Story*, *The Death of Bessie Smith* and *Virginia Woolf* are religious, social and cultural parables, respectively. Just below the conversational colloquy of *The Zoo Story* Albee evokes traditional Christian and classical myth and symbolism, as Rose Zimbardo[3] has pointed out. Finding that his parable of the dog has failed to break down his separateness from Peter, Jerry accepts a Christ-like death to save Peter's soul, to force him to feel his kinship with him and other outcasts. In *Bessie Smith*, which suffers from diffuseness and incompatible conventions, it is the Negro orderly who typifies the true existentialist saint. In contrast to the weak tyrannical nurse and the disillusioned intern, the orderly stoically accepts his fate like Camus's Sisyphus. He elevates himself above it by realizing what his destiny is. *Virginia Woolf*, as Diana Trilling[4] has suggested, is a parable of the threatened disintegration of Western society. It is set in a college town named New Carthage. The necessity for a drastic moral change, reflected in George's attacks on the amoral biological sciences, is pointed up by allusions to mock and serious utopias. History in the person of George has failed, the work of the professor rendered meaningless by events. Martha is the humane tradition, or maybe just plain humanity, older than history, helpless before her lost hopes, desperate in her dependence upon a failing historical destiny. Nick is the new man of science, in cold command of himself but impotent in his connection with humanity. Honey is the product of a dead religious faith which shored up the resources on which science now feeds and goes about its appointed task of destroying civilization. Mrs. Trilling concludes that the childlessness of both couples is our nightmarish possibility that all of us are without a future.

The title, which is sung to the nursery tune of "Mulberry Bush," literally refers to a joke Martha had made at a party earlier in the evening, a joke which is never clarified or restated. Although the famous woman novelist never figures in the action, the allusion establishes links for the knowing: George is a failed novelist obsessed with the impending destruction of civilization (Miss Woolf's last major work, entitled significantly "Between the Acts," treated the same theme). Albee also alludes to Poe, Spengler, Huxley, Freud, Lawrence, Coleridge, Wagner, some movies from the Thirties, several nursery rhymes, the *Odyssey*, the *Dies Irae* and the Roman Catholic *Requiem*, and Beethoven's *Seventh Symphony*. However, an unmentioned but crucial parallel is Eliot's "The Hollow Men." Both play and poem involve the themes of frustration; both utilize a nursery level of make-believe to mock the hopes of modern man; and the conclusion of "The Hollow Men" suggests the frustrations in *Virginia Woolf*: "This is the way the world ends / Not with a bang but a whimper." Most important, both works omit most logical connectives, relying instead on the direct perception of significance by the audience. Moreover, the action of both works is essentially paradoxical: at any moment we care to consider it, we can observe passion and lassitude, darkness and light, assault and withdrawal. Most ironic, perhaps, is Albee's sense that beneath the comic games of words, sex and war is a boding, angry, self-destructive layer of violence.

Dramatically, the action of *Virginia Woolf* has a concrete, realistic, recognizable setting and situation. It is constructed, like the bouregois drawing-room, around what amounts to a ceremonial social occasion. The play begins with Martha's party for a younger faculty member and his wife, Nick and Honey. Martha's husband George is first overruled in his objections to the party, disgusted by Martha's obvious attempts to seduce Nick, and finally humiliated by her stories revealing his past failures as teacher, novelist and man. In his use of the social ceremony — arrivals, departures, anniversaries, parties — Albee is close to Chekhov and James. His purpose in *Virginia Woolf* is to focus attention on an action which all the characters share by analogy: their perception of what it feels like to lose a child — the child that one once was, that one never can be again, that one never conceived. To assume, with many of the critics, that the device of the imaginary child is a cheap trick, is a misunderstanding. For the basic absurdity of the play is not the child's "existence," but the assumption that George and Martha could have concealed their secret for over twenty years, an absurdity no more odd that Oedipus's famous complex or Lear's world-weariness. Act I, "Fun and Games," ends with Honey's direct, intuitive perception of the senselessness of life: her vomiting parallels Camus's definition of the Absurd in *The Myth of Sisyphus*:

> This malaise in front of man's own inhumanity, this incalculable letdown when faced by the image of what we are, this "nausea," as a contemporary writer calls it, is the Absurd.

Act II, "*Walpurgisnacht*," is primarily the result, the extended suffering which ensues from the game-like mode of the play, which is directly linked to the title of Act I, to the sex games of Nick and Honey as children, and of Martha and Nick in the play itself, as well as to the crucial central game: "to tell the difference between truth and reality." The crisis, reversal and resolution of Act II proceed by a mode which Northrop Frye has called "ironic myth." It is primarily a "parody of romance, the application of mythic forms to a more realistic context which fits them in unexpected way."[5] This mythic game is essentially the "father-mother-baby" game which Nick and Honey once played, the basis of the trick which Honey had played on Nick, the game which George and Martha had played all their married life, and the trick which Martha and Nick try to play on George. Once we understand the conventions of "gaming" as Johan Huizinga has set them forth in *Homo Ludens*,[6] we gain a crucial insight into Albee's play as the "imitation of an action." For in all games played for their own sake, the players invent and obey rules which hold as long as the magic circle in which they exist remains unbroken. By revealing the "existence" of George's and her child to an outsider, and then trying to play the same game with Nick ("You be the father, and I'll be the mother"), she has released George from the rules of the game. Her action brings on the crisis of the play, a recognition scene which closes Act II, and the reversal of the action, extending George's recognition to all other characters in Act III, "Exorcism." The crisis is George's refusal to take the part of aggrieved husband in Martha's new game with Nick. He then reverses the action, adjusts his relationship with Martha and Nick, and shifts the balance of power by adopting the rules Martha had invented earlier: "If you existed, I'd divorce you." Thus, if Martha can pretend that George doesn't "exist" as a husband, he can pretend in turn that she doesn't exist either as a spouse or as a mother, and destroy their child.

It should be stressed, however, that George's brilliant improvisation of the "death" is a ritual purgation in a deeply religious sense, an act which re-enacts the destruction of Martha's first marriage by her father (thus dissipating the illusion of her father's love for her), and which destroys George's illusory guilt for the accidental death of his own father in an automobile accident. Moreover, despite the strong attractiveness of their child, his "existence" had fed their sadomasochistic relationship and its paradoxical, self-destructive urges: the attempt, on the one hand, to reduce the other partner to the helplessness of a child, and on the other hand, to recapture the childhood innocence symbolized by their son.

The peculiar qualities of the play rest upon the means by which it achieves its end: to demonstrate the difference between *knowing* something in the conceptual sphere and *experiencing* it as a living reality. For each of the characters, the quest for identity involves a coincident escape from false self-concepts. Initially, Martha embodies two polar types, deeply imbedded in American literary tradition: the masculine bitch-heroine who uses sex as a weapon, and the mindless, passive Earth Goddess type. When George realizes that his direct attacks on Martha merely extend the underlying conflicts, that expelling or exposing Nick or humiliating the bitterly frustrated Martha would only be cowardly evasions, he demonstrates ironically that he is too strong to be hurt by her infidelity, too secure to feel threatened by it, and too magnanimous to believe that her weaknesses outweigh her virtues. As a result Martha is led to recognize that she is a victim of her own contradictory desires, that the world is organized in absurd ways, and that her rejection of George stems from her own father's rejection of her. Through his sexual adventure with Martha, Nick learns that he has been a tool rather than the master of his emotions, that he has selfishly wronged an innocent man, and that he is neither capable of recompensing George nor of escaping his newly found self-knowledge. Like the typical Arthur Miller son, he has learned both that he is less than he thought he was and that he is capable of enduring that knowledge.

Honey plays both Jamesian *ficelle* and *naif*: although she elicits the revelations of truth without fully comprehending, she is too unhappy with the past to live in it any longer. Her perception of her and Martha's similar plights — loss of love from a corrupt father, drinking as an escape, the use of a child as a threat, false dreams of love and respectability — leads her to join in the destruction of Martha's and her own illusions.

George, protagonist and tragic anti-hero, is highly intelligent and sensitive, an idealist trapped into marriage with a demanding wife and into a job controlled by a man who insists on the destruction of meditative values and their replacement by standards of sterile conformity. (It is ironic that the two most grotesque, horrifying characters — male parents of female characters — never appear on stage, but hover ghost-like on its periphery.) George is also passionate, articulate and charitable, a man who finally surrenders his illusions for the dubious unknowns of reality and the responsibility for building a new life for himself and Martha on this basis. Moreover, he has had to learn, like Oedipus and Lear, that despite his age, his sense of history, and the supposed predictability of life, much of life must remain unknown. George finally reaches the perception of the Existentialist anti-hero: the intuitive penetration to "the marrow" of existence, man's capacity for essentially free choice. With it come some knowledge and a resolution to bring all the other characters to the same perception.

Although the play presents the themes of redemption, the stripping of illusion from reality, and of cosmic trial by ordeal which ultimately pits the forces of Historic Inevitability against those of Biological Determinism, its optimism is tempered by our sense of the fearful cost paid by its characters, in their abrasion by illusion, and their sense of loss at its destruction. The humanity of man emerges supreme, but only after the most demanding tests of his nerve, intelligence and endurance, within the last remaining institution of our society — marriage — be it ever so ephemeral, transitory and strained.

In a broad sense *Virginia Woolf* embodies Scott Buchanan's fundamental notions of tragedy: *hybris* and *nemesis*. Hybris involves the "arrogance that arises from blindness in human nature"; nemesis is that "eventual consequence of that blindness and arrogance."[7] Albee's play sets nemesis in motion before the force of hybris is entirely spent, resulting in the birth within George of the prime virtue of the tragic hero: irony, "the exercise of the capacity to discover and systematize clear ideas." The other characters, like George, are forced to perceive the dreams hidden behind their rationalizations, and to endure perception as an end of action. And that is why all our attempts to categorize the characters' motives neatly will fail: the suggestions that Martha wants Nick because she is a nymphomaniac, that Honey tricked Nick to get a husband, that Nick married Honey for money, that George finally "kills" their son for revenge are as melodramatic as the illusions which delude the audience and from which it must be purged in the catharsis it shares with the characters.

From the broadest perspective, Albee is a moralist, despite objections to the adultery, profanity and perversion in his play. Lionel Trilling[8] has pointed out that the artist who indicates degradation, sin, and vile language in his work is attacking not goodness, but *specious* goodness by revealing the corruptions which are concealed by a puritanical moral code, an observation rooted in Freud's *Civilization and Its Discontents*. Because the release of our inhibitions in dreams is often unpleasant, or in action is unsettling or even subversive, our frustrated impulses often emerge in ugly, but disguised ways. By allowing the dramatic expression of these frustrated urges, the artist is purging or "exorcising" the impulses which otherwise strengthen our self-destructive urges. Although Albee makes almost no overt comment on the shortcomings of our society (we cannot assume that George is an author *persona*), he has had to select his absurdities, and this act of selection is a moral act.

Notes

1. Martin Esslin, *The Theatre of the Absurd* (New York, 1961).

2. "On Broadway and Off," *Harper's Magazine* (March 1963), p. 104.

3. "Symbolism and Naturalism in Edward Albee's *The Zoo Story*," *Twentieth Century Literature* (April 1962), pp. 10–17.

4. "Who's Afraid of the Culture Elite?" *Esquire Magazine* (December 1963).

5. Northrop Frye, *An Anatomy of Criticism* (Princeton, 1957), p. 223.

6. Johan Huizinga, *Homo Ludens* (Boston, 1955).

7. Scott Buchanan, *Poetry and Mathematics* (Philadelphia, 1962), p. 147.

8. In an address entitled "The Anti-Hero in Literature," delivered at the University of Southern California, Los Angeles, May 17, 1964.

A Warp in Albee's *Woolf*   Bernard F. Dukore*

On numerous occasions, modern playwrights have gone to the classics for subjects or characters. Sometimes the borrowings are obvious, as in Sartre's *The Flies*. At other times the derivations are obscure; Eliot, for example, was so successful in disguising the classical source for *The Cocktail Party* that no one identified it until he himself pointed it out as Euripides' *Alcestis*. Such theft — if I may distort Proudhon's expression — is a playwright's proper cup of tea. Terence called his audience's attention to the fact that he did it, Shakespeare had no qualms about the propriety of doing it, few believed Shaw when he said he did it, and Brecht boasted of having had the sound judgment to find good authors to do it to. Every playwright may not be doing it, but many playwrights — bad as well as good — have. In 1920 Bernard Shaw wrote an article for *Hearst's Magazine* called, "I Am a Classic But Am I a Shakespear Thief?"[1] He replied that he was and concluded the article by ironically saying to the man who called him "a Shakespear Thief," "You would guess eggs if you saw the shells." From what looks like a shell, I should like to guess the classical egg that Albee hatched in his first full-length play, and also to suggest its relation to the authoress alluded to in the title.

In Euripides' *Alcestis*, the god Heracles brings Alcestis, wife of Admetus, back from the dead. In Eliot's *The Cocktail Party*, Harcourt-Reilly, a god-surrogate, brings Lavinia, wife of Edward Chamberlayne, back from a sanitorium where he had secretly sent her. A similar parallel exists between Albee's *Who's Afraid of Virginia Woolf?* and Euripides' *Medea*. In Euripides' play, Jason breaks the marriage vows he had made to Medea; in revenge, she kills their children. In *Virginia Woolf*, Martha breaks her vow of secrecy by telling outsiders of the imaginary son; in revenge, George "kills" that son.

Although the strongest parallel between Albee's play and *Medea* is the similar plot, there are others as well; *Virginia Woolf* appears to contain a broken line of references — some direct, some indirect — to the story of Jason and Medea.

Medea's ancestors had magical powers — her father was a sorcerer, her grandfather was Helios the Sun God, her aunt was Circe the enchantress — and she inherited supernatural powers from them. Albee has George attribute supernatural qualities to Martha's ancestors, though in a comic manner. "He's a God, we all know that," he says of Martha's father — who as president of a university has a position of authority that is suggestive of that of Medea's father, King Aetes. A few minutes later he adds, "the old man is not going to die. Martha's father has the staying power of one of those Micronesian tortoises. There are rumors . . . which you must not

*From *Southern Speech Communication Journal* 30 (Winter 1964):261–68. Reprinted by permission of The Southern Speech Communication Association.

breathe in front of Martha, for she foams at the mouth . . . that the old man, her father, is over two hundred years old."[2] Later, George describes Martha's mother as a rich witch who expired in a puff of smoke. In addition Martha herself has had the benefit of what might be called her father's magical restorative powers. Although she has been married before, "her father," she says, "put an end to that . . . real quick . . . annulled . . . which is a laugh . . . because theoretically you can't get an annulment if there's entrance. Ha! Anyway, so I was revirginized . . ." An additional suggestion of *Medea* occurs when George corrects Martha's claim to be an atheist: "Not an atheist, Martha . . . a pagan. (*To* HONEY *and* NICK) Martha is the only true pagan on the eastern seaboard." In another passage George presents her with a bouquet of flowers in the third act, she says, "Pansies! Rosemary! Violence! My wedding bouquet!" There even appears to be a reference to the golden fleece in George and Martha's description of their imaginary blond son:

> MARTHA: . . . and in the sun his hair . . . became . . . fleece.
> GEORGE: (*Echoing her*) . . . fleece . . .

One of Jason's trials was to sow dragon's teeth and to plough them into the earth. From these dragon's teeth, a crop of armed men rose and attacked him. Albee has George enact what may be a parody of this. In the third act, shortly before he reports the death of the son, he enters the living room holding some snapdragons before him, flourishing the flowers, and crying, "SNAP WENT THE DRAGONS!!" He then takes each snapdragon and throws it "*spear-like, stem-first*" at Martha, crying "SNAP!"

In both *Medea* (as in most extant Greek tragedy) and *Virginia Woolf*, the killing—real in the former play, fictitious in the latter—is performed offstage. In *Medea*, the murder of Creon's daughter is reported by a messenger; in *Virginia Woolf*, the murder of the imaginary son is reported, appropriately, by an imaginary messenger—a Western Union messenger ("the doorbell. . . . Chimed. . . . it was good old Western Union, some little boy about seventy. . . . crazy Billy . . . and he had a telegram" etc.).

Finally, it is possible to see a parallel in the concluding moments of the two plays: Euripides' ends with Medea appearing in a chariot sent to her by her grandfather, Helios the Sun God; Albee's ends at dawn.

Although Albee's play resembles *Medea* in these aspects, an important difference exists: the classical allusions are inconsistent sexually. The Jason references are used not only in connection with George but also with Martha; the Medea references are used not only in connection with Martha but also with George. In Albee's play, Medea's ruthlessness toward her family is echoed in George's tale of the boy who killed his parents—his mother by a shotgun and his father by an automobile accident—and it is implied several times that the boy was George. In Euripides' play the man is unfaithful; in Albee's the woman. In Euripides' play the woman kills her offspring; in Albee's, the man "kills" the son.

Not only is there sexual fluidity in the classical allusions, but Albee reverses the traditional marital characteristics of the two major characters. Martha is older than George. He, not she, is brought into the family home of the other. She admits, "I wear the pants in this house because somebody's got to." There are frequent references to George's emasculation. When Martha angrily says to him at one point, "I'll fix you," it is unlikely that the *double entendre* is accidental; and when she tells him that some men would give their right arm for the opportunity of being married to the daughter of the president of the university where they teach, he reminds her, "Alas, Martha, in reality it works out that the sacrifice is usually of a somewhat more private portion of the anatomy." There are neither such simple parallels as George-Medea, Martha-Jason, nor the attractively alliterative George-Jason, Martha-Medea. As the sexual roles of George and Martha are hermaphroditic, so are the classical echoes split between the sexes.

In addition to numerous revelations in the dialogue of Martha's masculinity and George's emasculation, Albee provides us with an onstage view of the castration ceremony. At the close of the first act, as she is busily emasculating her husband for the benefit of her next conquest, Albee provides appropriate images. Martha informs the guests that her father realized that her husband did not have any leadership qualities: "Georgie-boy didn't have the *stuff*. . . . he didn't have it in him!" Although George asks her to stop, Martha — *"Viciously triumphant!"* — replies, "The hell I will!" and continues: "he wasn't particularly . . . aggressive. In fact he was sort of a . . . (*Spits the word at* GEORGE's *back*) . . . a FLOP! A great . . . big . . . fat . . . FLOP!" At this point Albee makes the operation visually as well as linguistically symbolic: "CRASH! *Immediately after* FLOP! GEORGE *breaks a bottle against the portable bar and stands there, still with his back to them all, holding the remains of the bottle by the neck. There is a silence, with everyone frozen.*" George speaks, "(*Almost crying*) I said stop, Martha." But Martha completes the castration: "I hope that was an empty bottle, George. You don't want to waste good liquor . . . not on your salary." George then *"drops the broken bottle on the floor, not moving."* . . . and the ceremony is terminated with a chanting, almost ritualistic accompaniment:

MARTHA	GEORGE
. . . who's married to the President's daughter, who's expected to *be* somebody, not just some nobody, some bookworm, somebody who's so damn . . . contemplative, he can't make	I said, don't. All right . . . all right: (*Sings*) Who's afraid of Virginia Woolf, Virginia Woolf, Virginia Woolf, Who's afraid of Virginia Woolf,

anything out of himself, somebody without the *guts* to make
anybody proud of him . . . ALL
RIGHT, GEORGE!

early in the morning.

This brings us to the question of Virginia Woolf. Why Virginia
Woolf? Why not Thomas Wolfe? Why not simply The Big Bad Wolf
without any literary allusions? I do not believe that Albee selected his title
haphazardly or that he did so solely because of the pun. The change of
sexual roles in the play *Virginia Woolf* reminds us that the author Virginia
Woolf, spokesman for The Emancipated Woman (or "The Mannish
Woman," as opponents labeled her — and this reminds us of Martha) and in
that sense the Simone de Beauvoir of her day, is known not only for *The
Common Reader* but also for *Orlando*, whose title-bearing hero becomes
during the progress of the book a title-bearing heroine. At the beginning,
Orlando is a male teenager during the reign of Elizabeth I: "there could be
no doubt about his sex, though the fashion of the time did something to
disguise it,"[3] the author tells us. Later, in Constantinople near the close of
the seventeenth century, Orlando wakes up one morning to discover that
he is a woman.

> The trumpeters, ranging themselves side by side in order, blow one
> terrified blast: —
>   "THE TRUTH!"
> at which Orlando woke.
>   He stretched himself. He rose, He stood upright in complete naked-
> ness before us, and while the trumpets pealed Truth! Truth! Truth! we
> have no choice but confess — he was a woman.

The sexual change that occurs in Virginia Woolf's *Orlando* is in harmony
with the situations presented and the views demonstrated in *Who's Afraid
of Virginia Woolf?* and, I believe, was in Albee's mind when he gave his
play its title.

Now that some of *Virginia Woolf's* possible sources have been suggested,[4] one must ask what they tell us of the play.

In Albee's play, unlike Euripides', the explanation is everything.
Medea clearly tells the Chorus what she intends to do; we know what she
is doing as she does it; finally, we see the results of the deed. Euripides uses
the deed to focus on other matters (the social repercussions, the characters'
responses to each other as well as to the deed, Medea's proud and
wholehearted embracing of the crime); Albee uses other matters to focus
on the deed. Unlike *Medea, Who's Afraid of Virginia Woolf?* is essentially
a detective story: it hinges upon the revelation of a mystery, the explanation that the child is a fiction.[5] Albee does not show us *how* the lives of
George and Martha had been propped up by the lie; he merely tells us *that*
they had been so sustained — and since he offers no evidence (one can, in
fact, argue that the marriage is "sustained" not by the fantasy but by sado-

masochism), we are asked to accept his word that this is the case. In this respect, *Who's Afraid of Virginia Woolf?* may be compared with Harold Pinter's *The Lover*, in which an apparently sedate suburban couple also sustain their marriage by a fantasy. Each assumes a different identity (with appropriate costumes): he becomes a sensual stud, she a sexy whore (in his role as the very proper husband, he describes her as "a common or garden slut"). However, the audience knows all of this by the time the play is halfway through. Pinter explores the operation of the fantasy in the private lives of his couple and their response to the threatened destruction of their fiction. He is concerned not with giving a pat answer to a conveniently planted question, but with dramatizing the manner in which people employ fantasies in order to cope with their everyday lives and how these fantasies, upon which they are dependent, affect their relationship with each other. Albee, on the other hand, is concerned only with the pat answer: the shattering of the lie upon which George and Martha maintained their marriage is simply an answer to the question of what he will do to revenge himself on her.

A number of critics have found fault with what is intended to be one of the high points of the play (as its counterpart was one of the high points of *Medea*): the killing of the fictional child. Others, however, have put forth the view that Albee intends the child to be a metaphor for the illusions upon which we build our lives, and that he is saying that although our lives are desperate when they are built upon lies, we can find happiness by destroying those lies and facing reality.[6] Although this is probably the intention, Albee's play does not realize it. When Medea, outraged at the wrong done her by Jason, kills her children, we are horrified not only by the enormity of the revenge but by the fact that such an act is possible. Where there is a real child, a real murder may be committed, and such a crime is appalling. When George is humiliated to the degree to which Martha humiliates him, we can believe that he may react violently. However, the make-believe death of such a make-believe child should result, our common sense tells us, in make-believe tears unless the "parents" are hopelessly psychotic. Albee does not succeed in making us suspend our common sense. Although people do build their lives on illusions, the particular illusion upon which George and Martha build their lives is so fantastic that one questions whether even they themselves believe it. The fictitious child is too special to function as a symbol either for mankind in general or for Americans more specifically.[7] The structure of *Virginia Woolf* is built on too flimsy a foundation.

But while the "murder" may be a tepid Orlandization of the flesh-and-blood horrors of Euripides' play, it does not follow that Albee should be dismissed outright on this account. Although Albee may not have succeeded in shaping the classical story in contemporary terms (this appears to have been one of his attempts), he is obviously a serious playwright — and therefore deserves serious consideration. *Who's Afraid of*

Virginia Woolf? may not be an artistically successful play, but if one were to apply to the author Martha's words to Nick in the final act — "Your potential's fine. It's dandy. (*Wiggles her eyebrows*) Absolutely dandy. I haven't seen such a dandy potential in a long time. Oh, but baby, you sure are a flop." — one should emphasize the potential no less than the flop.

Notes

1. Reprinted in *Shaw on Theatre*, ed. E. J. West (New York, 1958), pp. 131–134.

2. All quotations from this play are from Edward Albee, "*Who's Afraid of Virginia Woolf?* (New York, 1963). Four periods (. . . .) indicate ellipses; three (. . .) indicate typographical devices in the text.

3. Quotations from this novel are from Virginia Woolf, *Orlando* (New York: 1946).

4. *Medea* is not the only story Albee seems to have drawn on. Robert Brustein points out that there may be "elements of the story of Aphrodite, Ares, and Hephaestus, mixed with pieces from the story of Aphrodite and Adonis" ["Theater: Albee and the Medusa-Head," *The New Republic*, CXLVII (November 3, 1962), 30.] In fact, there are scattered references which evoke a number of places and periods far removed from the present day. George, who is in the History Department, tells Nick that he is "preoccupied with history," and then, struck by the phrase, repeats it oratorically. The name of the New England town in which the action takes place is New Carthage, and at one point George refers to it — "*With a handsweep taking in not only the room, the house, but the whole countryside*" — as Illyria, Penguin Island, and Gomorrah. The house of Martha's father, wherein was held the reception which all our characters have just attended, is referred to as Parnassus. Further, George suggests that they should live on Crete, and insists that he once visited the Aegean Sea.

There are modern references as well. For example, Albee points at least twice to Tennessee Williams' *A Streetcar Named Desire*: at the beginning of the third act, Martha gives a title to the alcoholic and sexual activities of the evening: "THE POKER NIGHT" — which was the original title of *Streetcar* — and when George enters, preparing to announce the news of the son's death, he "(. . . *speaks in a hideously cracked falsetto*) Flores; flores para los muertos. Flores." — recalling the old Flower Woman of *Streetcar*.

5. Cf. Ionesco, who uses the term "detective story" in this sense (a mystery revealed) rather than in the sense of a whodunnit. In *Victims of Duty*, Choubert says, "Every play ever written, from ancient times up to the present day, has never been anything but a detective story. The theatre has never been anything but a theatre of realism and of detective stories. Every play is an inquiry carried to a satisfactory conclusion. There is an enigma which is revealed to us during the final scene. Sometimes before. First you seek, then you find." [Eugene Ionesco, *Théâtre* (Paris, 1954), Vol. I, p. 179.]

6. The most convincing exposition of this view has been given, I think, by Harold Clurman in his very provocative second review of *Virginia Woolf*: "Many marriages and lives, Albee may be saying, become miserable because they are based on chimeras, on an evasion of facts. Only when reality, howsoever painful, is faced, when life's wretched disappointments are steadfastly confronted, can there be many hope of sanity and strength. George, the husband, breaks through his wife's illusion by the fiercely determined declaration, 'Our son is dead': we must kill the lie." ["Theatre," *The Nation*, CXCVI (March 9, 1963), 213–214.]

7. Albee evidently meant to reinforce the metaphor by the parallel of Nick and Honey (to whom I have made no direct reference because they only touch upon the Medea-Jason parallel: Martha attempts adultery with Nick). The marriage of Nick and Honey is, among other things, also an example of a marriage built upon a lie; and the imaginary pregnancy echoes the imaginary child. However, their relationship seems to me to be at least as special as

that of George and Martha, and instead of extending the situation they call attention to its uniqueness and emphasize its limitations.

It has also been suggested [e.g., Lee Baxandall, "Theatre and Affliction," *Encore*, X (May-June, 1963), 12] that the names George and Martha are intended to recall George and Martha Washington, thereby serving as symbols for the American man and woman. Although this may be the intent, the significance seems to me to be strictly one of nomenclature.

Albee's Great God Alice   Mardi Valgemae*

Critics who have grappled with Edward Albee's *Tiny Alice* have conjectured about its possible sources. These range from *Alice's Adventures in Wonderland* to the plays of Noel Coward, T. S. Eliot, Jean Genêt, and several other European playwrights. Surprisingly, no one has mentioned Eugene O'Neill. Albee himself has repeatedly admitted being "an enormous admirer" of "late O'Neill." "By late O'Neill, do you mean *Long Day's Journey Into Night?*" asked an interviewer. "Yes," replied Albee, "and *The Iceman Cometh* and those of that period when he started writing good plays." The interviewer: "Do you mean after he got over his gimmicky period?" Albee: "Yes."[1] Yet it is precisely the O'Neill of the "gimmicky period" who seems to have influenced the Albee of *Tiny Alice*.

Tiny Alice, said Albee at a press conference, was "something of a metaphysical dream play which must be entered into and experienced without predetermination of how a play is supposed to go."[2] Since Albee was not so much explicating his play as lecturing the New York critics, his warning about "predetermination" in all probability referred to thinking conditioned by the conventions of theatrical realism. For by calling *Tiny Alice* "a metaphysical dream play," Albee placed his own play in the tradition of dramatic expressionism that goes back to Strindberg's dream plays and eventually became naturalized, as it were, with the experiments of O'Neill. Thus we are justified, I think, in approaching *Tiny Alice* as an expressionistic objectification of Brother Julian's nightmare or hallucination.[3] Further external evidence to support this contention is found in Albee's statement that "Brother Julian is in the same position as the audience. He's the innocent. If you see things through his eyes, you won't have any trouble at all."[4]

"Things" are seen through the eyes of the protagonist also in O'Neill's expressionistic plays, where the action on the stage is distorted in order to capture a character's subjective view of the world. In *The Great God Brown*, the most complex and imaginative of O'Neill's experimental plays, the most salient expressionistic device is the mask. Masks are worn by all the major characters, thus objectifying the duality between their outer

*From *Modern Drama* 10 (1967):267–73. Reprinted by permission of the journal.

and inner selves, between illusion and reality. Most of the characters in *Tiny Alice* from time to time don metaphoric masks, Butler refers to the Cardinal as having to "wear a face,"[5] and when Julian first meets Miss Alice, she appears in a matted wig as well as the mask of an old hag. By removing both mask and wig, Miss Alice is suddenly transformed into an attractive woman. Yet this is not her real identity, either. For as we discover later in the play, she is the symbol of the abstraction Tiny Alice. The transformation of Miss Alice from an old crone into an attractive woman — an action that has puzzled critics[6] — suggests that all is not as it appears to be on the surface and foreshadows the stripping away of illusions that Julian must undergo in order to confront the abstraction, or Alice, which derives from the Greek word for truth.

Miss Alice's seemingly surreal transformation brings to mind Strindberg's "expressionist manifesto" — his preface to *A Dream Play* — in which he proclaims that in a play governed solely by dream logic, "Characters divide, double, redouble, evaporate, condense, float out of each other, converge."[7] Albee's debt to Strindberg has been investigated by Marion A. Taylor[8] and Robert Brustein, in his *New Republic* review of *Tiny Alice*, has suggested parallels between that play and Strindberg's *A Dream Play*.[9] Yet Miss Alice's unmasking is also reminiscent of the action in scene ten of O'Neill's *The Fountain*, where an old woman appears to Juan. *"In a flash,"* read the stage directions, *"her mask of age disappears"* and the beautiful Beatriz stands before the hero.[10] More indirectly, Miss Alice, masked and unmasked, brings to mind the objectification of the split personality of John and the masked Loving in O'Neill's *Days Without End*. And like Billy Brown in *The Great God Brown*, who at times wears the mask of Dion Anthony, Butler and the Lawyer in *Tiny Alice* assume for a while the personae of Julian and the Cardinal.

Related to the mask as an expressionistic device in *Tiny Alice* is the castle, which contains an infinite number of proportionately smaller models of itself. The castle can easily be related to the more traditional House of God, thus forming yet another link with *The Great God Brown*. In *Tiny Alice* the Lawyer suggests that the very foundation of the castle is "a wreck" (p. 81). As Butler phrases it, "Something *should* be done about the wine cellar. I've noticed it — as a passerby would — but Brother Julian pointed out the extent of it to me: bottles have burst, are bursting, corks rotting . . . something to do with the temperature or the dampness. It's a shame, you know" (p. 77). The connection between the house of mouse-god Alice and a more conventional if similarly metaphorical House of God is established by the Lawyer, who says: "When Christ told Peter — so legends tell — that he would found his church upon that rock. He must have had in mind an island in a sea of wine. How firm a foundation in the vintage years" (p. 143). The parallels between the rock of Peter in a sea of wine and Dion's cathedral, into which he has concealed a blasphemous, wine-loving Silenus, are equally apparent.

Dion's cathedral, argues Doris Falk in her study of O'Neill's plays, "is a metaphor of the neurotic process . . . which O'Neill seems to have understood thoroughly throughout the play. Man's normal need to transcend himself, to build spires toward the infinite, is blasphemed and travestied when its energies are all diverted inward to the struggle with masks of self."[11] Professor Falk's observation suggests an interesting point of comparison between the two plays, especially in the light of Brother Julian's erotic hallucinations. For the castle, like the cathedral in *The Great God Brown*, has certain affinities with the neurotic process occurring within Julian's mind. Hence the fire in the chapel serves as an objectification of Julian's physical passion for Miss Alice, which threatens to destroy the tenuous order he has established for himself as a lay brother. The scene opens with Miss Alice running away from the Lawyer, telling him to "KEEP OFF ME!" To the Lawyer's "Don't be hysterical, now," she replies, "I'll *show* you hysteria. I'll give you *fireworks!*" (p. 69), thus linking *fire* and the Greek *hysteria* for *womb*. When the actual fire breaks out in the chapel, it guts the altar area, just as Brother Julian's sexual fantasies destroy his attempts to come to grips with religious experience. For Brother Julian's road to religious ecstasy is paved with sexual hysteria (to use Albee's own terminology[12]), and before he can embrace his God in a not so metaphoric marriage, Julian must be seduced. As Butler remarks at the beginning of the next scene, referring to Julian and Miss Alice, "the fire in the chapel . . . brought them closer" (p. 95), after which the lovers go picnicking and partake of an almost O'Neillian "Montrachet under an elm" (p. 96). (Also decidedly O'Neillian is a conversation between Brother Julian and Butler. The former states that he dislikes being left alone. "Like a little boy?" questions Butler, "When the closet door swings shut after him? Locking him in the dark?" (p. 126) In *The Great God Brown* Dion Anthony speaks similar words about his mother: "I remember a sweet, strange girl, with affectionate, bewildered eyes as if God had locked her in a dark closet. . . ."[13])

The union of Brother Julian and Miss Alice is consummated in the flesh, but the fusion of their bodies is merely a further concretization of abstract states. For as in *The Great God Brown*, the characters in *Tiny Alice* are not merely individuals but rather expressionistic types: the Cardinal, the Lawyer, and Butler, the butler. The parallels between the protagonists of both plays are fairly obvious. In Dion Anthony, as his name implies, struggle "the creative pagan acceptance of life" and "the masochistic life-denying spirit of Christianity."[14] Brother Julian, who narrates at length his erotic experiences, has a Christian martyr complex: he has "dreamed of sacrifice" (p. 120). O'Neill's protagonist experiences a four-way tug of war between the Christian, pagan, aesthetic, and materialistic forces within him (and within society). So Julian's soul is at the mercy of the Cardinal, the Lawyer, Butler, and Miss Alice. Julian, like "Dion Brown" (as Cybel calls the composite of the Dion Anthony-Billy Brown multiple personality in *The Great God Brown*), who is shot by a police officer, is killed by a representative of law and order, in his case, the Lawyer. Similarly, O'Neill's statement to the press about Brown: "in the end out of this anguish his soul is born, a tortured Christian soul such as the dying Dion's, begging for belief, and at the last finding it on the lips of Cybele"[15] could almost describe Julian's death scene. He, too, is a "tortured Christian soul" begging for affirmation of his belief.

Miss Alice, in turn, displays similarities not only to Cybel but also to Margaret, both of whom represent aspects of the *Ewig-Weibliche* in the O'Neill play. In the fire scene in *Tiny Alice*, where she speaks in her *"little-girl tone"* (p. 90), Miss Alice approaches O'Neill's "girl-woman" Margaret. When Julian is dying, Miss Alice cradles him in her arms, the two forming "something of a Pietà" (p. 167), which is one way of describing Cybel's and Brown's relationship at the end of *The Great God Brown*. And just as Brown gratefully snuggles against Cybel as he dies, saying, "The earth is warm,"[16] so the dying Julian finds comfort in Miss Alice: "Closer . . . please. Warmth" (p. 168).

The constant putting on and removing of masks in *The Great God Brown* not only objectifies the characters' inner states but also creates a ritualistic pattern. In *Tiny Alice* the "ceremony of Alice" concretizes Julian's distorted view of the Eucharist and combines it with a sinister *rite de passage* that portends Julian's death and links him to Alice. Against a background of carefully positioned characters and considerable patterned movement, Butler, whose name derives from the Old French *cupbearer*, serves Julian his symbolic Last Supper. But since the God of Wrath has become literally mousy, the more substantial traditional red wine has now been diluted into a quickly staling, though deceptively bubbly, champagne.

In this scene Albee throws a little more light on the basic allegory in *Tiny Alice*. While Miss Alice is trying to tell Julian that she is merely an agent of the mouse that lives in the model of the castle, Butler links the mouse to God: "Do you understand, Julian?" asks Miss Alice. "Of course not!" replies Julian. Miss Alice: "Julian, I have tried to be . . . *her*. No; I have tried to be . . . what I thought she might, what might make you happy, what you might use, as a . . . what?" "*Play* God," says Butler. Miss Alice continues: "We must . . . represent, draw pictures, reduce or enlarge to . . . to what we can understand." Julian's next speech returns us to his basic metaphysical dilemma: "But I have fought against it . . . all my life. When they said, 'Bring the wonders down to me, closer; I cannot see them, touch; nor can I believe.' I have fought against it . . . all my life . . . All my life. In and out of . . . confinement, fought against the symbol" (pp. 155–156).

In *The Great God Brown* Dion Anthony dies unmasked at the feet of his alter ego, the crass, materialist Billy Brown. With his last breath, Dion speaks the first two words of the Lord's Prayer. Julian also dies at the mercy of materialistic forces. He, too, struggles to accept the god in the model while the Lawyer and the Cardinal banter over the two billion in the briefcase. And here, in the final scene of *Tiny Alice*, we once more encounter the mask. Dying, Julian asks of God, "How long wilt thou hide thy face from me?" (p. 173) A few moments later the Lawyer enters with Miss Alice's wig and places it on a phrenological head. (In William Ball's highly acclaimed American Conservatory Theatre production of *Tiny Alice* the mask was used more extensively than the published text warrants, and it remained attached to the wig throughout the play.) Phrenology is supposed to tell us something about the mind inside the skull, but here is an empty mannequin. To the accompaniment of the gradual crescendo of the audible heartbeat, an effective borrowing from O'Neill's *The Emperor Jones*, Julian notices the wig on the phrenological head, crawls toward it, and half kneels in front of it. He is alone with this inscrutable dummy, and he addresses it as if it were the mouse-god Alice:

> Thou art my bride? Thou? For thee have I done my life? Grown to love, entered in, bent . . . accepted? For thee? is that the . . . awful humor? Art thou the true arms, when the warm flesh I touched . . . rested against, was . . . nothing? And *she* . . . was not real? Is thy stare the true look? Unblinking, outward, through, to some horizon? And her eyes . . . warm, accepting, were they . . . not real? Art thou my bride? (p. 182)

It is ironic that Julian, who has "fought against the symbol" all his life, should now turn to the mask, as does Margaret in the final moments of O'Neill's "gimmicky" *Great God Brown*: having never really understood Dion, she worships his mask even in death.

Both Albee and O'Neill, like most modern writers, grapple with the meaning of life and religion in a materialistic world. Albee has said that *Tiny Alice* "is essentially an attack on modern institutions, modern materialism, and the illusory nature of modern life, indicating much of the evil caused by the misuse and misunderstanding of the institutions."[17] Albee's statement brings to mind O'Neill's widely quoted remark to George Jean Nathan about the playwright's having to "dig at the roots of the sickness of today as he feels it—the death of the old God and the failure of science and materialism to give any satisfying new one for the surviving primitive religious instinct to find a meaning for life in, and to comfort its fears of death with."[18] These fears are comforted in both plays. Dion Brown dies, *"exultantly"* repeating the words of Cybel: "Our Father—? . . . Who art!"[19] Julian accepts Tiny Alice. Albee has said that "Once Julian accepts the existence of what does not exist, his concept (his faith) exists for him. Or, if one does not accept God, then, there is nothing. Since Julian accepts Tiny Alice, his God becomes real."[20] O'Neill would probably have agreed.

O'Neill would certainly have agreed with Albee's discarding the old implements of dramatic realism in his attempt to dig at the roots of the sickness of today. For most serious playwrights have by now grasped the more imaginative tools of expressionistic dramaturgy in order to hack through "the banality of surfaces," as O'Neill put it, and penetrate into "the characteristic spiritual conflicts which constitute the drama—the blood—of our lives today."[21] The parallels between *Tiny Alice* and *The Great God Brown* suggest that in breaking away from the realistic mode, Albee has been influenced not only by Strindberg and recent European playwrights but also by Eugene O'Neill.

Notes

1. "An Interview with Edward Albee," in *The American Theater Today*, ed. Alan S. Downer (New York, 1967), p. 121. See also Thomas Meehan, "Edward Albee and a Mystery," New York *Times*, December 27, 1964, Sec. 2, p. 16; and "Theater: Talk with the Author," *Newsweek*, LX (October 29, 1962), 52.

2. Quoted in Louis Calta, "Albee Lectures Critics on Taste," New York *Times*, March 23, 1965, p. 33.

3. That the entire play may take place in the mind of Brother Julian has been suggested by Lee Baxandall ("The Theatre of Edward Albee," *Tulane Drama Review*, IX [Summer, 1965], 33–34) and Leighton M. Ballew ("Who's Afraid of *Tiny Alice?*" *Georgia Review*, XX [Fall, 1966], 299).

4. "Broadway: A Tale Within a Tail," *Time*, LXXXV (January 15, 1965), 68. Albee sustains Brother Julian's subjective point of view by means of images of deafness. Julian tells us in Act I, scene three, that his "periods of hallucination would be announced by a ringing in the ears, which produced, or was accompanied by, a loss of hearing." If the characters around Julian are presented as if perceived through the protagonist's mind and the entire play is his hallucination, then these characters should be subject to the sensations experienced by Julian himself. A close reading of the text reveals that loss of hearing, a failure to respond to what other people are saying, characterizes not only Miss Alice when she masquerades as an old and deaf woman but also the Cardinal, the Lawyer, and Butler at various times throughout the play.

5. Edward Albee, *Tiny Alice* (New York, 1966), p. 99. Subsequent references will be to this edition.

6. See, for example, Bernard F. Dukore, "Tiny Albee," *Drama Survey*, V (Spring, 1966), 63. Cf. Howard Taubman, "Theater: Albee's 'Tiny Alice' Opens," New York *Times*, December 30, 1964, p. 14.

7. August Strindberg, *The Father, A Dream Play*, trans. Valborg Anderson (New York, 1964), p. 62.

8. "Edward Albee and August Strindberg: Some Parallels between *The Dance of Death* and *Who's Afraid of Virginia Woolf?*," *Papers on Language and Literature*, I (Winter, 1965), 59–71. See also Taylor's "A Note on 'Strindberg's *The Dance of Death* and Edward Albee's *Who's Afraid of Virginia Woolf?*," *Papers on Language and Literature*, II (Spring, 1966), 187–188.

9. "Theater: Three Plays and a Protest," *New Republic*, CLII (January 23, 1965), 34. It might also be pointed out that *Tiny Alice*, like Strindberg's *The Ghost Sonata*, involves a conflict between hedonism and religious restraint, and both plays introduce the image of horseback riding to suggest sensual pleasures. It may be more than a coincidence, furthermore, that at least one part of the Student's final prayer in *The Ghost Sonata*, "may you be greeted . . . in a house that gathers no dust," is granted in *Tiny Alice*, where Butler announces that the model of the castle is "sealed. Tight. There is no dust." (p. 25)

10. *The Plays of Eugene O'Neill* (New York, 1955), I, 442.

11. Doris V. Falk, *Eugene O'Neill and the Tragic Tension* (New Brunswick, N.J., 1958), p. 103.

12. Paul Gardner, " 'Tiny Alice' Mystifies Albee, Too," New York *Times*, January 21, 1965, p. 22.

13. *Nine Plays by Eugene O'Neill* (New York, 1954), p. 333.

14. Eugene O'Neill, "The Playwright Explains," New York *Times*, February 14, 1926, Sec. 8, p. 2.

15. *Ibid.*

16. *Nine Plays by Eugene O'Neill*, p. 374.

17. Prospectus to the backers of *Tiny Alice*, quoted in Sam Zolotow, "Box-Office Queue for 'Tiny Alice,' " New York *Times*, December 31, 1964, p. 14.

18. Quoted in Joseph Wood Krutch, "Introduction," *Nine Plays by Eugene O'Neill*, p. xvii.

19. *Nine Plays by Eugene O'Neill*, p. 374.

20. Gardner, p. 22.

21. Eugene O'Neill, "Strindberg and Our Theatre," Provincetown Playbill for *The Spook Sonata*, January 3, 1924; reprinted in *O'Neill and His Plays*, ed. Oscar Cargill et al. (New York, 1961), pp. 108–109.

Edward Albee and Maurice Maeterlinck: *All Over* as Symbolism

James Neil Harris*

Edward Albee's play *All Over* clearly is about death and dying. It is literally a deathwatch: an unseen man lies dying, surrounded by his wife, mistress, best friend, children, doctor, and nurse; they talk around him and about him; at the end of the play, the man dies. It is a drama, as Richmond Crinkley has observed, "in which nothing much happens . . . a prolonged doldrums, measured by the apocalypses which don't occur, by the conflicts which are never resolved, and by the rhythms which are repetitive rather than dynamic."[1] Like Albee's earlier avant-garde *Box and Quotations From Chairman Mao Tse-Tung*, *All Over* utilizes an entropic vocabulary, employs similar primary themes and motifs, and gives the nihilistic impression — as its title aptly indicates — of being all over before the action has even begun. Unfortunately, most critics who saw the play's production when *All Over* opened in New York in March, 1971, applauded Albee's ingenious choice of title — but with an ironic twist. As far as they were concerned, the sooner the play's run was all over, the better; *All Over* was denounced as — to give just a quick sampling — "deadly dull,"

*From *Theatre Research International* 3 (1978):200–208. Reprinted by permission of the journal.

"an arrogant display piece, puffed up with sophomoric diction," "self-indulgent," "a depressing event in an enigmatic career," and a "Death Prattle."

Some of the reason for its rapid, ruthless critical rejection may be the playwright's own fault, since he was reported in *The New York Times* to have "admitted" in rehearsal that the play supposedly "was more natural-istic, perhaps closer to *A Delicate Balance* than to his other works."[2] Thus, when most of the reviewers debunked the play as being overly abstract, impersonal, and unbearably dull, they were apprehending the play from the naturalistic *point d'appui* which its author had given them.[3] But this perspective — understandably employed in the wake of *Tiny Alice* — is unsound when applied to *All Over*, since the play owes much more to *Box-Mao-Box* than to *A Delicate Balance*. Albee's statement (if he ever made it) is misleading. *All Over* is not naturalist drama but symbolist drama, develops not from action but exists in stasis, functions not as much on the personal plane as on the level of abstraction.[4] Harold Clurman seems to have discerned this in his note that "*All Over* seems written from a tomb, a world on the other side of existence. Its people, though recognizably contemporary, produce the effect of wraiths recalled from a bygone life. The play conveys an existential shudder which has its origins in the soul's dark solitude."[5]

It also may have origins in Samuel Beckett's *Waiting for Godot*, a work which Albee has always admired. To begin with, *Godot* and *All Over* share a major character — Godot and the dying man — who is never seen, never heard, definitely never arrives, and yet defines all those on-stage by his very non-presence. In addition, within *Godot*, there is a brief episode which clearly ties the two plays together even closer: in Act II there is a beat of dialogue which begins when Estragon, asleep in a fetal position to the cooing of Vladimir's "Bye," suddenly has a nightmare and

> *wakes with a start, jumps up, casts about wildly. Vladimir runs to him, puts his arms round him.*) There . . . there . . . Didi is there . . . don't be afraid . . .
>
> ESTRAGON: Ah!
> VLADIMIR: There . . . there . . . it's all over.
> ESTRAGON: I was falling —
> VLADIMIR: It's all over, it's all over.
> ESTRAGON: I was on top of a —
> VLADIMIR: Don't tell me! Come, we'll walk it off.[6]

Estragon's dream about falling — in other words, dying — and his startled "Ah!" seems echoed in *All Over* by The Wife's dream about death and her startled "Ha-ah" (74)[7] upon awakening bolt upright. Tellingly, *Box-Mao-Box* has employed the image of falling repeatedly, particularly in relation to The Wife's direct predecessor, the Long-Winded Lady. In that play, the

Long-Winded Lady not only falls off an ocean liner but also spends two pages talking of how she has dreamt of "falling straight up . . . or out, all in reverse."[8] Certainly, Beckett's "it's all over" is partly behind Albee's choice of title and can be said to carry much the same existential impact, an attitude which Clive Barnes—in writing of Albee's play—has nicely tagged "death without transfiguration."[9]

The second source for Albee's *All Over* is, unexpectedly perhaps, Maurice Maeterlinck. Albee, unlike some other dramatists, has never been in the habit of mentioning other playwrights by name within his own drama; surprisingly, he makes a point of mentioning Maeterlinck's name twice within the first minutes of this play. It is difficult to dismiss this as name-dropping, using the Belgian symbolist as literary froufrou, since it is plain by the nature and manner of his allusions to Maeterlinck that Albee is familiar with Maeterlinck's life and, as we shall see, his work. The Mistress mentions Maeterlinck first when she recalls that just before her now dying lover had observed the ontological and semantic distinction between "dying" and "death," the two of them had been discussing—and apparently for no good reason—"Maeterlinck and that plagiarism business" (4); the second reference comes when The Wife queries, at the end of The Mistress' speech, "Maeterlinck?" instead of logically picking up on her cue line "But could not . . . be . . . dead" (4). Albee does seem to be going a bit out of his way to slip these references to Maeterlinck in; this is easily perceptible; but why so much emphasis on a man who seemingly does not have anything to do with the rest of Albee's play?

To begin with, Maeterlinck and the unseen dying man of *All Over* are biographical analogues. For example, Maeterlinck and the dying man share the same attitude toward death as a finality sans any postulate of God, loving or merciless; both wish to be cremated; both die at home; both have lived in France—though not Frenchmen—and both have travelled a great deal (96, 101); finally, both exemplify public figures who have outlived their usefulness. Bettina Knapp has stressed that "Maeterlinck was indeed a nineteenth-century man";[10] The Mistress in *All Over* indicates much the same thing when she says that "we [the older characters] keep the nineteenth century going for ourselves" (36). As The Daughter spitefully declares about her father, "The dust bin: anachronism" (59).

Ironically, both have had mistresses. In fact, "that plagiarism business" discussed by The Mistress concerned Maeterlinck's own mistress Georgette Leblanc and her charge that Maeterlinck has secretly plagiarized her work. As W. D. Halls, Maeterlinck's most modern English biographer, tells us: "The thread of grievance that runs through the *Souvenirs* [Georgette Leblanc's *Memoirs*, (1931)] is that Maeterlinck refused to recognize how greatly she inspired his work, particularly *Le Trésor des humbles* and *Sagesée et destinée*. Inevitably the partnership of Willy and Colette springs to mind, but the comparison is inexact. . . .

[but] Georgette Leblanc's role was [that] . . . She helped him to develop, to discover his other self; she brought him out, she fussed over him like a mother. . . . This is a long way from a literary partnership."[11] Albee plays with a charge of "plagiarism" in *All Over*, too — although it is only hinted at, merely suggested. In the play, there is conflict between The Wife and The Mistress over funeral arrangements: The Wife wants her husband buried; The Mistress insists that her lover had expressed the desire to be cremated. The Wife, unless given written proof, refuses to take The Mistress at her word, to which The Mistress — in a sentence reminiscent of George's explanation to Martha about the imaginary telegram in *Who's Afraid of Virginia Woolf?* — replies "It was a verbal . . . envelope" (22) and adds, "Oh, Christ; you people! You will go by what I tell you; finally as I have told you" (23). In the end, whether the dying man had or had not demanded to be cremated is left as open as whether Maeterlinck had or had not plagiarized a sentence or two from Madame Leblanc. And, in an ironic reversal, it is the mistress who is accused of fraud in Albee's play rather than her lover.

But Maeterlinck's influence on *All Over* extends much deeper than biographical data; more influential is Maeterlinck's work. And, in this regard, *Le Trésor des humbles* — that same book which Madame Leblanc felt had been plagiarized from her — deserves particular attention. In this volume of essays published in 1896, is *"Le Tragique Quotidien"* ("The Tragical In Daily Life"), Maeterlinck's most developed discussion of his theory of "static theatre."[12] According to Maeterlinck, static theatre eschews conventional dramatic action and plotting in order to reveal symbolically the true state of the unconscious, or "the soul, self-contained in the midst of ever-restless immensities; to hush the discourse of reason and sentiment, so that above the tumult may be heard the solemn, uninterrupted whisperings of man and his destiny" (TofH, 98). Instead of action per se, the playwright urges "psychological action — infinitely loftier in itself than mere material action, and truly, one might think, well-nigh indispensable" (TofH, 108); in lieu of "bloodshed, battle-cry and sword-thrust," (TofH, 103), theatrical spectacle and adventure, Maeterlinck proposes a drama which "eliminates words which merely explain the action, and substitutes for them others that reveal, not the so-called 'soul-state' but I know not what intangible and unceasing striving of the soul towards its own beauty and truth" (TofH, 112). In short, Maeterlinck's "static theatre" emphasizes the inner life, the constant drama of the emotions, the symbolic conflict of states of feeling. As the most famous passage of the essay states:

> I admire Othello, but he does not appear to me to live the august daily life of a Hamlet, who has time to live, inasmuch as he does not act. . . . I have grown to believe that an old man, seated in his armchair, waiting patiently, with his lamp beside him, giving uncon-scious ear to all the eternal laws that reign about his house, interpreting,

without comprehending, the silence of the doors and windows and the quivering voice of the light, submitting with bent head to the presence of his soul and his destiny . . . that he, motionless as he is, does yet live in reality a deeper, more human and more universal life than the lover who strangles his mistress, the captain who conquers in battle, or "the husband who avenges his honour." (TofH, 105–06)

In order to reveal this "deeper, more human and more universal life," Maeterlinck propounds that the modern dramatist place his characters within a stasis suffused with ritual and symbol.

Maeterlinck does follow his own theory of drama remarkably well within three of his early plays—*L'Intruse* (The Intruder, 1890), *Les Avengles* (The Blind, 1890), and *Intérieur* (Interior, 1894). Like *All Over*, these plays deal thematically with death, belong to the *drame d'attente*, employ a minimum of plot, are tragical in tone, and are based on gesture and ritual. Bettina Knapp, in the concluding pages of her critical study, *Maurice Maeterlinck*, has summarized their common denominators:

> The conflict in dramas such as *The Intruder*, *The Blind*, *Interior* . . . is experienced as an inward journey. The exteriorization of the protagonists' moods and feelings is effected by their physical demeanor and by the incantatory quality of their speech. Maeterlinck's language, punctuated with silences, relies heavily on repetition of sounds and phrases that frequently take on the power of a litany, a melopoeia, rediscovering in this form the original function of language . . . gone are the platitudes and banalities. Words . . . [arouse] a multitude of associations and sensations that act and react viscerally upon the onlooker—not by brash or obvious means but rather by imposed restraints, nuances, and subleties.
>
> Everything within Maeterlinck's plays works toward a cohesive whole. The drama is tightly structured, adhering to the formulas of French classical theater; unity of time, place, and action. Language, lighting, peripeteia, and gesture flow into one central image. Its impact, accompanied by powerful feeling tones, has a cumulative effect on the audience; nuances flay; feelings pain—until the weight of the experience becomes almost unbearable.[13]

Albee's play follows the ideas and dictates of Maeterlinck's static theatre closely. First, *All Over*—as most critical response has indicated—is nearly plotless and particularly static physically. Second, unity of time, place, and action is strictly observed. Third, the language—which Clurman has described as a "frozen fire . . . with every phrase carefully shaped in congruence,"[14] and Barnes has observed as "consciously operatic"[15] is deliberate, repetitive, sometimes even melopoeic, and functions not to resolve conflict but to elucidate mood and feeling. Fourth, the play is heavily symbolic and transparently ritualistic: for example, the set—with its coffin of a bed, a *"huge, canopied four-poster on a raised platform"*—is as dominating a symbol as the transparent cube from *Box-Mao-Box* which

it resembles; the deathwatch itself is so selfconsciously played that even
The Doctor likens himself to a priest (25), The Mistress refers to it as a
rather unpleasant "ritual" (37, 39, 71), The Nurse calls it a "procession"
(72), and The Best Friend defines it as a necessary "custom" (6). Finally,
the overall effect of *All Over* is one of waste, loss, inaction — of stasis —
whereas the effect of the play is nearly negligible, having been predeter-
mined by the very first line ("Is he dead?" [3]). It seems clear that
Maeterlinck's theory of static drama and the general characteristics of his
early work have impressed Albee profoundly.

However, Maeterlinck's influence does not stop here: if his work has
impressed Albee generally, his play *The Intruder* has molded *All Over*
specifically. John Gassner, in his introduction to an English translation of
The Intruder, has stated his belief that this work is "the purest expression"
of Maeterlinck's aesthetic aims and "If the play has no external conflict
and approaches a condition of stasis, it nevertheless progresses from point
to point in representing the growing apprehension of the characters.
Although they obviously cannot cope with anything so intangible as death,
their plight does represent the oldest and most universal of all conflicts.
Conflict, moreover, has its equivalent here in tension . . . and death . . . is
an intensely dramatic reality."[16] Like *All Over*, *The Intruder* is a *drame
d'attente* in which an exhausted family conducts a ritualized deathwatch,
and, just as *All Over*, Maeterlinck's play unfolds in a symbolic and
timeless present, takes place in a gloomy room set in shadow, and has very
little physical movement. The major characters of *The Intruder* — like the
major characters of *All Over* — are identified in the script by their family
relationship, i.e., The Grandfather, The Uncle, The Father, and so on. Its
dialogue also resembles the dialogue of Albee's play in that it describes
characters' feelings but does not alter the play's situation nor create any
new source of dramatic action. Finally, as in *All Over*, *The Intruder*
focuses on an unseen, mute, and bedridden character who brings the play
to its close by dying.

Evidently, then, Albee's mention of Maeterlinck in the first minutes
of *All Over* is neither trivial nor unrelated. Indeed Maeterlinck's life,
aesthetic, and early drama so pervade the framework of Albee's play on
death that it should indicate — no matter what Albee may have said to *The
Times* — that *All Over* does not function as naturalism. On the contrary,
like *The Intruder*, *All Over* must be approached as a symbolic drama if it
is to be approached properly at all. Here, one is reminded that C. H.
Whitman once casually dismissed Maeterlinck's early plays — *The Blind*,
The Intruder, and *Interior* — as "little more than plotless 'mood-
pictures.' "[17] Of course the choice is ours to make.

If we do choose to address *All Over* as symbolism, we see that it
operates simultaneously on a number of different levels. On one plane, the
drama is a thorough examination of interpersonal withdrawal, a withdrawal which contains cataclysmic connotation. The Mistress refers to this

"faint shift from total engagement" (14) and describes it as essentially an act of will: "It's when it happens calmly and in full command: the tiniest betrayal . . . and it can be anything, or nearly nothing, except that it moves you back into yourself a little, the knowledge that all your sharing has been . . . willful [sic], and that nothing has been inevitable . . . or even necessary" (16). This willful disengagement from others has always been portrayed in Albee's drama as the final failure of nerve, as a denial of one's basic humanity, and as a form of dying in itself. On this level, the man hidden in the boxy four-poster is not the only character who is dying—all of them are. His death is also theirs.

To be strictly precise, however, these betrayals, these failures of love, have crystallized long before the weary deathwatch has even commenced. The Wife, who has been separated from her now dying husband for years, has only mean contempt for her ineffective son and is estranged totally from her bitchy daughter; The Son—overweight, withdrawn, and impotent—has apparently never been capable of communicating with his parents and cannot muster the strength even now to face his comatose father; The Daughter consciously alienates everyone in the room, suffers from an extreme Electra complex, has been carrying on a masochistic affair with a married hoodlum who beats her regularly, and is most concerned with "the guilt I can produce in those that do the hurting" (62). The other characters have also failed in vital ways: The Best Friend has just divorced his wife—an act which is compared to murder (32)—and committed her to an insane asylum; The Mistress, whose only ties are to an unseen man, feels put off by the familial ritualism; The Nurse hides her emotions behind a mask of professional cynicism; The Doctor either sleeps or delivers treatises on death (30–32, 99). In a way, we are given *Huis Clos* reserved for a larger party of still-transient guests.

And, like *No Exit*, *All Over's* thrust is existential. Trapped outside of normal considerations of time in the static ritual of a deathwatch, each character must await not only the unseen man's corporal death, but must attempt to face his or her own symbolic death as well. Here, the occupant of the coffin-like container is not important so much as an individual as he is as an abstraction, a point of focus for each character's personal brand of fear and trembling; here, the slow ritual forces an *"existential awareness"* (48), a kind of Heideggerean "being unto-death" (*Sein-zum-Tode*) in which one must recollect one's past, appraise one's future possibilities, and accept one's death in the *now*. But in Albee's play it is a self-examination which comes too late for those who have the courage to accomplish it. The Wife recognizes this paradox at the end of the play when she tonelessly states "All we've *done* is think about ourselves. Ultimately" (110). Truly, The Best Friend's comment that "You end up with what you start out with" (25)—an aphorism which sounds as though coined by Camus' Sisyphus—is a fine summation of each character's own deadly anguish.

On other symbolic levels the anguish expressed in *All Over* is also representative of historical, societal, and generational pain. The emphasis is bleak: the characters worth saving (if any really are) are all well on their way to the grave; the ones worth murdering all have a number of years left to them. As C. W. E. Bigsby has pointed out in his essay "To the Brink of the Grave: Edward Albee's *All Over*," "Time is running out, not only for the dying man but for a dying civilization . . . The connection he [Albee] seeks is that between the body and the body politic, as society reflects the dissolution, the failure of human relationships, the abandonment of responsibility and the callous indifference, observable on an individual scale."[18] Within this context the dying man symbolizes "the Puritan moral soul . . . the sturdy group" (59), the invisible *paterfamilias* of Lee Baxandall's generational scenario who personifies the positive values, energies, and ethos of nineteenth century America. He is, as Baxandall puts it, "the dynamic principle of the vanishing generation,"[19] a patriarchal society which is far superior to the matriarchal perversions of the present (or 'now') generation. However, unlike Martha's imperial father in *Virginia Woolf?* who has the "staying power of one of those Micronesian tortoises" and is "never going to die,"[20] the paterfamilias of *All Over* hasn't a prayer of surviving and is taking the liberal values of an over-idealized nineteenth century right down into the grave with him. Waiting to fill the ensuing vacuum — camped right outside the door, as a matter of fact — is Albee's heinous *nowhere* generation, the "sad and shabby time we live in" (42), the technological and corrupt twentieth century with its TV, "tubes and wires! Like a fungus" (40). *All Over* is here but a few actual breaths removed from that spiritual death exemplified so emptily by the massive cube of Albee's absurdist liturgy *Box-Mao-Box*. Indeed one might say that when The Doctor announces gently "All over" (111) at the close of the play, the playwright really means "ALL OVER!!!"

Finally, let us get back to the title of Albee's pessimistic play. Since Albee has shown himself to be more than a little familiar with Maurice Maeterlinck's life and work, and the dictates of static theatre and symbolist drama, it should be no more than reasonable to assume that Albee is also conversant with Maeterlinck's death. W. D. Halls has related it in some detail:

> About nine o'clock he [Maeterlinck] decided to go to bed. . . . But about ten o'clock the following evening a new crisis occurred. . . . In the throes of a violent heart attack, he murmured, "It's all over with me." Mme. Maeterlinck tried to reassure him. He replied in a whisper, "I have only one regret, that of leaving you." A half-smile played about his lips and he uttered a few unintelligible words. By eleven o'clock on the night of 6 May [1949] he was dead.[21]

"It's *all over* with me" — a coincidence. But does it not seem perfectly fitting that Maurice Maeterlinck's last words turn up as the title and last line of Edward Albee's play on death, a play so weighted by him.

Notes

1. Richmond Crinkley, "The Development of Edward Albee," rev. of *All Over*, by Edward Albee, *The National Review*, 24 Jan. 1967, p. 100.

2. Mel Gussow, "Albee's New 'All Over' in Rehearsal," *New York Times*, 9 Feb. 1971, p. 32.

3. Walter Kerr wrote that "The exercise at the Martin Beck is extraordinarily remote, detached, noncommital" (*New York Times*, 4 April 1971, Sec. 2, p. 1); Jack Kroll echoed this objection when he stated that "abstraction has the windpipe of the play in a death grip" (*Newsweek*, 5 April 1971, p. 52).

4. Clive Barnes noted about *Box-Mao-Box* that "in the 20th century when every art form has moved to the abstract, or at least the impersonal, it is curious how long it is taking the drama to catch up" (*New York Times*, 1 Oct. 1968, p. 39). Later, when reviewing *All Over*, Barnes indirectly refers back to this point when he observes that *All Over* "has been very much influenced by his [Albee's] experiment in theatrical abstraction, *Box-Mao-Box*" (*New York Times*, 29 March 1971, p. 41).

5. Harold Clurman, rev. of *All Over*, by Edward Albee, *Nation*, 12 April 1971, p. 476.

6. Samuel Beckett, *Waiting For Godot*, trans. by Beckett (New York: Grove Press, 1954), p. 45. Albee has read *Godot* a number of times and has said publicly that "There's no self respecting playwright writing today who hasn't been influenced by Samuel Beckett" (*The New Yorker*, 5 June 1974, p. 30). Albee's latest play, *Seascape* (1975), has also been influenced by Beckett — in this case, Beckett's *Happy Days*.

7. Edward Albee, *All Over* (New York: Atheneum, 1971), p. 74. All further references to *All Over* will be given parenthetically, with no abbreviation for title.

8. Edward Albee, *Box and Quotations From Chairman Mao Tse-Tung* (New York: Atheneum, 1969), p. 31.

9. " 'All Over,' Albee's Drama of Death, Arrives," rev. of *All Over*, by Edward Albee *New York Times*, 29 March 1971, p. 41.

10. *Maurice Maeterlinck*, Twayne's World Author Series, No. 342 (Boston: Twayne Publishers, 1975), p. 53.

11. *Maurice Maeterlinck: A Study of his Life and Thought* (London: Oxford University Press, 1960), pp. 123–4. This book, because of its singularity as the only full biography of Maeterlinck thus far in English and its date of publication, may well have been read by Albee.

12. Maurice Maeterlinck, *The Treasure of the Humble*, trans. Alfred Sutro (New York: Dodd, Mead & Co.; London: George Allen, Ruskin House, 1905), p. 106. All further references will be cited parenthetically, with the abbreviation "TofH."

13. Knapp, *Maurice Maeterlinck*, pp. 175–6.

14. Clurman, p. 477.

15. Barnes, *New York Times*, 29 March 1971, p. 41.

16. *A Treasury of the Theatre* (1935; rpt. New York: Simon & Shuster, 1959), p. 266. *The Intruder* can be found in this volume.

17. *Representative Modern Dramas* (1936; rpt. New York: MacMillan, 1958), p. 406.

18. "To the Brink of the Grave: Edward Albee's *All Over*," in *Edward Albee, A Collection of Critical Essays*, ed. C. W. E. Bigsby, Twentieth Century Views (Englewood Cliffs, N.J.: Prentice-Hall, 1975), p. 172.

19. Lee Baxandall, "The Theatre of Edward Albee," *Tulane Drama Review*, 9, No. 4 (Summer, 1965), p. 20. Baxandall discusses Albee's generations on pp. 19–40.

20. Edward Albee, *Who's Afraid of Virginia Woolf?* (New York: Atheneum, 1962), p. 41.

21. Halls, *Maurice Maeterlinck: A Study of his Life and Thought*, p. 164.

CRITICISM

Morality, Absurdity, and Albee Wendell V. Harris*

He who sets himself up as arbiter of literary morality engages in a perilous undertaking. However enlightened the critic may be, and however much a work may seem to deserve censure, there are so many dangers for the knight-errant who attacks immorality in literature that he is lucky if he comes off no worse than Don Quixote with the windmill. The adoption of a tone too righteous produces the effect of self-parody; the attempt to be moderate in denunciation prompts the question, "What's all the fuss about?" And then there is always the painful possibility of falling into the most egregious of Bowdler's errors, that of revealing one's naïveté through missing the meaning of some of the most deliciously off-color passages.

Such reflections on the hazards of the literary censor, official or self-appointed, are brought to mind by the recent objections to the morality of Albee's *Who's Afraid of Virginia Woolf?* The Boston city censor, Richard J. Sinnott, after asking that "abuse of the Lord's name" be deleted in twelve places, added that some fifty other "remarks and epithets" were questionable. W. D. Maxwell, a member of the Pulitzer Prize advisory board which refused to accept its drama jury's nomination of *Who's Afraid*, announced simply, "I thought it was a filthy play."

The unfortunate error of these critics consists in their choosing for attack a play which is not only in its presuppositions and implicit philosophy the most cheering and morally hopeful of Albee's plays, but which contains much more assurance of the possibility of meaningful moral choice than has generally been offered by recent drama. It is hardly necessary to note the impossibility of judging the morality of a play by the vocabulary employed or the openness with which certain human actions and relationships are presented. However, it is important to recognize that the criticisms of Sinnott and Maxwell are unusually wide of the mark, that they indicate a total failure to comprehend the significance of the play, and that there is an especial irony in such charges having been made

*From *Southwest Review* 49 (Summer 1964): 249–56. Reprinted by permission of the author and the journal.

against this particular play at this point in the history of twentieth-century drama. The moral significance of *Who's Afraid* is best made clear by contrasting it with Albee's previous plays. Those which seem to belong to the "theater of the absurd," like most of the other plays generally described by that loosely used term, in effect deny or ignore the fundamental condition for the existence of morality: the very possibility of making a choice between good and evil. Since morality and all other evaluative concepts depend on the existence of discernible alternatives and the possibility of choice between them, these plays deny not only those standards which conventional morality's keepers rush to defend, but all value systems whatever.

Let us consider *The American Dream* and its sequel, *The Sandbox.* . . .

Although the two plays are generally described as American contributions to "the theater of the absurd," like numerous other plays so classed they can as well be analyzed as twentieth-century variants of the genre of satire. Satire proceeds, to a great extent, by making the follies it attacks unmistakably visible through magnification. The creation of a fantastic world which turns out to present in grotesque form certain follies and vices strikingly like those of the society satirized (Lilliput, Erewhon) is one of its favored devices; equally common is a lenslike distortion of the society itself with follies and vices at the center of focus. Now it is obvious that *The American Dream* is a satire directed against the emasculated men and domineering women, the heartlessness, the glitteringly hollow goals and ideals which Albee seems to see on every side in contemporary America. It is equally obvious that the play presents its satire through immense distortion—Mommy, Daddy, the Young Man, and to a lesser extent Grandma are so exaggerated as to become abstractions inhabiting an unreal world. (Albee depends heavily upon this unreality to make possible various techniques for livening up the play: everything from Mrs. Barker's bland removal of her dress to the unreal cleverness of parts of the dialogue is licensed by the play's distance from the real world.) In *The Sandbox* the process of exaggeration is carried one more step, so that the entire scene has become fantasy, though the usual devices for effecting a transition from the world we know to its hyperbolic equivalent are omitted.

However, although Albee is attacking what he believes to be false values, there is an enormous difference between the operation of such twentieth-century satire and that of the traditional genre. Both plays combine denunciation and humor, using the humor as a vehicle for the denunciation in the approved satiric manner. However, one of the recognized qualities of almost all satire but that directed at specific persons is that it allows each reader or viewer to excuse himself from the indictment while seeing that the satiric whip is deserved by those all around him. As Swift says in the preface to *The Battle of the Books*, "satire is a sort of glass, wherein beholders do generally discover everybody's face but their own; which is the chief reason for that kind reception it meets with in the world, and that so very few are offended with it." Yet at least in my own discussions of these plays with those who have seen them performed, a substantial number admitted to a most uneasy feeling of identification with the objects of the plays' satire. The handling of relationships between parents and children, attitudes toward death, and failure to assert one's individuality as satirized in the plays seemed all too close to home.

The reason for this is not far to seek. Ordinarily, those characters upon whom satire falls are seen as aberrants, as having departed from established values. Such is true even when the satire would seem to be aimed at the majority of the members of a given society; that which is being attacked in such cases is departure from a norm which is recognized though not adhered to. Even Swift's supposedly misanthropic attack on the human race in the fourth book of *Gulliver's Travels* is no exception, for not only had *Swift* already supplied the ideal in his description of the Brobdingnagians and Houyhnhnms, but the eighteenth-century belief in the attainability and value of rationality provided the norm. In contrast, no quality of the twentieth century has been more often cited than the lack of assured values, the search for some code to replace all those standards which disintegrated during the latter half of the nineteenth century. A contemporary satire simply cannot assume the existence of universally recognized norms existing outside itself.

It is from this normlessness that the term "theater of the absurd" has of course been derived. To explain the application of "absurd" to much of modern drama, Martin Esslin, the best-known analyst of the "movement," quotes Camus: "Absurd is that which is devoid of purpose. . . . Cut off from his religious, metaphysical, and transcendental roots, man is lost; all his actions become senseless, absurd, useless." Esslin thus distinguishes his use of the word from its common meaning of "ridiculous." However, it becomes clear in the body of his book that, like the existentialists themselves, Esslin trades on both senses of the word: that is, characters and actions which are absurd in the sense of ridiculous are employed to portray a world which is absurd in the sense of meaningless. But in any case, to say that the world is meaningless is to say that there is no system of interpretation which can establish meaning and thus no possible pattern of action which can be meaningful.

Such a situation undercuts the whole question of the freedom of the will, making that once hotly contested issue irrelevant. For what does it matter whether one may unconditionally make choices or decisions if there is no standard by which to judge the correctness of those choices? The most dramatic recent expression of this radical denial is *Waiting for Godot*. As Vladimir and Estragon wait, passing the time by pointless dialogue and by making decisions they don't carry out, it becomes apparent that although these two tramps can indeed make choices and decisions, they are unable to determine whether a given choice is good or bad, for they have no criteria by which to judge. Were Godot to appear, he presumably would provide such criteria, but he has not come, is not coming.

The audience is to be drawn into the situation portrayed on "the theater of the absurd" then, not in the traditional manner through an illusion of reality, but by each beholder's identification of his own lack of certainty and direction with that underlying the action on the stage. The audience has no set of values against which to contrast, or through which to give perspective to, the chaos on the stage. Such an analysis of the relation between audience and play is not peculiar to myself; support from a very different point of view is to be found in Lionel Abel's fascinating little volume, *Metatheatre*. First, in his analysis of Jack Gelber's *The Connection*, Abel discovers the source of the play's power precisely in the manner in which it traps the audience into feeling as rootless and directionless as the dope addicts the play presents. The member of the audience who knows what his values are and believes himself possessed of more strength than the addicts will be able to leave the play at any point, says Abel. But, those who are not sure that their values are better than heroin stay to the end, though only to find that the end provides no revelation. What the play has to say is simply that there are no superior values, or at least if there are, few can find them. Similarly, Abel discovers an ancestor for such plays in Cervantes' *The Marvellous Pageant*, a play which, says Mr. Abel, "charms at once." In Cervantes' play, a stage audience is shown watching a ludicrous performance which it has been told will be fascinating to all except Jews and bastards. Everyone in the stage audience of course feels the necessity of enduring the performance to the end — one did not care needlessly to proclaim oneself either Jew or bastard in seventeenth-century Spain. But what attracts Abel to the play is that he feels Cervantes was relying on each member of the real audience to feel the same compulsion to endure the play to the end for fear of being himself stigmatized as bastard or Jew. Now although I dissent from Abel's praise for such plays, it seems to me that he has accurately identified the rather morbid fascination of the modern "theater of the absurd," "metatheater," or "theater without norms."

Secondly, Abel insists that the kind of drama written by Beckett, Ionesco, Genet, and Albee (as well as their forerunners) depends on the world's being seen as an illusion; that is, it depends on our not feeling the reality of the events on stage, but seeing everything presented there as dramatic construction. This explains these playwrights' fascination with plays within plays and roles within roles (especially noticeable in Genet). The paradoxical effect of all such devices is that while the characters on stage become so distanced that they do not seem human beings capable of sincere or deep feeling, members of the audience find, despite their laughter, that they are feeling painful emotions, the source of which is the realization, at one level of consciousness or another, that the grounds of all values are being denied.

What the "absurd" plays of Albee essentially satirize, then, is the human condition itself, not deviations from an ideal. Gilbert Highet has argued that those aspects of human life which are essentially horrible or pathetic cannot be satirized, Edgar Johnson that one does not satirize a man dying of cancer, or any other irremediable evil. But it is just here that the work of such dramatists as Albee most obviously breaks with traditional satire: Albee attempts to satirize a situation which he sees as both painful and irremediable.

Further, Albee's earlier realistic plays, *The Zoo Story* and *The Death of Bessie Smith*, are in fact brutal attacks on humanity itself. *The Zoo Story* is effective drama, and parts of the dialogue are truly comic, but the choices it seems to postulate are simply those of being so sensitive as to be more than a little mad, or compromising, priggish, and finally contemptible. There may be a middle ground, but no hint of its existence is to be found in the play itself. In *The Death of Bessie Smith* Albee has abandoned almost all comic resource, grimly analyzing the odiousness of human motivation. Bessie's driver wrecks the car because he has drunk too much while boasting of his connection with her; the white nurses refuse to aid in order to show power and superiority; the intern is prevented from immediately exercising his humanity by fear and a last touch of desire for one of the nurses.

The essence of drama—satiric, tragic, or comic—is revelation. The revelation of *The American Dream* and *The Sandbox* is that human life is selfish and unavoidably, even disgustingly, trivial and animal-like. The revelation of *The Zoo Story* is merely that eccentrics on the verge of suicide are more interesting than the ordinary cowed and compromising citizen. The revelation of *Bessie Smith* is that the determining motives of human action are largely base. All represent satire at its farthest boundary, that of the sardonic grimace which Northrop Frye has described as "the seamy side of the tragic vision" constituting "a universal negation that cheapens and belittles everything."

It is precisely because Albee's earlier work is so largely a negation of the possibility of meaningful human action that *Who's Afraid* is so significant. Amidst all the violence and bitterness of the play, for the first time Albee gives us three-dimensional human beings. More important, the illusions which the play presents are confined to the stage characters; it does not assert that life is as much an illusion as that which occupies the stage. And most important, by the conscious exercise of a willed choice, one of the characters, George, finds it possible to dispel those illusions, to reconstitute the world in which he lives, not merely by subjectively assuming a role or adopting a new illusion, but objectively, by finding a meaning in the human relationships which surround him and moving toward a goal which he, the other characters, and the audience all can recognize as meaningful.

It has been objected that the whole play hinges on a trick, the discovery by the audience that George and Martha's child is imaginary. That the child proves a product of the imagination is of course the heart of the play, but it is far more than a trick. In the first place it is prepared for by a series of hints that there is some secret about the child; these begin with the initial reference, George's "Just don't start in on the bit about the kid, that's all." Thus the moment at which it becomes apparent that the child never existed is not only dramatically impressive, but explains the incubus which has hovered over the action of the play to that point — and shows that it can be exorcised. And more importantly, the imaginary child is a symbolic assertion that at least a great part of the turmoil and the feeling of futility in human life results not from an unalterably tragi-comic human dilemma, but from remediable human error compounding itself.

The childless couple in their frustration had indeed made themselves parents, parents of a mind-and-soul-destroying illusion. Once they have recognized the destructiveness of their creation, however, a new relationship between themselves and with the world becomes possible, a relationship which will necessarily be imperfect, at times painful, at times perhaps foolish, but which will not be merely "absurd." That is the revelation of *Who's Afraid*.

[Albee in Protest]   Michael Rutenberg*

Why has Albee been embraced as the single hope for an almost ossified Broadway theatre? Unquestionably it is his supreme ability to present plays of shocking social protest which reflect present-day thinking. These plays, rich in verbal texture and poetic rhythms, display his uncanny genius for theatricalizing human conflict and speak to a modern generation determined to break through the deadly apathy of the fifties. It is a television generation that has been horrified by the assassinations of John and Robert Kennedy, Martin Luther King, Malcolm X, and Medgar Evers; a generation of dissidents appalled at this country's intervention in Vietnam, and angered by a war budget of thirty billion dollars a year while Congress quietly cuts back federal funds for the maze of domestic poverty programs to a token two billion dollars a year; a generation that has read the President's *Report of the National Advisory Commission on Civil Disorders*, and agrees with its indictment of our historically irrational and inhuman racist credo.

*From *Edward Albee: Playwright in Protest* (New York: Drama Book Specialists, 1969), 5–11. Reprinted by permission of the author.

Albee speaks to these dissentients who are united in their fervor to churn up a social cataclysm that will bring about needed reforms. He speaks to those who have stood up to the huge, previously unshakable urban Boards of Education, and are now forcing them to decentralize in order to give more community control over ghetto schools. He appeals to those kindred youth who have watched their elders dissociate themselves from the plight of the American Indian and the migratory farm worker and look the other way while ten million people in this wealthy nation suffer the effects of malnutrition because they are too poor to buy the proper food. Albee relates to a new student generation that has seen first-hand evidence of CIA subversion of the National Students Association and recognizes the *faux pas* Congress made when it exempted this undercover agency from normal legislative surveillance and the General Accounting Office[1], a student generation that is beginning to question those institutions of higher learning that advocate the right to teach *in loco parentis* and disallow students a voice in campus administration or shaping curriculum — a rationale that has also punished male students for long hair and fanciful clothing. . . .

Contemporary writing turned about and soon began to reflect this new surge of social commitment. The *New American Review* (of fiction, essays, and poetry) devoted its summer 1968 edition to a socio-political dialogue between writer and reader. National magazines and scores of paperback books whose main themes examine the domestic and foreign scene have entered bookstores and newsstands across the country. In the theatre Edward Albee writes reformist plays of social protest which unflinchingly reveal the pustulous sores of a society plagued with social ills. His first decade of playwrighting has consistently displayed an unyielding social commitment as he experimented with varying dramatic styles and playwriting techniques. Realism served admirably for the shocking events of *The Zoo Story, Who's Afraid of Virginia Woolf?*, and *A Delicate Balance*; surrealism provided the form for the socio-political didactics of *The Sandbox* and *The American Dream*; impressionism was the major style of social protest in *The Death of Bessie Smith*; symbolist mysticism permeated the theological metaphysics of *Tiny Alice*; and theatrical revolution prompted the polyphonic, nonnarrative design of *Box-Mao-Box*.

Albee's early plays from *Zoo Story* through *American Dream*, though vastly different in theatrical form, are all protests in defense of those outcasts of society who have been victimized by the stupidity and bias of the successful elite. In *Virginia Woolf* his sociological vantage point changes, and he attacks the hypocrisy and corruption in some critics of the intelligentsia of our society, stripping all comfortable illusion from the protagonists in an effort to make them face the truth of their barren lives. The later plays, *A Delicate Balance* and *Tiny Alice*, continue the destruction of individual illusion, but go further into an exploration of modern man's very real sense of isolation and estrangement from society and his God. The adaptations, *Ballad of the Sad Cafe* and *Malcolm*, though certainly not up to the level of his indigenous works, support his defense of the misfit — society's outsider — while the last of these, *Everything in the Garden*, continues his assault on an affluent society gone amoral. His newest theatre piece is actually two short but highly original plays of The New Theatre. The first, *Box*, a post-holocaust requiem for the dead, performed in monodic fashion, is carefully interwoven into the second, *Quotations from Mao Tse-Tung*, a contrapuntal score for voices whose main theme is man's impending doom.

Albee's plays of social protest work because they touch the pulse of change in our time. He is into what is happening. The anti-realistic revolution going on in today's New Theatre had its start with men like Jarry, Artaud, Beckett, Ionesco, Genet, and Pinter, but its social commitment was influenced by Edward Albee and his English counterpart, John Osborne. Young American playwrights such as Rochelle Owens, Sam Shepard, Paul Foster, Megan Terry, Leonard Melfi, Lanford Wilson, Jean-Claude van Itallie, LeRoi Jones, Rosalyn Drexler, and many, many others, came out of Albee's Playwrights Unit and other Off-Off Broadway hostels, notably: Joe Chaiken's Open Theatre (which is an outgrowth of the Beck's Living Theatre), Ellen Stewart's Cafe La Mama, Al Carmine's Judson Memorial Theatre, Ralph Cook's Theatre Genesis, and the late Joe Cino's Cafe Cino. These innovative artists have in part helped to create the mixed-media play — a genre more stirring and more raucous than its prototype, The Living Newspaper of the Federal Theatre.

It is apparent in any historical overview of dramatic writing in this country that it has been Edward Albee (though Miller should be included, but to a lesser degree) who has shown the new theatre writers that they can no longer remain aloof to social and political commitment as their predecessors did for more than a quarter of a century after the demise of social drama in the late thirties. . . . .

Some *have* dropped out, frantic to induce an LSD psychosis or narcoticize themselves into vegetative oblivion, rather than admit to the boredom of an uncommitted life. But Edward Albee has not left the scene. Unwilling to accept the perpetuation of a *pastiche* theatre, he refuses to compromise his personal vision, vindicating this new generation's belief in him. All across this country, with the sole exception of Shakespeare, he is the most produced playwright in colleges and universities. It is because Edward Albee has never believed — as do his European contemporaries — that man is a helpless pawn caught in the capricious grip of an absurd and indifferent universe. Writing out of the social ferment and societal unrest which surrounds his very existence, Albee has given a resurgence to the history of social protest in the theatre, a tradition that has its roots in Aristophanes' criticism of the Peloponnesian War. Albee is, and has always been, a social protester, deeply moral, and committed to the cause of human dignity in an ethically moribund age. He has said of the artist's work, ". . . the responsibility of the writer is to be a sort of demonic social critic — to present the world and people in it as he sees it and say, 'Do you like it: if you don't like it change it.' " As Alan Schneider has declared, Albee "speaks and feels for the American moment that is *now*, and he's a talent that has only started."[2]

Notes

1. Marver H. Bernstein, Robert K. Carr, and Walter F. Murphy, *Essentials of American Democracy* (New York: Holt, Rinehart, and Winston, 1968), pp. 484–85.

2. Interview by Richard Schechner entitled "Reality Is Not Enough: An Interview with Alan Schneider," *Tulane Drama Review*, 9 (Spring 1965), 118–152.

Evasions of Sex: The Closet Dramas

Foster Hirsch*

The anti-female strain in Albee's work is nakedly obvious. In *The American Dream*, Mommy destroys her son, almost literally gobbling him up. Martha in *Virginia Woolf* is almost a parody of female lechery. The Nurse in *Bessie Smith* is a demon of negative energies. In these early plays, Albee unleashed his misogyny in bitter, hilarious tirades; his intense feelings were expressed in great waves of fierce rhetoric. These wildly funny female gorgons are the most spectacularly written roles in the canon. They are each presented with the kind of theatrical overstatement that is severely chastened in the later chamber plays of more intimate focus. Manic, extroverted, on the warpath, Albee's rampaging women established his reputation.

Mixed with Albee's evident disgust with these women, however, is a kind of complicity, even a certain sly, grudging admiration for their strength, or for their triumph over their weakness. It is too simple to describe Albee as an out-and-out misogynist. In *Seascape*, he creates a wise, relaxed woman, and his matrons in *A Delicate Balance*, in *All Over*, and in *Quotations from Chairman Mao Tse-Tung* are not vicious. They are forbiddingly formal, but they uphold rather than destroy their families. Their commitment to order and decorum provides shelter and necessary, if rather sombre, comfort. Albee clearly intends us to respect them, if not exactly to regard them with warmth. He admires their steadfastness, their stern WASP morality.

The women Albee reserves his sharpest satiric jabs for are the ones

*From *Who's Afraid of Edward Albee?* (Berkeley, CA: Creative Arts Book Co., 1978), 101–35. Reprinted by permission of the publisher.

who unravel, like the Nurse and Mommy, the hysterics who want everyone to collapse along with them. Women rule the roost in Albee's households; sometimes they govern wisely if icily, sometimes their power is clearly threatening and emasculating. It is significant, though, that women are typically presented as maternal rather than romantic figures.

Sexual fear of powerful women, a theme which is sounded obliquely in almost all the plays, is a major element in two dramas, *Tiny Alice* and *Malcolm*. In these two works, men who are weak enough to be seduced by aggressive women pay with their lives for their moral lapse. In his scathing review of *Tiny Alice*, "The Play That Dare Not Speak Its Name" (*The New York Review of Books*, February 25, 1965), Philip Roth accused Albee of writing a disguised homosexual play in which the gay man's fear of sleeping with a woman is presented as an allegory about faith and doubt, appearance and reality. . . .

Although Roth's harsh reading was attacked at the time as simplistic and reductionist, it is in fact eminently sensible. Roth cuts through the play's topheavy religious and philosophical masquerade to focus on the sexual frustration that is at the core of Albee's fable.

A lay Brother, on an errand for his church, goes to the mansion of Miss Alice, who plans to make a donation of two billion dollars. Brother Julian is unknowingly being used as a scapegoat, since the bequest will be made only if he is sacrificed to the deity Miss Alice represents. In the course of the play, Miss Alice seduces, marries, and then abandons the innocent go-between. Seeing that Julian is really a terrified child, Miss Alice skillfully controls her sexuality beneath displays of matronly concern. Julian is soothed, caught off-guard. He confesses to Miss Alice that he may once have slept with a woman at the time he was confined to an asylum. His possible lover was a religious hysteric, a woman with delusions that she was the Virgin Mary. Julian himself suffers from an acute Christ complex. He is a masochist, enamored of a voluptuous vision of himself as a martyr. "I have longed . . . to be of great service," he announces to Miss Alice. "When I was young—and very prideful—I was filled with a self-importance that was . . . well disguised. Serve. That was the active word! . . . I WISH TO SERVE AND . . . BE FORGOTTEN."

For Julian, humiliation and pain are deeply sexual. His fantasy of Christian martyrdom, in which the Romans "used the saints as playthings," produces orgasmic release:

> Oh, when I was a child and read of the Romans . . . I could entrance myself, and see the gladiator on me, his trident fork against my neck, and hear, even hear, as much as feel, the prongs as they entered me; the . . . beast's saliva dripping from the yellow teeth, the slack side of the mouth, the . . . sweet, warm breath of the lion; great paws on my spread arms . . . even the rough leather of the pads; and to the point of . . . as the great mouth opened, the breath no longer warm but hot, the fangs on my jaw and forehead, positioned . . . IN. And as the fangs

sank in, the great tongue on my cheek and eye, the splitting of the bone, and the *blood* . . . just before the great sound, the coming dark and the silence. I could . . . experience it all. And was . . . engulfed. Oh, martyrdom. To be that. To be able . . . to be that.

Julian's notion of martyrdom is a thinly disguised gay fantasy, in which the weak lay Brother is vanquished by a rough gladiator — nelly gay sodomized by butch leather stud.

When Julian gives himself to Miss Alice, it is because of his desire to serve God and Church through the exquisite pleasure of self-sacrifice. Driven by a compulsion to debase himself, enticed by fantasies of physical torture and degradation, Julian makes an excellent patsy, primed for rape. On one level (its lowest), *Tiny Alice* is an overexcited sadomasochistic fantasy, with Julian the willing, quivering masochist to the sadism of the Church. Like the characters in Genet's *The Balcony*, Julian cannot take his sex straight; he can achieve orgasm only through elaborate ceremonies of self-debasement. Sex for him, as for Genet's gamesplayers, must be heavily ritualized.

Albee's methods are as indirect as his character's tortured sexuality. He presents Julian as a man of austere religious scruples who is unable to reconcile an ideal concept of God — God as pure abstraction — with man's limiting, anthropomorphic concept of divinity. Throughout most of the drama, Julian is ravaged by religious doubts, by a crisis of faith. The character's religious confusion — his ache to serve the Church, his struggle to understand the infinite — is, however, only a mask for his sexual hysteria. Between his terror of women and his temperamental inability to be actively homosexual, Julian is sexually traumatized, and Albee has constructed a flamboyant fable in which the scared lay Brother is tricked into heterosexuality.

Julian's "punishment" for sleeping with a woman is extreme: he is betrayed by Miss Alice, by his Cardinal, and by a Lawyer, who is the worldly emissary between Miss Alice and the Church. In the play's allegorical scheme, he is seduced and abandoned by Women, Religion, and Society. And all because he had sex with a woman!

Albee has cleverly elaborated this perverse sexual tale into a multi-focus drama, which is at once a busy religious allegory about one man's loss and recovery of faith; a satire on the worldliness, the corruption, and greed of the Church; a parable about appearance and reality, the symbol and the substance, the abstract and the concrete; a morality play about man's inevitable defeat in reaching for the Platonic Ideal. Since its theatrically charged surface, its overheated drama of religious and philo-sophical conflict, masks its sexual trauma, the play itself becomes part of the dialectic between appearance and reality that is one of its persistent themes.

As in virtually all of Albee's work, sex is handled evasively, kept at a distance from the play's ostensible focus of dramatic interest. For Julian, the religious and the sexual impulse are hopelessly entangled. Though linked to the character's spiritual quest, sex remains concealed throughout the play. In *Tiny Alice*, the sexual masquerade is more elaborate and more highly charged than in any other Albee drama because the concept of the mask, of subterfuge, is built into the play's method as well as its theme. Everything here is merely a front for something else. Miss Alice is only the earthly representative of the deity Tiny Alice, who is in fact infinite. Miss Alice first confronts Julian in the disguise of an old woman, and, though she takes off this mask, she remains in "costume" for the rest of the play— Julian never does learn exactly who and what she is. Miss Alice, Lawyer, and Butler, the three guardians, are controlled by the mysterious and omnipotent Force of Tiny Alice, and so their behavior is never free or genuine; they're puppets. Inside the mansion is a model of the mansion, and inside that model is another replica. When a fire breaks out in the chapel in the full-scale mansion, there is a facsimile fire in the model, or miniature mansion. Examples of the real and the fake multiply dizzy-ingly—the play is a mosaic of reflections and replications. Each character and event is therefore seen in symbolic double focus; for Julian, the mansion is a treacherous place because nothing in it is what it seems to be; everything is both smaller and larger than its actual dimensions, thereby hopelessly confounding Julian's romantic quest for the Absolute.

In the fantastic world that the play constructs, then, reality is maddeningly elusive, confusing, hostile. The play itself is confused and confusing, cunning in its slipperiness. Albee, on one level, doesn't want his audience to get it, and his symbolic scaffolding is designed to push us off the track, to keep us away from the central, inescapable theme of the fear of powerful women. The allegorical embellishments keep the sexual neuroses at a distance. (This same kind of self-created aloofness is evident in Albee's recent mannerist work, where affected language and format build screens against unmanageable feelings.)

Despite the skillful diversionary tactics, *Tiny Alice* contains the ultimate image of enveloping, devouring Womanhood in the canon. The play raises the domineering woman figure that recurs obsessively in Albee's writing to the exalted position of rapacious, all-consuming Deity. Miss Alice, who has been both mother and mistress to Julian, abandons him to the dark powers of the ironically misnamed infinity, Tiny Alice. As he lays dying in the empty mansion, as the force of Tiny Alice overwhelms him, Julian, the abandoned Brother, resembles the many other abandoned, mistreated, fatally maimed children in Albee's work. Like the mutilated child in *The American Dream* and the imaginary child in *Virginia Woolf*, he has been used by his "parents," cruelly manipulated by them for their own self-serving needs. But even in Brother Julian's orgasmic final soliloquy, Albee links the sexual resolution—Tiny Alice overtakes Julian, female force overwhelms male weakness—to the spurious philosophical theme: Julian, we are meant to understand, has been finally united with that Abstraction he has struggled to experience and to visualize:

> You . . . thou . . . art . . . coming to me? ABSTRACTION? . . . ABSTRACTION! . . . Art coming to me. How long wilt thou forget me, O Lord? Forever? How long wilt thou hide thy face from me? . . . Consider and hear me, O Lord, my God. CONSIDER AND HEAR ME, O LORD, MY GOD. LIGHTEN MY EYES I SLEEP THE SLEEP OF DEATH. BUT I HAVE TRUSTED IN THY MERCY, O LORD. HOW LONG WILT THOU FORGET ME? How long wilt thou hide thy face from me? COME, BRIDE! COME, GOD! COME! Alice? Alice? ALICE? MY GOD, WHY HAST THOU FORSAKEN ME? The bridegroom waits for thee, my Alice . . . is thine. O Lord, my God, I have awaited thee, have served thee in thy . . . ALICE? ALICE? . . . GOD? I accept thee, Alice, for thou art come to me. God, Alice . . . I accept thy will.

At the end, as throughout the play, Albee sets up a network of correspondences: Julian's lust for union with abstraction is both religious and sexual; the language is both mock-sexual (the punning use of "come") and mock-religious (the echoes of Christ's crucifixion); God and Alice are hopelessly enmeshed in Julian's ravings; Julian's martyrdom is equated, in language and iconography, with Christ's. Philip Roth scoffed that Julian's death has "as much to do with Christ's Passion as a little girl's dreaming about being a princess locked in a tower has to do with the fate of Mary Stuart." Julian is likened to Jesus Christ, Roth suggests acidously, "because he has had to suffer the martyrdom of heterosexual love."

Written in Albee's early, exuberant style, *Tiny Alice* is exciting hocus-pocus. It has enormous theatrical imagination and audacity — it is something of a put-on, a coded gay drama about what happens if you get seduced by a woman. The writing has the verve and attack, the manic energy, evident in the one-acts. The play's opening dialogue between Lawyer and Cardinal, universally admired for its crackling, venomous wit, sets the campy but evasive tone. The exchange between these two poseurs suggests, glancingly, that they were schoolboy lovers. They understand, and are skillful in exposing, each other's nastiness. . . .

Mocking each other's homosexuality, the characters express themselves with campy sarcasm and irony; their arch, mock-imperial tone (Cardinal uses "we") has unmistakable elements of stereotypical gay humor. The scene establishes a connection that runs throughout the play between the priesthood and homosexuality: "The more urbane of us wondered about the Fathers at school," Lawyer recalls, "about their vaunted celibacy . . . among one another. Of course, we were at an age when everyone diddled everyone else . . . and I suppose it was natural enough for us to assume that the priests did too." Later, Butler's calling Lawyer "Dear," and his insinuating, flirtatious manner toward Julian underscore the veiled homosexual milieu. In outmoded gay jargon, *Tiny*

Alice is a code term for the anus. Has Albee played a sly in-joke on straight audiences?

Aggressively heterosexual critics like Robert Brustein, Richard Schechner, Philip Roth, and Stanley Kauffmann have accused Albee of writing closet dramas in which hidden gay motifs sneak by the unsuspecting bourgeois crowd that comprises most of the playwright's audience. Philip Roth summarized the impatience of critics with gay masquerades when he asked, at the end of his review of *Tiny Alice*, "How long before a play is produced on Broadway in which the homosexual hero is presented as homosexual, and not disguised as an angst-ridden priest, or an angry Negro, or an aging actress, or worst of all, Everyman?"

Homosexual imagery and character types are presented indirectly in Albee's plays. One of Albee's many screens as a writer is the one he erects between himself and the subject of homosexuality. Apart from the special case of *Tiny Alice*, only his early plays, *The Zoo Story*, *The Sandbox*, and *The American Dream*, and his adaptations of the work of other writers, *Malcolm* and *The Ballad of the Sad Cafe*, contain gay motifs, and these are treated circumspectly, almost surreptitiously. Homosexuality is never called by its rightful name, but, as in *Tiny Alice*, is introduced as both something else and something *more* than simple homosexuality. Brother Julian isn't presented as a gay man for whom sleeping with a woman is a fate not worse than but exactly equal to death; he is a tormented seeker after union with a pure, abstract divinity. Similarly, Jerry in *The Zoo Story* doesn't want simply to pick Peter up, he wants to sacrifice himself as a kind of perverse testimonial to human isolation. He is not a cruising gay (Albee hardly confronts this level of the action), he is a haunted, brooding loner with a Christ fixation. Like Brother Julian, Jerry compulsively seeks martyrdom.

Typically, sexual drives in Albee become transfigured into mock-religious acts of sacrifice, penitence, and immolation; sex is incorporated into a lofty symbolic framework. Sex in Albee's work is not a healthy, gusty sport — the happiest celebration of sex in the entire canon is the memory of a long ago summer affair spoken by the Mistress in *All Over* in which, distanced by time, a teen-age passion is eulogized. Albee's characters customarily use sex either as a deadly weapon in ferocious marital battles, or else abstain from it altogether, like the withered middle-aged couples that figure prominently in the recent plays.

Jerry in *The Zoo Story* is representative of Albee's evasions of sex. . . .

Albee presents Jerry's agonizing loneliness as a universal condition, rather than a specifically gay one. At the end, Jerry impales himself on a dagger that he has thrust into Peter's hand. The character's self-willed crucifixion is intended to give the park bench encounter allegorical dimensions. The lesson that Jerry learned at the zoo — the one he keeps threatening to reveal to Peter — is that, like the animals, we all occupy our separate cages. Jerry immolates himself on Peter's knife as a testament to that dark truth; but on a less exalted level, does that swift thrust of the dagger suggest sexual penetration as well? "I came unto you," Jerry laughs, faintly, "and you have comforted me. Dear Peter." Sexual climax and crucifixion, as in *Tiny Alice*, are inextricable; death and sexual release mingle in dark alliance.

Homosexual imagery is more blatant, though even less relevant thematically, in *The American Dream* and *The Sandbox*. A bikini-clad young man, a male model type, is a prominent icon in both short pieces. *The American Dream* is a longer version of material first articulated in *The Sandbox*—both plays use the same family consisting of bossy Mommy, namby-pamby Daddy, and acerbic Grandma, and in both the Young Man is an emissary of death, his perfection of form a reminder of mortality. Albee's symbolic use of the beautiful male figure is thus highly charged as well as ambiguous. The body beautiful is placed center stage for the approval of the characters as well as the audience. But the character's physical perfection is associated, as in the work of Tennessee Williams, with death. Albee's Young Man, like Williams's stud figures in play after play, and especially in *The Milk Train Doesn't Stop Here Any More*, is an angel of mercy who guides old women to their end. The Young Man, the American Dream, comes to "call" on Grandma. He treats her with gentleness. He is sensitive and patient, and in some undefined way he is a source of salvation: he represents, for Grandma, an alternative to the confinement and indignity of life in her mean daughter's house. The Young Man himself has a more negative interpretation of his beauty, his physique being merely a shell, a thin cover for emptiness. His external perfection is the objective emblem of the American Dream—the Young Man, who is himself a "dreamboat," is both symptom and result of a national addiction to superficial values; his unblemished form and his supreme passivity, his absence of feeling, indicate a bankrupt national sensibility, a corrupt infatuation with plastic surfaces.

Typically, as a social dramatist, Albee is undistinguished, a mere dabbler in generalizations about false values and deceptive appearances. His use, though, of a curiously de-eroticized hustler-like figure is richly ambiguous. The character is both gentle and vacant, both innocent and cynical. His youth is a reminder of Grandma's age. Albee seems to respond positively to the character's beauty and at the same time to resent him for it, to undermine the beauty as a mask for inner emptiness. Youthful beauty is enshrined as powerful and beckoning, and then attacked for its spiritual vacancy; and so, in ways that remain unresolved and even to some extent unexplored, the American Dream is both admired and satirized, both applauded for his pleasing facade and scored for his festering insides.

Although the Young Man is an image of ripe sexuality, Albee presents him as being sexless. He merely triggers the sexual desires of others. Like the popular notion of the cool hustler, whose Narcissus-like admiration of his own form is self-sufficient, the American Dream does not, cannot, reciprocate. As an icon, the American Dream is a blatantly gay fantasy figure, but Albee avoids presenting the character as specifically gay. The dark world of the sexual outlaw, the urban landscape of John Rechy's *City of Night*, with its compulsive sex-seekers, is only faintly suggested in Albee's play. As a creative writer, Albee is clearly more comfortable in the heterosexual suburban drawing room than in the homosexual underground. Sexual tensions aren't as taut in his work as in Tennessee Williams's, where there is often a conflict between the heterosexual surface and the homosexual undercurrents.

Williams's work often follows the Proustian Albertine strategy, where, because of social pressures, the writer plays it safe by transforming a male figure into a female. Proust transferred his own feelings for a man into a fictional counterpart, who was, for propriety's sake, female. Williams's plays contain the same kind of transference. Hungry women who desire beautiful men are imaginative transformations of the writer's own impulses. There is a deep psychic connection between the playwright, concealing his own sexual identity, and a character like Blanche Du Bois, hiding her sexual rapacity beneath a mask of ladylike gentility. In many ways, Williams benefited from the pressures of social convention, which set limits on what kind of sexuality would be acceptable in the commercial theatre for which he wrote. Williams's sense of restriction creates the explosive sexual tension that bursts through his writing even in his less flavorful later work. Williams is a poet of homosexual longing that is expressed and released through nominally heterosexual characters. The resulting clash between surface image and subtextual resonance has been useful to Williams as a creative artist, if not perhaps always healthy for his psyche. Williams feels, in fact, even after he has publicly come out, in *Memoirs*, and now that it is not only safe but "in" to write an openly gay play, that homosexuality is not a promising subject for him as a dramatist. He fears the results might not have the coiled tensions, the layered quality of the plays that to some extent are masked and coded. Williams thrives on the subterfuge and masquerade that social attitudes have forced on him.

Albee doesn't have Williams's exhibitionistic flair, his great generosity, his openly hungry sexuality. He is a cooler, far more cerebral writer for whom sex is always treated at a distance, usually ironically. Williams celebrates sex, despite that the fact that it can also bedevil his characters; Albee never sees the body as a means of salvation. Albee's writing does not have the tension, demonstrated in Williams's work, of an underground sensibility struggling both to express and to conceal itself within a conventional sexual context. Gay imagery appears around the edges of the frame in several plays, and Albee chooses to keep it there.

Albee is entirely at ease with the tone and the rhythms of the Westchester families whose homes he exposes—he grew up in one. Some critics and audiences, however, have read his continuously hostile and at times almost savage portraits of family life as masked, insidious put-downs of straight ideals, though the notion that fear of overpowering women and pleasure in puncturing the value of family life automatically render a writer's work "homosexual" is wildly prejudicial. In this light, however, *Virginia Woolf* has been read as a masked play about two extraordinarily bitchy gay male couples. Straight people don't treat each other like this, with such irony, such rapier wit, such quick repartee, the argument foolishly runs. Heterosexual couples aren't this decadent! Those who see Martha as a man in drag point to the famous opening lines in which she says "What a dump!", thereby parodying the dialogue from a Bette Davis movie. Since Bette Davis has long been a cult figure in the gay world, and since she is one of the favorite targets of female impersonators, doesn't this only underline the play's essentially camp sensibility? Martha's sexuality is thus read as a parody of female desire rather than the thing itself—her interest in sex is mocked, and so she can be seen as an ironic gay projection of what real women are really like. In this interpretation of the play, Martha is the butch gay, Honey is the nelly, and they both conform to gay stereotypes just as much as the campy boys in the band do. And because they are really men in drag, playacting their way through acid portraits of women who are either impossibly domineering or impossibly silly, the two nominally female characters are childless. There are no children in the play because there are no women to produce them! And this is the true explanation for that troublesome imaginary child!

Albee has always dismissed such a reading. He nixed a proposed Broadway revival with males playing Martha and Honey. The camp humor is abundant, certainly, aimed at the knowing but in no way undermining the play for an unsuspecting straight audience. Middle class audiences have laughed at and recognized aspects of themselves in the two ghastly marriages the play dissects, and whatever else they may be, Martha and Honey are convincing as recognizable women, just as much as Blanche or any of Williams's fluttery belles "play" as particular kinds of neurotic females.

Significantly, the plays in which homosexual motifs are most openly treated—*Malcolm* and *The Ballad of the Sad Cafe*—are those adapted from the work of other writers. Like *Tiny Alice*, *Malcolm* is about the corruption of an innocent. Malcolm is a golden young man, another version of the American Dream, who is ogled by both the male and female characters. . . .

Like *Tiny Alice*, the play is bewitched by the notion that sex with demanding women is lethal. The acquisitive, super-sophisticated Madame Girard, and the hot to trot Melba—both merciless parodies of female sexuality—promote Malcolm's deterioration. Sex with a nymphomaniac spells his final undoing, his ultimate loss of innocence. Behind the play's mocking treatment of sex is a kind of adolescent terror of normal adult sexuality. Purdy's fable is about the consequences of "doing it" with a woman—sex with Melba coarsens Malcolm, fatally contaminates him.

Albee worked on Purdy's parable of the loss of innocence right after he had completed his own version of the theme in *Tiny Alice*. Purdy's story is much simpler, although the homosexual currents remain as submerged. The play's opening image of blond, ethereal Malcolm seated primly on a golden bench is gay imagery of a particularly romantic and sentimental kind. But Malcolm never has sex with a man, although it is implied that Mr. Cox "used" him. In his devastating review, Robert Brustein noted the "masked, guarded nature" of the play, concluding that *Malcolm* was (in 1966) Albee's "most deeply homosexual work." As Albee gets closer and closer to his true subjects—the malevolence of women, the psychological impact of Mom, the evolution of the invert—he tends to get more abstract and incoherent until he is finally reduced, as here, to a nervous plucking at broken strings.

But whether gay or straight, sex in the play is presented as distinctly unsavory. All of the marriages—Malcolm's own, as well as the ones he is sent by Mr. Cox to observe—are dramatized as wounding, destructive perversions of human need. Married people are treated with outright contempt.

Malcolm is Albee's most resounding failure. Even his customary verbal deftness falters here. He flattens the spare, cadenced diction of the Purdy novel, and his heavy underlining of the allegorical framework coarsens what is at best a wry cautionary tale for susceptible, handsome young gays.

The Ballad of the Sad Cafe is a more robust treatment of gay characters. Though it is never labeled this exactly, the play concerns a homosexual triangle in which a woman, Amelia, and a man, her former husband Marvin Macy, fight over a midget, Lymon, who has a crush on Marvin. The play is certainly unliberated in its imagery since its lesbian heroine is a big strapping woman who moves like a wrestler, and its homosexual hero is a flirtatious, petulant midget who falls in love with a Marlboro Country fantasy figure. . . .

Through the presence of a narrator, who acts as a screen between the audience and these fantasms of McCullers' sad, lyrical imagination, Albee keeps his distance from the material. Typically, he does not examine the characters' coiled, loaded sexuality. The homosexuality is implicit, as in the novella. Amelia's intense aversion to Marvin's strutting maleness is never explained, never defined as specifically lesbian. Her hatred of male sexuality is palpably rendered, however, and when she and Marvin fight at the end, she seems to be going to battle against all self-regarding studs.

Albee retains the lilting rhythms of McCullers's language, its mellow, nostalgic tone. But these tapestry-like figures, and the strange sexual ritual in which they participate, which develops over a long period of time, are not comfortable on the stage. Seeing their combat enacted in the manner of a Western movie showdown threatens to turn them simply into freaks. The delicacy and poignancy of McCullers's fable cannot really be transferred to a more physical medium. As in *Malcolm*, Albee's literal rendition of symbolic action blunts the original material.

Edward Albee — The Anger Artist   Sharon D. Spencer*

America's most fervently discussed playwright, Edward Albee, has been the target of passionate acclaim and equally passionate contempt. He appears stranded midway between the "middlebrow" critics, who scold him for his "nastiness," and the "highbrow" critics, who shout the news that Mr. Albee is really a sneaky conformist who has learned how to exploit Broadway by offering it tasteless, but palatable, imitations of the latest Absurdist innovations. All agree that he at least *appears* angry, that his imagination is activated by hatred, his insights sharpened by contempt, his language inflamed by malice. But so far no one seems to have commented on the quality of his anger, its esthetics, the source of its immense appeal, or on the very strong parallel between the work of Edward Albee and the flamboyantly outrageous comic mode of the "Sick" or "Black" comics. The public's reaction to Mr. Albee's plays resembles its ambivalent reaction to the routines of the "Sicks": "While the new comics have been repudiated as nihilistic, hostile, destructive, degenerate and confused, they have also been hailed as the welcome bearers of a long-overdue and desperately needed catharsis. That their savage satire touched off a deep response in the smothered emotional life of Americans is evident from their success. . . ."[1] Although the ruthless anger of Mr. Albee's work makes the public and the critics squirm, they go right on rushing to openings, lavishly rewarding him with production opportunities, public appearances, and — now — Hollywood success. His vitriolic portrayals of American life are receiving a deep, though perhaps unconscious, sympathetic welcome from audiences that are profoundly gratified by his display of rage, despite their apparent shock. Similarly, millions who thought they were scandalized by the bitter routines of the "Sicks" flocked to nightclubs to see them and bought their records by the tens of millions. (The "Sicks" include comedians like Mort Sahl, Shelley Berman, Mike Nichols and Elaine May, Dick Gregory, and the late Lenny Bruce; improvisatory groups like The Compass, The Second City, and The Premise; magazines like *Mad* and *Help;* and recently the flood of comic fantastic novels that includes Jeremy Larner's *Go*, Terry Southern and Mason Hoffenberg's *Candy*, and many others descended from Joseph Heller's *Catch 22.*)

*From *Forum* (Houston) 4 (Winter/Spring 1967): 25–30. Reprinted by permission of *Forum* and the University of Houston.

Starting in the early 1950's in nightclubs on the West Coast, "Sick" humor sped across the nation, taking over one popular entertainment form after another. Certainly Mr. Albee is not a part of the "Sick" movement (for one thing, he is an artist, not an entertainer); nevertheless, it is very likely that he owes both the immediacy and the wide range of his popularity to the fact that his work taps exactly the same infected mass of repressed rage and frustration that has been drained again and again by the "Sick" comics.[2] "Forced by lessons of history to give up the previous generation's faith in politics as the key to Utopia, bewildered and helpless among the grinding pressures of the age of BIG . . . millions of Americans are the victims of a paralyzing tension — on the one hand, there is the reality — on the other, the smooth, glossy, sugar-coated surface. This tension is both maddening and crippling because it constantly gnaws away at the individual's sense of his own reality (he sees a festering black sore; society sees rosy-cheeked, bright-eyed health); it makes him question his every move. And ultimately it makes him frustrated, cynical and enraged. Sick comedy is an eruption of this rage. . . ."[3]

And so — on a higher plane — is the work of Mr. Albee. The sting of his plays, with their slashing anger and their irreverence for supposedly forbidden topics, is similar to the bitter violence of the "Sicks," who attack all the most sentimental subjects: deformity, motherhood, religion, minority groups, and sex (especially the more exotic varieties). Second, like the comic style of the "Sicks," whose leading exponent, Lenny Bruce, had to fight at least ten obscenity indictments, Mr. Albee's style is often fiercely scatological ("Who's Afraid of Virginia Woolf?"), and at times filled with so-called "toilet" humor ("The Death of Bessie Smith" and "The American Dream"). Finally, this new brand of humor differs from more traditional comic styles in its intensity, its extremism. With the "Sicks" Mr. Albee shares deep estrangement from American life, contempt for its values, defiant hostility toward the middle-class American family, an obsession with the sado-masochistic patterns of life in our machine society (in which one apparently either runs the machine, or is run by it), and, finally, a sense of repugnance associated with sex.[4] And, like the "Sicks," Mr. Albee is ferociously determined to expose the diseased guts of the "Great Society"; he is like a sadistic surgeon, coldly, but nevertheless furiously, slicing up the cancer-riddled patient.

In one crucial respect, however, Mr. Albee's work is the opposite of that produced by the entertainers working in the "Sick" vein. While their material is often carelessly improvised, repetitious, crudely articulated and structured (even the best of the novels, *Catch 22*, has the strung-together shape of a stand-up comic's flow of gags), the plays of Mr. Albee demonstrate the control provided by the sublimation of the artist's raw emotion into highly organized broadly meaningful expressions of that same emotion. Consequently, the finished monuments of his anger — while performing the same exorcism of rage achieved by the "Sick" comics —

articulate more completely and more lastingly the despair and rage that are typical of post-war generations.

Anger is the key to Mr. Albee's work, his ability to harness and use it the crucial factor that provides the motivation toward expression, the originality of insight, his special power. And since anger is also one *subject* of his plays, it is both the content and the crackling current of response between the playwright and the audience. Mr. Albee performs two valuable functions, and both depend for their success on his skill in manipulating anger: the first is medicinal, the cathartic release of hostile, violent and self-destructive impulses; the second, the self-revelation offered by Mr. Albee's exposures of the various delusions (sometimes neuroses) which we erect as "safe" realities, despite their smothering of our emotional and sexual lives. . . .

In "Who's Afraid of Virginia Woolf?" the use of rage to create a viable human relationship has a relative degree of success, however, and for a time seems to provide the essential organizing and binding cement of George and Martha's marriage; eventually, though, the set of hostile games on which they subsist, breaks down and is exposed as a negativistic delusion. Just as Jerry's visit to the zoo and resultant decision to force someone to "connect" with him is self-consciously formulated, so George and Martha consciously invent a number of games, each of which is a display of controlled use of anger. Since they are much more imaginative than Jerry, their hostile games and contests temporarily "work" as a basis for their relationship to each other and to the world. When the curtain goes up, they are testing each other's memories of tunes from old movies (incidentally, parodies of the films of the thirties and forties are a major target of "Sick" and "Black" humor). After George's abortive attempt to strangle Martha (who has been "riding" him about his novel), the stage directions call for the four principals to move around "like wrestlers flexing after a fall."[5] And to regain social equilibrium after the choking episode, George says, "Well. That's one game . . . let's think of something else. We've played Humiliate the Host . . . we've gone through that one . . . what shall we do now?" (138) "Hump the Hostess" and "Get the Guest" follow, and they lead to a public exposure of the most crucial game of all — the pretended existence of the son who is the focal point of the fantasy life George and Martha have erected together to protect themselves from the disappointments of reality and from the necessity of confronting their own neuroses.

The gamesmanship of the play is a protection against the frightening aspects of adult sexuality. The baby talk, the childish "yah-yah" taunts, the "tricks" (for example, the Japanese gun with which George arouses Martha sexually by pretending to kill her), the homosexual overtones conveyed by Martha's masculinity, by George's waspish nastiness, his occasional coy attitude toward Nick, and — most important — the make-believe son — all these features of infantilism are part of George and

Martha's fantasy, a sort of virtuoso performance based on variations of hostility that enables them to construct a bogus reality that is less terrifying than reality itself. Their ditty "Who's Afraid of Virginia Woolf?" opposes "Virginia Woolf" as the reality that must be avoided, while the "big bad wolf" represents a pretended reality that can be magically disposed of and rendered harmless through their games.[6]

The life of fantasy which regulates George and Martha's existence is actually a form of neurotic adjustment, and like all neuroses, it is partially effective as a protection against feared actualities, but ultimately inadequate, a mechanism of diminishing returns which eventually threatens their marriage far more savagely than would reality itself. Their fantasy is like comedy itself — a way of taming situations that terrify and frustrate one; but if carried too far and used too consistently, the comic attitude itself can become an emotional prison — nonseriousness a tough hide insensitizing its wearer to experiences of genuine emotional significance. This is what is happening to George and Martha when the play begins. Martha "gives away" her perhaps unconscious knowledge that the games are losing their power when she tells Honey about the imaginary child. George, however, takes the initiative in destroying the fantasy, and his apparently brutal insistence on the death of the child represents his refusal to continue living out a delusion, his determination to confront "Virginia Woolf" instead, and, finally, his consciously willed rebirth as a man. . . .

Midway through the play George shouts, "The game is over!" (136) — and from this point on he sets out to destroy virtually every image of his and Martha's regressive fantasy. Nick and Honey (representatives of everything George and Martha detest in themselves) have to be destroyed along with the imaginary son. These ritualistic "murders," in addition to the apparent cruelty of George's forcing Martha to let go of "the one light in all this hopeless . . . darkness . . . OUR SON" (227), are all necessary stages along the path to an increasing acceptance of reality (signified by the titles of the play's three acts: "Fun and Games," "Walpurgisnacht," "The Exorcism"). At the end of the play Martha, exhausted and heartbroken, still terrified of "Virginia Woolf," is subdued and submissive, for the first time willing to let herself give in to George's control. There is at least hope for their marriage, since they have "struck through the mask" of their hatred-activated fantasy.

Seen within the total context of Mr. Albee's work, the bewildering "Tiny Alice" would seem to be a parody of Christian martyrdom, as well as a vitriolic attack on any beatification of suffering. Julian's steps along the path of unfolding truth (that Tiny Alice — representing materialistic power and sensuality — and God are indistinguishable) corresponds to the gradual destruction of the controlling fantasy that is the central action of "Virginia Woolf." However, for Julian truth (the ambiguous "I accept" of the death scene) comes too late to be put into operation, and he dies — like Jerry, a foolishly eager victim of his own delusions, in Julian's case, delusions that lead him to offer himself up to his victimizers in the name of "service" to God. Julian (mankind) is trapped between sometimes competitive and sometimes cooperative (but essentially identical) power complexes: the Church under God and the play's vicious Cardinal; and secular or materialistic power under Miss Alice and her "priests" — a sadistic, dishonest Lawyer, a charming, but alternately haughty, alternately generous and always faithless representative (Miss Alice); and a Butler, a cynical but unfailingly cooperative underling.

The play's key metaphor (corresponding to the anecdote of the zoo and to the gamesmanship of George and Martha) is the notion of "play-acting." Each character is a representative of someone else, an actor playing a role in the so-called "service" of some higher, but hidden, reality. Ironically, however, the characters do not serve in the expected ways, but in other ways which they do not choose, but which they accept. Thus, the Butler hardly ever waits on any one, but patiently attends his former mistress, Miss Alice, whom he seems to love in his decidedly casual manner. The Cardinal, who is supposed to be serving the Church, is actually serving the secular power of Alice, while the Lawyer, who is supposed to be serving Alice, is actually forwarding the interests of the Church. Miss Alice, whose role is to be an instrument of the god of materialism and the life of the flesh, is to some extent an instrument of her personal and private pleasure in so far as she sincerely cares for Julian. The Lawyer correctly accuses her of being "*Too* human; not playing it straight."[7] She both is and is not involved with Julian on the level of individual feeling (a Freudian interpretation would probably see her as a small boy's vision of his mother — seductive but untrustworthy). Together Alice and God seem to symbolize a grotesque celestial "Mommy" and "Daddy" who conspire to destroy their child. Julian appears to be a symbol of mankind in its capacity for self-delusion and its inability to accept passion (especially sexual passion) as a self-justifying good. To the very end, Julian insists on exonerating sexuality as a token of "service" (a crude pun) to some supposed eternal verity.

The central symbol of the notion of "service" and of "play-acting," Julian (who ironically is the only character who refuses to admit he is playing a role) is innocent, sweet and likable, a sort of delightful fool who is easily destroyed by his overwhelming need to believe passionately in something *beyond* reality. His sexual "problem" is obvious; though not a priest, he has taken vows of chastity (perhaps symbolizing not only a Roman Catholic but a Puritan society's refusal to accept sexuality as a self-justifying good). While in a mental institution during a period of temporary loss of faith (without which Julian cannot sustain his life), he *perhaps* has sexual relations with a mad woman who imagines herself the Virgin Mary and "gives birth" to a cancer which kills her. The grim parody of this joke at the expense of the Christian myth (essentially an example of "Sick" humor) is further enhanced by the absurdity of Julian's *not being certain* whether he has had sexual intercourse. (Clearly, this is intended as a wry comment on modern man's capacity for sensual response.) The major point, however, is that Julian can accept a sexual relationship only when he is caught up in some religious fantasy. Consequently, since he believes his engagement to Miss Alice to be part of some mysterious form of "service" to his Cardinal and his Church, he is quite gracious about permitting himself to be seduced. Mr. Albee uses Julian's inability to hold out for very long as a further twist on the inherent faithlessness of Julian's ostensible devotion to a master. In fact, once initiated into the rites of Miss Alice (sex), Julian rather naughtily threatens to whip her: "Shall I take my crop to you?" (114) The association here is between repression and sadism, and its ramifications regarding the sexual health of Julian (mankind) are even more devastating when it turns out that Julian finds no difference between religious ecstasy and sensual ecstasy! After his wedding night, he bubbles to the Cardinal: "I can't tell you, the . . . radiance, humming, and the witchcraft, I think it must be, the ecstasy of this light, as *God's* exactly; the transport the same, the lifting, the sense of *service* [italics added], and the EXPANSION. . ." (140).

The sexual puns of this devastating passage prepare the way for the absolutely ludicrous mock crucifixion scene—replete with parodies of Christian devotional objects such as the "model" or "replica" of Alice's castle (a joking reference to a cathedral, or perhaps a reliquary) in which "miracles" occur; the phrenological head rakishly topped off by Miss Alice's wig, the signs of the "presence" (the shadow and the "thumping"); and, finally, the caricature of the Pietá formed by the principals after the Lawyer has shot Julian. In death Julian gasps, "Alice? Alice? My God, why hast thou forsaken me?. . . . Alice? . . . God?. . . . I accept thee, Alice, for thou art come to me. God, Alice . . . I accept thy will." (189–190). All of this adds up to an absolutely wildly irreverent joke, and yet there is pathos in Julian's death. . .

But he is never able to accept the fact that the only reality is life itself, to face the truth that to devote oneself to the "service" of something that does not exist (or if it exists, is evil), is to destroy oneself, or that his own martyrdom is nothing more than an exceedingly cruel and meaningless joke, for which he in his pride is just as responsible as the other more evil, but more realistic, characters. Like Jerry, Julian commits a sort of suicide, but his death is complicated by clouds of metaphysical and psychological inferences about the nature of man's ability to accept what is at hand without "ennobling" it with overlays of supernatural significance.

A playwright with a scalpel, Mr. Albee repeatedly wields it to strip away the delusions of his contemporaries. This is not in itself so unusual as is the special quality of white-hot, controlled rage that emanates from all of his plays. Chief among his surgical instruments, as among the weaponry of contemporary comedians and comic-fantastic novelists, is the free-wheeling application and manipulation of anger. A critic of the popular arts has recently compared the comedian Lenny Bruce to a witch doctor, or *shaman:* "In every primitive tribe we find the *shaman* in the center of society and it is easy to show that he is either a neurotic or psychotic, or at least that his art is based on the same mechanisms as a neurosis or psychosis. The *shaman* makes both visible and public the systems of symbolic fantasy that are present in the psyche of every adult member of that society. They are the leaders in an infantile game and the lightning conductors of common anxiety."[8] The comparison of a comedian to a *shaman* is equally appropriate as a description of Mr. Albee's function — particularly in an age when there cannot be too many public exorcisors of "common anxiety." But the plays of Edward Albee — in addition to their cathartic feature — provide much more than an opportunity for the audience to "get off its rocks." Eventually these works lead to forceful revelations of our most familiar and sterile delusions, our national fantasies, our spiritual pretensions; these plays encourage us by indirection to throw off spurious dreams and escapist illusions. Mr. Albee is not only the *shaman* who "makes both visible and public the systems of symbolic fantasy," he is a "hatred artist" in the fullest sense, since he not only displays his own anger, but uses it; and in using it, he gains mastery over it, forcing it to yield — not pain and death — but the vivid lives of his plays.

Notes

1. Albert Goldman, 'Sick Comics from Birth to Death," *Nugget Magazine* (June, 1964), p. 54.

2. My intention is not to imply that "Sick" comedy is responsible for the favorable reception of work that would otherwise have been ignored, but rather that the audience's adjustment to "Sick" humor paved the way for a much *faster* acceptance of Albee's plays than would otherwise have occurred.

3. Goldman, *ibid.*, p. 52.

4. Interestingly, Lenny Bruce's autumn, 1964, obscenity conviction was based on the opinion that he "debased" sex by describing it in foul language, a reversal of the usual charge of arousing prurience. If anything, his routines made sexual activity seem ugly and frightening.

5. Edward Albee, *Who's Afraid of Virginia Woolf?* (New York, 1963), p. 138. (Numbers in parentheses after quotations from this play refer to pages in this edition.)

6. An allusion may be intended to the difficulty of "Virginia Woolf's" characters in working out harmonious sexual lives and also perhaps to the sexual metamorphosis that is depicted in *Orlando*.

7. Edward Albee, *Tiny Alice* (New York, 1965), p. 98. (Numbers in parentheses after quotations from this play refer to pages in this edition.)

8. Gézá Roheim, quoted by Albert Goldman, "The Comedy of Lenny Bruce," *Commentary* (New York, October, 1963), p. 315.

Language of Movement in Albee's
The Death of Bessie Smith   Paul Witherington*

The Death of Bessie Smith seems more social, more obvious, and looser in form than Albee's other plays, and it is therefore often regarded as an inferior work.[1] I believe the neglect and abuse the play has suffered come from a misunderstanding of Albee's methods and purpose. On the surface *Bessie Smith* is an oversimplified protest drama in which the general inhumanity of White to Negro reflected in Bessie's needless death is unrelieved by the stereotype, the farcical and absurd dimensions of violence, or the masks of allegory Albee manipulates so charmingly in the later plays. Moreover the play appears to be split into several parts: that dealing with Nurse's home life, that dealing with Bessie and Jack, and that dealing with affairs at the hospital. The last two plots seem joined only accidentally by the crash of Bessie's car, whereas Nurse's home life, as well as the initial scene in which Jack talks with his friend Bernie about going north, as well as the mayor's convalescence seems thematically irrelevant. The key to the play's structure—a juxtaposition of seemingly unrelated scenes and characters—and to its meaning which is broader than the immediate race issue is the language of its characters, a rich, suggestive language which forms an atmosphere of stasis and misdirected action.[2]

The central imagery of *Bessie Smith* is that of movement on the one hand and rest, inertia, and fixity on the other. Values of movement and lack of movement are mixed, however, for what appears to be the one is often the other. Albee partially establishes this ambiguity by forms of the verb *go*. A sense of action and even initiation is strong in *go* but we use the verb often in an almost contrary sense. Consider, for example, the following statements: boys like to *go* barefoot; mustard *goes* with hot dogs; books *go* on shelves; those colors *go* well together; how does that line *go*; we *go* by the book here. In dictionaries such usage is described with words like *specified, allotted, suitable, habitual, fitting, certain, established, in accord with, in harmony with*; suggested here is fixity, not movement, or if there is movement at all, a habitual, unchanging, and predictable movement, one that suggests complacency. Another "contrary" sense of *go* is that of intention or expectation; the progressive form *going* used with present infinitive indicates a state of inaction potentially quite far removed from motion (consider "going to go"). Both of these antitheses to what might be called organic action are dramatized in the language of *Bessie Smith*; the latter could be thought of as purpose without action, and the former as action without purpose. These categories will be examined in more detail.

All the characters are *going* to do something, but execution is almost

*From *Twentieth Century Literature* 13 (July 1967):84–88. Reprinted by permission of the journal.

always lacking. In just two pages of Scene Two in which Nurse and Father are arguing about their car, *going* in the sense of intention appears thirteen times, and the effect emphasizes their inertia. There is no indication the car is used by either Nurse or Father despite their conflict over it; Nurse evidently takes the bus, and she accuses Father of merely watching the car: "You going to sit here with a shotgun and make sure the birds don't crap on it . . . or something?" In Scene One Jack is going to go up north, but he cannot resist sitting instead with his friend Bernie and talking about going, a procrastination that establishes the mood of inertia for the rest of the drama. Bessie is lying on the bed throughout Scene Three while Jack tries to get her up and moving. Orderly speaks of "going beyond" his present role as errand boy, but Nurse taunts him (my italics): "Just what do you think is *going to happen* to you? Is His Honor, the mayor, *going to rise* out of his sickbed and take a personal interest in you? Write a letter to the President maybe? And is Mr. Roosevelt *going to send* his wife, Lady Eleanor, down here after you? Or is it in your plans that you are *going to be handed* a big fat scholarship somewhere to the north of Johns Hopkins?" (Scene Four) Nurse appears to be able to execute her purposes better than the other characters who live in fear of her power, but her threats (here, to Intern), "I am going to get you . . . I am going to fix you . . . I am going to see to it that you are *through* here," become at the end just as meaningless as the others' purposes. Nor is lack of action attributed only to circumstance: Father is a hypochondriac, Bessie a fat, lazy has-been, Orderly an addict to the safe status quo. The general inertia in the play extends to authority itself, the mayor, who is laid up after an operation (Nurse tells Second Nurse in a lazy scene neatly counterpointed by sounds of Jack and Bessie's crash), "his ass in a sling." Only Intern is capable of organic action at the end of the play, but throughout most of it he is as fixed as are the other characters who serve as a control group against which his final movements can be measured. "Everything is promises," Nurse says, "and that is all there is to it."

Conflict between intention and performance is supported by Albee's imagery. Intern dreams of Nurse's stabbed arm bleeding while he merely holds it; Nurse envisions Intern sitting on a horse, his neck in a noose while she waits with a whip; Intern describes his affair with Nurse as an "infuriating and inconclusive wrestling match"; several times Jack says Bessie is "free as a bird," but this metaphor becomes ironic when Bessie must be goaded from bed and driven by Jack (all the characters need, it seems, to be acted upon); finally there is the furious stasis described by Jack after the wreck, "We were stopped . . . my motor running," which could describe all the characters' frustrations. Intern is a white knight and great white doctor to the sarcastic nurse, but white here as in the case of the "white" (segregated) hospital ambiguously connotes sterility and isolation as well as purity. White, like cool which appears several times in the play, indicates a lack of motion as opposed to the red (and hot) vitality of blood which eventually covers Intern's uniform, and the blazing sunset he symbolically enters. The hospital itself is, as Intern says, stagnant; a second-rate institution, it caters nevertheless to the wealthy and to authority, to the "system" as it is. Nurse, talking on the phone to Second Nurse (Scene Five), reveals the rigidity with which she runs her own position and, ironically, her inhumanity: "Mercy Hospital! Mercy, indeed, you away from your desk all the time. *Some* hospitals are run better than *others*; some nurses stay at their posts." Nurse's criterion for a smoothly running operation is, evidently, the least possible motion.

Purpose without action is complemented by action without purpose. Whereas the former is an attempt to ignore present needs, the latter is an attempt to escape present involvement. For Nurse and Father — Father, like George in *Virginia Woolf*, is an historian — movement is toward the past; *go* becomes *gone*. Intern tells Nurse, "Your family is a famous *name*, but those thousand acres are *gone*." Nurse echoes this loss later talking to Orderly: "Our knights are gone forth into sunsets . . . behind the wheels of Cord cars . . . the acres have diminished and the paint is flaking . . . that there is a great abandonment." Divided between the vulgar present which she apes in her loose sensual talk and the genteel past she tries to re-create by the ritual of her actual sex behavior, Nurse endures life on her own terms of fancy and regression by becoming, in Intern's words, "king of the castle." The ritual infantilism of her verbal assault and inhibited behavior is thus an effort — as it is by Martha in *Virginia Woolf* — to avoid mature human contact. An intended parallel is Bessie's loss of popularity as a blues singer. The motif of lost folk art is united to the strain of lost aristocracy near the end of the play symbolically when Nurse, after hearing that the hurt Negro (by then actually dead) is Bessie Smith, identifies briefly with Bessie and her severed arm by reflecting on her own bleeding arm in the vision described by Intern. (Nurse likes stereotyped Negro music because it suggests the uncomplicated past.) The irony is that she cannot for more than this instant admit the similarity of their present losses, their common displacement in the changing South. Bessie's record-ings — that is, Bessie at a distance — are acceptable, but Bessie's armless arrival at the hospital cannot be tolerated for it brings Nurse a sense of her own fragmented situation.

Escapism also takes the form of directing others' affairs, a kind of vicarious participation in life; in this respect Nurse is an early Mommy, Peter, Martha, or Miss Alice, for each Albee play seems to have its own built-in director who controls life by distancing himself as if it were an external drama. This sense of motion is a rigid and impersonal imperative: *go*, or *don't go*. Significantly Nurse is at the admissions desk; she controls the going and coming of patients, admits and dismisses. But her admis-sions are only nominal and theoretical, for she never admits any particular involvement with patients such as a floor nurse would have. She gets their names — this is what she demands of Jack while Bessie lies outside (Intern, by contrast, says at the end he does not want Jack's name) — for she is impressed by names, but she keeps personal distance. Nor can she admit any form of reality, though she is continually telling others to face facts; her own split between past and present is never breeched. "How do you manage to just dismiss things from your mind?" Intern asks her; at the end she dismisses both Jack and Intern and indeed the entire external world as she becomes physically what she has revealed herself to be emotionally, rigid and unfeeling.

Nurse speaks often of fixing characters by which is implied not only revenge but the placing of characters in set roles or patterns. Orderly and Intern are put in their places, she says, "as I have done before . . . and as I shall do again." Both are told to walk a straight line, Orderly's being that of antebellum body servant, Intern's that of antebellum suitor. They are to be what their names indicate — stereotyped, not real. (Intern, as the name suggests, is not to go outside himself.) Intern, Nurse says, must be to her as tangent to circle, never as radius; in other words, as the heavily loaded sex imagery of Scene Six indicates, Nurse rejects full human interaction, sexual or otherwise, and the drive home each evening with Intern will be a fruitless ritual. Orderly is told to go north which is a tangential direction with regard to the symbolic burning circumference (human involvement) of the western sun. The tangent, then, is metaphoric for action without purpose; it is the prescribed pattern for those who only skirt commitment and do not wish to go anywhere at all.

Neither tense inaction nor aimless, habitual, or vicarious motion can solve the unique present emergency. When Jack goes to the first hospital with the dying Bessie he is told to wait, to sit, to cool his heels. When he goes to the second hospital (where Nurse and Intern are) he is told to move on. Neither waiting nor moving on can save Bessie. The question in *Bessie Smith* is whether there is a real alternative to stasis or lost, misguided action. Intern goes outside to see Bessie despite Nurse's commands to stay inside, and he returns covered with blood from the severed arm (significantly he dreamed earlier of bandaging an arm in Spain and of refusing to bandage Nurse's arm — indications that he, like Nurse, prefers people at a distance), but his involvement has been with a dead woman, a final irony that seems to cancel the effect of his commitment. "Maybe he thought you'd bring her back to life," Nurse scoffs as she tells Intern his career at the hospital is over. But one remembers that the hospital itself is a kind of stagnancy, and so for that matter — granting Albee's play on words — is the position of Intern. Moreover the closing symbols of the play indicate Intern's commitment has not been futile. His final movement is a backing from the room into the glaring sunset. Nurse, on the other hand, perhaps because she has had a glimpse of her own inadequate response to life, remains (Albee's stage directions tell us) "frozen." The fact that Bessie has been dead for some time reveals that the drama is not about a particular emergency or about Negro and White as such, but about the larger issue of human commitment. Imagery of movement unifies the play thematically, dramatizing in each scene humanity's prevailing inertia and purposelessness but also humanity's occasional chance to act with direction and force.

Notes

1. Most critical opinion of *The Death of Bessie Smith* has been unfavorable and has failed to recognize its complexity and unity. Wendell Harris in "Morality, Absurdity, and Albee," *Southwest Review*, XLIX (1964), 249–256, speaks of the play's revelation "that the determining motives of human action are largely base" (p. 255); Emil Roy in "*Who's Afraid of Virginia Woolf?* and the Tradition," *Bucknell Review*, XIII (1965), 27–36, calls the play a social parable which "suffers from diffuseness" (p. 31); Charles T. Samuels in "The Theatre of Edward Albee," *Massachusetts Review*, VI (1964–65), 187–201, says the play is "split between a private and a public drama only dimly analogous." (p. 190)

2. A few critics have recognized the importance of language in Albee's plays, most recently Arthur K. Oberg in his article "Edward Albee; His Language and Imagination," *Prairie Schooner*, XL (1966), 139–146. Oberg believes, however, that in the early plays words become ends in themselves and often cloud rather than illuminate the issues.

The Verbal Murders of Edward Albee
Ruby Cohn*

. . . Satiric caricature is Albee's main technique in *The Sandbox* (1959) and *The American Dream* (1960). Both monologues and thrust-and-parry exchanges contain the clichés of middle-class America. The implication is that such clichés lead to the death of Grandma, who represents the vigorous old frontier spirit. In her independence, Grandma resembles Jerry or the Intern, but age has made her crafty, and she has learned to roll with the punches. In both *The Sandbox* and *The American Dream*, Mommy delivers these punches verbally, and yet she does not literally kill Grandma.

Of the relationship between the two plays, Albee has written: "For *The Sandbox*, I extracted several of the characters from *The American Dream* and placed them in a situation different than, but related to, their predicament in the longer play." *The Sandbox* is named for the grave of Grandma, the first-generation American, and *The American Dream* is named for the third-generation American, a grave in himself; in both plays, murderous intention is lodged in the middle generation, especially Mommy. In *The Sandbox*, Mommy and Daddy deposit Grandma in a child's sandbox, as Hamm deposited his legless parents in ashbins in

*From *Dialogue in American Drama* (Bloomington: Indiana University Press, 1971), 137–40. Reprinted by permission of the publisher.

Beckett's *Endgame*. Half-buried, Grandma finds that she can no longer move, and she accepts her summons by the handsome Young Man, an Angel of Death.

In *The American Dream*, Ionesco is a strong influence on Albee. Like *The Bald Soprano*, *The American Dream* thrives on social inanities. Like Ionesco, Albee reduces events to arrivals and departures. As in *The Bald Soprano*, a mock-recognition scene is based on circumstantial evidence — husband and wife in the Ionesco play, and in the Albee play, Mrs. Barker and the American family for whom she barks. Albee also uses such Ionesco techniques as proliferation of objects (Grandma's boxes), pointless anecdotes (mainly Mommy's), meaningless nuances (beige, wheat, and cream), cliché refrains (I don't mind if I do; how fascinating, enthralling, spellbinding, gripping, or engrossing.).

Within this stuffy apartment of Ionesco motifs, Albee places a family in the American grain, with its areas for senior citizens and its focus on money. When Mommy was eight years old, she told Grandma that she was "going to mahwy a wich old man." Sterile, Mommy and Daddy have purchased a baby from the Bye-Bye Adoption Service, that puns on Buy-Buy. Mommy spends much of her life shopping (when she isn't nagging Daddy or Grandma). In *The Sandbox*, Mommy and Daddy carry Grandma to *death*, but in *The American Dream*, Mommy nags at Grandma's *life*. She informs a feebly protesting Daddy that he wants to put Grandma in a nursing home, and she threatens Grandma with a man in a van who will cart her away. Mommy treats Grandma like a naughty child; she discusses Grandma's toilet habits, warns her that she will take away her TV, worries about her vocabulary: "I don't know where she gets the words; on the television, maybe."

And Grandma, who is treated like a child, repeats the phrases we learn as American children: "Shut up! None of your damn business." Grandma tells the story of the family child to Mrs. Barker. Since "the bumble of joy" had eyes only for Daddy, Mommy gouged his eyes out; since he called Mommy a dirty name, they cut his tongue out. And because "it began to develop an interest in its you-know-what," they castrated him and cut his hands off at the wrists. Our acquaintance with Mommy has prepared us for Grandma's account of Bringing up Bumble. But more painful than the mutilations are the ailments it subsequently develops, because we can hear in them Mommy's cruel American platitudes: "it didn't have a head on its shoulders, it had no guts, it was spineless, its feet were made of clay." This is Mommy's more insidious castration, nagging the child into a diminutive Daddy, who is "all ears," but who has no guts since he "has tubes now, where he used to have tracts." Daddy's organs are related to housing, on the one hand, and television, on the other — both mass produced in modern America, and both part of the modern American dream life. In *The American Dream*, like father, like son. Daddy "just want[s] to get everything over with," and his bumble-son does get everything over with, by dying before Mommy can complete her murder of him.

In *The American Dream*, it is an off-stage bumble that predicts Grandma's death, as an off-stage rumble announces Grandma's death in *The Sandbox*. Like the bumble, Grandma escapes Mommy's murderous malice by a kind of suicide. As Jerry turns Peter's reluctant threat into the reality of his death, Grandma turns Mommy's repeated threats into the reality of her disappearance from the family. Mommy is even more conformist than Peter, so that she cannot perform deeds of violence herself. Daddy has been devitalized on an operating table, so that Grandma has to be threatened by a proxy murderer — the man in the van.

When a handsome Young Man arrives, Grandma is alone on stage, and she instantly recognizes the American Dream shaped by Mommy. He shares only appearance and initials with the Angel of Death in *The Sandbox*, but he has the same meaning. The American Dream is an Angel of Death who is linked to both the mutilated bumble and to Grandma. In a confessional monologue, the Young Man tells Grandma of a twin "torn apart" from him, so that it seemed his heart was "wrenched from his body," draining him of feeling. As his twin brother was mutilated physically, the American Dream is mutilated emotionally.

When Mrs. Barker intrudes upon this confrontation of the numb young modern man with the vigorous old frontier spirit, Grandma introduces him as the man in the van, Mommy's bogey-man. Asking him to carry her boxes, Grandma follows the Young Man out. Boxes and sandbox are coffin and grave; the American Dream leads but to the grave, and Grandma, accepting her fate, goes out in style — escorted by a handsome swain whose gallantry replaces feeling.

Though minatory Mommy later admits that "There is no van man. We . . . we made him up," she readily accepts the American Dream as a replacement for Grandma. Thus, the "comedy" ends happily, though Grandma is dead to Mommy: "Five glasses? Why five? There are only four of us." In spite of Mommy's malice — expressed in the clichés of contemporary America — Grandma and bumble manage to die their own deaths.

In the conversation between a sympathetic Grandma and an ambiguous American Dream, Albee dilutes his satire. In spite of Grandma's pithy frontier comments and her asides on "old people," Grandma does not openly oppose Mommy. Since the Young Man is first caricatured, then sentimentalized, his long speeches sag. He will "do almost anything for money," and he tries to sell us the sad story of his life. Apparently ignorant of the mutilations to his twin brother, he describes his parallel loss of sensation that has resulted in his inability to love. In spite of Albee's rhythmic skill, this abstract statement of losses is duller than Grandma's pungent summary of the mutilation of his twin, and this dulls the edge of Albee's satire. In spite of the Young Man's warning that his tale "may not be true," the mutual sympathy of Grandma and the American Dream is incongruously maudlin. Albee makes an effort to restore the comic tone by bringing back Mommy and Daddy with their mindless clichés, and the play ends with Grandma's sardonic aside: "everybody's got what he wants . . . or everybody's got what he thinks he wants." The word "satisfaction" has threaded through the play, and the American family finally snuggles into its illusion of satisfaction.

The Mystique of Failure: A Latter-Day Reflection on *Who's Afraid of Virginia Woolf?*

John Kenneth Galbraith*

Failure is man's most nearly universal experience. It is also a deeply preoccupying concern and, unlike love and hate, one that he does not readily avow. Most men live anxiously but silently with the thought of failure and the wonder of how, in the end, it will come to them. . . .

I was in India when *Virginia Woolf* opened, and I did not see it until a few weeks ago. I did hear the explanations for the profound interest it aroused both here and more recently in London—the piercing dialogue, the ingenuity with which Mr. Albee rings and changes and contrives the situations which retain interest through that long evening in the academic living room, the riddle over what is real and which is the game which George, the middle-aged history professor, and his wife play with each other's sanity, the novelty of fornication, even unsuccessful, just offstage. I am sure the fascination lies in the exposed nerve of anxiety which the play touches in every reasonably conscious person who attends, anxiety over how failure will come to him and when. At *Death of a Salesman*, everyone carried Willy Loman's huge suitcases for an evening. At *Virginia Woolf*, everyone faces the greater horror of the day when he is discovered to be an empty shell.

For the study of failure, the selection of an academic community, and especially a small one, was nearly perfect. Failure in most of its forms short of death is highly objective and circumstantial—the crowd does not come, the cops do come, the book does not sell, debts increase and assets dwindle, the prostatitis or carcinoma is palpable, there is a letter, a notice in the pay envelope, a bulletin on the board. The bitch goddess has the vi ·e of candor as she announces her departure. But an academic community is the exception; here failure is subtle and intensely subjective. l continues. The students remain deferential and may even applaud. Colleagues are affable. It is only that the community has reached a consensus that the man is done. The once-promising young scholar or

*From *Show*, May 1964, 112. Reprinted by permission of the journal.

scientist is now known to be a hopeless pedant or a minor fraud. The academic eagle of the Truman years is really a hopeless bore. The man who was once an exciting teacher is a classroom Barnum. These decisions are made by a jury of intimates. Once made, they cannot be reversed. There is no appeal. The conviction is only gradually communicated to the man concerned. By showing concern, he affirms the decision against himself. No arrangement could be more ingeniously cruel or better serve Mr. Albee's purpose.

In ordinary academic life, the victim comes only gradually to the knowledge of failure. His spouse, poor soul, usually resists the knowledge to the end. "You have no idea how hard Henry works. And the students just love him." In *Virginia Woolf*, George's wife telescopes this gradual process by relentlessly translating the estimate of the community to her husband. This is a brilliant solution, and I thought that she was, by a considerable margin, the most expert creation of the play. Every member of a university or college faculty knows this woman. She is assertive, rowdy and rough-talking and often quite rotund. In the tightly knit family of teachers and scholars, people who live close to each other and their work, she is determined that, while her sex may keep her out of classrooms and faculty meetings, it damn well won't keep her out of conversations and academic politics. (I am happy to report that I never encountered one who was able to drag men off to bed.) As the daughter of the president, George's wife has a special claim to a proprietary role in local affairs. She is in every respect a fine specimen. The hipless little girl of the false pregnancy and her equally insipid scientist are also well drawn and serve admirably as audience for the searing exposure of the older couple's failure. The principal problem of the play, so it seems to me, is George.

George no longer has any chance of becoming president of the college. Nor will he be chairman of his department—a post which he filled on an emergency basis during World War II. He will serve his life as a permanent associate professor, a title which many colleges and universities (including Harvard) use, also with exquisite cruelty, to brand their errors in according permanent tenure.

But, at least as played by Donald Davis, George does not resemble the failures one encounters in academic life. Invariably they are insecure, protesting and very dull. They know that the consensus of the community has turned against them. They may dwell compulsively on the injustice of the decision. Or, more commonly, they are impelled to work the offsetting evidence into their conversation—they are devotedly deep in fascinating research, they are brilliantly destroying some mountebank in controversy, they are being pressed very hard by students, they got very drunk with the very great at the last meeting of the Modern Language Association. None of this makes for very interesting company, and all such tendencies are exaggerated by alcohol.

In the play, however, George is clever, interesting and rather self-assured. He has written a novel; the failures I have known have never got beyond well-advertised intentions. He drinks like a fish, which is alto-gether faithful to my experience in Cambridge — supplemented by obser-vation in Princeton and Berkeley — but this leads him neither to dull self-pity nor transparent self-promotion.

Nor is it clear that such a man would be terribly perturbed by his failure to achieve what scholars condescendingly call "an administrative post." On the contrary, New Carthage, where he teaches, is something of an autocracy of its president, George's father-in-law. All college faculties that are worth anything have at least a latent instinct to revolt. The fact that George's father-in-law had put a hex on the career of such an intellectually alert and attractive man would have made him something of a hero — a rallying point for like-minded colleagues. As a result, George would have been largely invulnerable to his wife's game. Failure is not accidental; it is for a reason.

But a failure — a vulnerable and rejected man — would not have held the play together and, more to the point, he wouldn't have held the crowd together through a long evening and certainly not after that much booze. A failure at New Carthage could not be a success on Broadway. Lear would spoil Lear.

This kind of contradiction and contrivance does not happen in a very great play. But neither does it keep *Virginia Woolf* from being an extremely interesting one.

Exorcisms: *Who's Afraid of Virginia Woolf?*

Anne Paolucci*

. . . It is a peculiarity of Albee's and a trademark of his that the protagonists of his plays are at one and the same time distinctly themselves and just as distinctly Everybody Else. In Martha and George, Nick and Honey, this identity is perfected dramatically, so that the play appears — from one point of view — a psychoanalytic "happening" in which the audience is intimately involved. The strength of such a play lies in this immediate and growing identification of the audience with the protago-nists on stage; the difficulties of the characters, though rooted in mystery, are simple enough to grasp in their social implications.

As in the earlier plays, Sex is the dynamo behind the action. But in this case, instead of an oversimplified statement about homosexuality and who is responsible for it, or a brief reminder of how private sexual

*From *From Tension to Tonic: The Plays of Edward Albee* (Carbondale: Southern Illi-nois University Press, 1972), 46–63. Reprinted by permission of the publisher.

indulgence turns into prurient lust, or an unsympathetic suggestion of how heterosexual demands within a materialistic society corrupt and destroy the individual, we have for the first time an examination of the various phases through which a sexual relationship passes in its normal, or rather, its inevitable development. Like Shaw, who shocked a good many of his contemporaries, and still shocks a good many of his readers today, by insisting that love and sex don't mix easily in marriage, Albee is here reminding us of the deterioration which even the best-matched couple will suffer in their sexual relationship if love is not properly distinguished from it and nurtured apart from it. There is almost an Augustinian conviction in Albee's insistence on what sex in marriage is *not*.

St. Augustine long ago described the paradox when he noted that the outgoing altruism of love is always destroyed in the act of sex, which by its very nature is a selfish and private affair, even when it corresponds with its selfish and private expression in the other person. It was his view — and the view of the Church from earliest times — that, for a marriage to succeed, the concupiscence of sex had gradually to be transformed into the sacrifice of love. The sacrifice becomes embodied in the child born of sex; in the attention and care the child requires, the selfish and very human demands of the parents are turned into selfless giving. In their offspring, the parents really become one; the children's claims give them the opportunity of rising above themselves, of losing themselves lovingly in the desire they have made flesh. Where this transformation does not take place, sex seeks other outlets, searches for excitement, gratifies the normal desire for self-sacrifice in all kinds of perversions. In *Tiny Alice* this theme will be beautifully elaborated in Brother Julian's despairing search for martyrdom — which turns out to be an erotic indulgence. In *Who's Afraid of Virginia Woolf?* the theme is examined within the context of a marriage grown stale.

Albee is no Augustinian, and he might even reject Shaw; but what he succeeds in doing is giving their view added authority. He has depicted in this play the excruciating agony of love as it struggles to preserve the fiction of its purity through a mass of obscenities and the parody of sex. The Son-myth is the embodiment of that fiction. It is the frustration around which the action of the play revolves.

Albee plays on the theme a number of ways, one of which is the introduction of a kind of Shakespearean subplot, in the story of the second couple. Honey and Nick have some kind of sex together, but little love and no children. Honey confesses, late in her drunken stupor, that she doesn't want children. Her fear of pregnancy is also a fear of sex, basically, and throws new light on the story of her courtship and marriage. The hysterical pregnancy which "puffed her up" and made Nick marry her has its own complicated explanation, no doubt; but at the time it took place, it served — in part at least — as a guard against sexual abandonment and a way back into conventional and acceptable relationships. Honey's predicament is characteristic of Albee's handling of complicated human motivation. He neither blames nor prescribes a moral "cure." His dramatic instincts keep him from easy labels; not once does he betray his characters into clinical diagnoses of the kind that O'Neill was prone to. Honey is anything but a case history; in her own way she is pathetically attractive and appealing. There is a kind of strength in her not wanting to keep up with the others. Her childlike trust looks ridiculous in that company, but it is incongruous in the same way that the impossible purity of Martha's fictional son is incongruous. When she returns from the "euphemism," after George's vicious Get the Guests, she says simply, "I don't remember anything, and you·don't remember anything either." Her despair, though different from Martha's, is just as intense and real to her. Like the fictional son of her hosts, her innocence is already compromised. The *Walpurgisnacht* is her initiation party. Her childish decision not to remember unpleasant things has to be put to the test.

Honey, like Martha, is childless; but the parallel is propped up by contrast. Martha wanted children and hasn't any; Honey doesn't want them and manages to keep from having them — or, rather, she doesn't want to go through the pains of childbirth. At the end she confesses pathetically that she fears the physical labor connected with childbirth and reveals a very different kind of impulse. The two stories move toward the same psychological vacuum. The hysterical pregnancy and the fictional son are conceived in different ways, but they are essentially the same kind of birth. Both are the result of impotence, or rather, of a willful assertion which proves abortive. George fails to measure up to Martha's ambitions for him as the son-in-law of the college president; Nick fails to measure up to Honey's romantic dream. Both women give birth to an unsubstantial hope.

Sex is the name of the game; but around Martha — the embodiment of Mother Earth — everything sexual seems to collapse. Men are all flops, and she herself a fool to be tempted by them:

> I disgust me. I pass my life in crummy, totally pointless infidelities . . . WOULD-be-infidelities. Hump the Hostess? That's a laugh. A bunch of boozed-up . . . impotent lunk-heads. Martha makes goo-goo eyes, and the lunk-heads grin, and roll their beautiful, beautiful eyes back, and grin some more, and Martha licks her chops, and the lunk-heads slap over to the bar and pick up a little courage . . . so, FINALLY, they get their courage up . . . but that's all baby! Oh my, there is sometimes some very nice potential, but, oh my! My, my my. . . .

In spite of appearances and what she says in her verbal skirmishes, George is the only man who has ever satisfied her sexually. Even the suggestion of physical impotence is canceled out in the end, when George proves that the ultimate power of life and death lies with him.

The parallel between the two couples is strengthened by other contrasts. Nick and Honey are just starting out and have something of the hopes and energies that George and Martha had when they first came together; but where George failed, Nick might well succeed. He is willful in a petty way, knows exactly what he wants, and is callous enough to reach out and grab it. His plans are clear and realizable. He is much more practical and less idealistic than George, but lacks George's potential to adjust to what the world calls failure. George's *failure* is incomprehensible to Nick: would anyone, in his right mind, turn down a high administrative post simply to indulge a passion to write the great American novel? The irony is that Nick wants what George had in his grasp and turned down. In this context, Nick's designs seem downright petty, while George's worldly failure takes on heroic colors. For George, money means compromise; for Nick, it is the one sure sign of success. His decision to assume the "responsibilities" of marriage was in large measure determined by the fact that Honey was rich; but already he has failed in his role, unable to share his wife's fears and hopes. He is absolutely callous to her emotional needs, bent on humoring her in order to get what he wants. His relationship with Honey is an excellent barometer of his relationship with the rest of the world. He will very likely get everything he wants; but the world will hold his success against him, for his ambition is utterly transparent. George and Martha have understood this and are contemptuous of him; Honey suspects it but cannot bring herself to face the truth.

These ironic oscillations produce something resembling the oppressive emptiness of the plays of Beckett and Sartre. The inescapable dialectic builds up to the recognition, on the part of each of the protagonists, of what he is not and cannot ever be. Each absorbs as much as he is capable of taking in; the rest of the lesson is there to be heard and carried away in the memory. In their hell, the will continues to assert itself in impotent frustration. The exorcism which finally comes about is a vacuum — stylistically, the play reflects the collapse of the will in a quick staccato of monosyllables which brings the action to its close. The exhaustion of pretense is caught neatly in the tired jingle which earlier in the evening, at Daddy's party, brought down the house. Nothing happens in the play, but reality is changed completely in the gradual discovery and recognition of what is inside us all. Whatever else Martha will hit on to substitute for Junior, it can never be confused again with the real condition of her life. This is not necessarily an advantage; confession craves absolution, but all Martha can hope for (and George) is compassion.

The existential mood is caught by means of ambiguous explanations, unfinished or incomplete stories, emotional climaxes suddenly deflated into absurdity. The scene where George "shoots" Martha is a striking example of the explosion of emotional tension into frivolity. Martha is playing up to Nick, as George watches; when she brings up the story about the boxing match in which she managed to stun George, he leaves the room. Martha goes right on — it's all part of their repertory — and George eventually returns with a shotgun which he raises, aims . . . and shoots. But what bursts out, without a bang, is a Chinese parasol. The tension breaks; there is a moment of hysterical relief — but it is only the prelude to a new emotional buildup.

The parasol is perhaps the neatest symbol of George's impotence in his destructive relationship with Martha. It is given sexual overtones by Martha's exchange with Nick, a few moments later — "You don't need any props, do you baby?" "Unh-unh." "I'll bet not. No fake Jap gun for you, eh?" Nick too will turn out to be another "pointless infidelity," and will be relegated to the humiliating role of "houseboy" at the end. No one can match George, but George cannot altogether satisfy her shifting moods. He understands them and adjusts to them — but at his best he must appear weak. He is her scapegoat, the articulate challenger who keeps Martha on her toes, the constant reminder of her own inadequacies. Martha needs victims, and she can pick them up anywhere; but George is the only one who rises to the occasion each time she lashes out. There is some secret understanding between them; she has ruined him with her excessive demands and her domineering ways; but he has not been crushed. His strength reassures her, even when she forces it against herself. George is her conscience and her accuser. In her soliloquy she admits that all the things he says are true — even to Daddy's red eyes — but she fights him for having said them. In some strange way, their fighting is their only means of real communication. George's obstinacy is the reassurance that he has understood the script and can play it out. Martha accuses him of wanting the flagellation she inflicts, but the statement is only partly true. He wants it because he knows she needs it as excuse. She herself can't say this, but there is every reason to believe that she has grasped and accepted that conclusion. She comes close to confessing it in the soliloquy.

> I cry all the time too, Daddy. I cry all the time; but deep inside, so no one can see me. I cry all the time. And Georgie cries all the time, too. We both cry all the time, and then, what we do, we cry, and we take our tears, and we put 'em in the ice box, in the goddam ice trays . . . until they're all frozen . . . and then . . . we put them . . . in our . . . drinks.

In this summing up of the vicious cycle which is the aimless habit of their life, Martha turns a commonplace into a poetic image. The futility of all that frustrated energy is beautifully captured in those ice cubes which will go into furnishing new energy for new recriminations and fresh tears.

In his verbal agility and his instinctive grasp of things, George has a Hamlet-like appeal. Somewhere in his soul, his aimless puns have meaning. His verbal fencing with Nick on at least two occasions succeeds in humiliating the younger man, who thinks he *knows*. But *knowing* means being married to Martha and being able to fence in that way. *Knowing* means weaving in and out of irrelevancies and coming back each time to the sore spot; it means indulging in confusion which is not altogether accidental. Even his absentmindedness seems to have a purpose. With a kind of fixation, George keeps coming around to the subject of the History Department and his own abortive role in it. His failure is a challenge hurled at his potential rival. Nick may be more likely to succeed, but he cannot hold his own in the hard-hitting duel of words.

The only worthy challenger is Martha. Both have an uncanny gift for turning obvious disadvantage into victory through wit, ad-libbing where the familiar script seems to repeat itself monotonously and turning the unexpected into an integral part of the dialogue. The game is brilliant and vicious when they indulge in it together; it takes on a sad, pathetic quality when one or the other indulges in it with Nick or Honey. Honey is, on the whole, too naïve to be an effective foil, but Nick is just self-conscious enough to draw blood. And George and Martha are always ready to catch the faintest suggestion of hypocrisy, any hint of weakness that can be turned into a weapon. They enjoy the game as only experts can. If at times others are hurt, it isn't so much that they enjoy inflicting pain but that their nature demands satisfaction. In his insistence on false pragmatic values, in his false dignity, Nick repeatedly invites such cruelty. The verbal parrying is inspired by the recognition of humbug; irony and sarcasm cut into the surface of things and expose the raw nerves of the offender. The urge is the urge to grasp reality.

All this talk serves, paradoxically, to underscore the incommunicability which is the heart of the play. Nick tolerates his wife and uses her—and, presumably, her money—for his own private ends; Honey is too preoccupied with her own puffed-up fears to realize what is going on and face up to the difficulties in her marriage; George and Martha prefer to indulge in private games and public hostility rather than face their shared loneliness. Occasionally, some attempt is made to reach out—as when George warns Nick about the danger of being overconfident and using people callously to get what he wants. To Nick, George is simply a jealous husband, the impotent male wounded in his vanity.

Frustration is the dramatic impulse of the play. The invitation to Nick and Honey is a frenzied attempt at oblivion through a kind of saturnalia; the verbal skirmishes are frustrated attempts at communication; the history of the two couples is the story of frustrated love; the accusations are frustrated attempts at understanding; a frustrated prayer celebrates the end of the nightmare.

The climax of the play is the high point of frustration, where George's anger presents an immediate threat and—miraculously—is turned instead into the inspiration which gives focus and purpose to the aimless action up to that point. Nick and Martha are in the kitchen; and George, in his lonely despair, throws the book he has been reading across the room, hitting the door chimes which are set off by the impact. Honey returns from the bathroom at this moment and George's frustration is turned full blast on her. He lashes out cruelly, trying to enlighten her about the hard realities she chooses to ignore—

> There are a couple of people in there . . . they are in there, in the kitchen . . . Right there, with the onion skins and the coffee grounds . . . sort of . . . sort of a . . . sort of a dry run for the wave of the future.

Honey's desperate retreat into ignorance enfuriates George; he has found her weak spot—"you simpering bitch . . . you don't want CHILDREN?"— and all his accumulated hatred is turned on her. Honey has managed to find a way to avoid pregnancy without Nick's knowing—but Nick is out in the kitchen trying to "hump the hostess" while the host struggles to contain his anger. The moment is explosive. Both Honey and George are aware at that moment of the demonic force which has been let loose and which threatens to destroy them all. It is at this point that Honey, in her childish attempt to distract her enemy, reminds him about the chimes ringing. To George—who must adjust to the change—it is "the sound of bodies" at first; but his feverish imagination is quick to answer the challenge and he shapes the sound into a purposeful plot meant to punish Martha:

> . . . somebody rang . . . it was somebody . . . with . . . I'VE GOT IT! I'VE GOT IT, MARTHA . . . ! Somebody with a message . . . and the message was . . . our son . . . OUR SON! . . . It was a message . . . the bells rang and it was a message, and it was about . . . our son . . . and the message . . . was . . . and the message was . . . our . . . son . . . is . . . DEAD!

With characteristic resiliency, George manages to turn chaos into meaningful reality. Impotence is transformed into creative purpose; the two separate vectors—Honey's desperate demand for reassurance and George's demonic spite—come together at this crucial moment to give new direction to the action. From that moment on, George is in command, a providential agent calling the moves right up to the resolution and fulfillment of his plan.

In resolving to destroy the fiction of the son, George is responding to his own impotent spite; but there is a certain tragic justice in the plan. Martha keeps changing the rules of the game, after all; and although George has gone along up to that point ("learning the games we play as quickly as I can change the rules" as Martha says), she has gone too far, stepping over some invisible line; she has betrayed some tacit agreement. George's plan to punish her is, by her own admission, the fulfillment of her paradoxical impulses: she needs his love but does not deserve it; she hates him for his idealism but acknowledges her weakness in exposing him; in taunting him she is expressing disgust at her own shortcomings; she will not forgive him "for having come to rest; for having seen me and having said: yes; this will do; who has made the hideous, the hurting, the insulting mistake of loving me and must be punished for it." In hatred, as in love, they are indissolubly bound; in punishing Martha, George is also punishing himself. This paradox is the source of their frustration: it gave birth to the Son-myth and will now destroy it.

Martha's fictional son is the child of her will, the symbol of potency and virility, the imaginative embodiment of all the masculine roles idealized and idolized. He is the perfect lover, the perfect son and husband, the successful breadwinner, the creature of all her hopes. George points up the erotic implications of Martha's obsessive interest in the boy:

> He's a nice kid, really, in spite of his home life; I mean, most kids'd grow up neurotic, what with Martha here carrying on the way she does: sleeping 'till four in the P.M., climbing all over the poor bastard, trying to break the bathroom door down to wash him in the tub when he's sixteen, dragging strangers into the house at all hours. . . .

Martha herself suggests a very different picture. With nostalgia she recalls all the vivid details of the child's discovery of the world, the cane headboard he wore through with his little hands, the croup tent and the shining kettle hissing in the one single light of the room "that time he was sick," animal crackers, and the bow and arrow he kept under his bed, her beautiful boy walking "evenly between us . . . to protect us all from George's . . . weakness . . . and my . . . necessary greater strength . . . to protect himself . . . and us." Martha's child is perfection and George the "drowning man" who threatened repeatedly to destroy that perfection. Instinctively, we understand that this exchange marks the moment of destruction—Martha's recollections are the examination of conscience that precedes confession and the entire cycle of purification. George—who has always stopped her from bringing up the subject—this time has actually encouraged her to do so. It is part of his plan.

Martha's moment of grace is short-lived. Having named George in her reminiscences, she turns her full attention to describing his negative influence on the child and the boy's shame at the "shabby failure" his father has become over the years. The quarrel resumes with these accusations and recriminations, rising to a pathetic climax with Martha's claim that the child is "the one thing, the one person I have tried to protect, to raise above the mire of this vile, crushing marriage; the one light in all this hopeless . . . DARKness . . . OUR SON." Against her stark accusations, we hear the funeral service for the dead, intoned in Latin by George; both end at the same moment. There is a brief interruption by Honey, at this point, and then George's triumphant announcement that sunny-Jim is dead.

Martha's account almost convinces us, but there is no sunny-Jim, of course. By the time the exorcism is over even Nick has seen the light. Martha's furious "YOU CANNOT DO THAT! YOU CAN'T DECIDE THAT FOR YOURSELF!" leaves no more room for doubt. George has killed the myth and Martha finally has to accept the fact. But the reasoning behind the fact is a private understanding, a tacit agreement between George and Martha.

MARTHA: [*Great sadness and loss*] You have no right . . . you have no right at all. . . .

GEORGE: [*Tenderly*] I have the right, Martha. We never spoke of it; that's all. I could kill him any time I wanted to.

MARTHA: But why? Why?

GEORGE: You broke our rule, baby. You mentioned him . . . you mentioned him to someone else.

The tacit agreement was that the boy remain their private dream, not to be shared with anyone else, not to be corrupted by exposure to an unsympathetic world. Martha's indulgence in confiding to others, her breaking the rules and telling "the bit" about their "son" is the cue that private communication is breaking down. George's decision was not so much punishment as necessity. It had been "an easy birth . . . once it had been . . . accepted, relaxed into"; presumably it will be an easy death, once it is accepted in the same way. Martha must give him up because the myth has taken over and entered into her public life. Private necessity has turned into a public joke. George has tried to protect her from this moment; but when the shared myth turns into a stunted fact, he destroys it. Like an inexorable agent of fate, he guides Martha through the long reminiscences and the subsequent "confession." Having been exposed, the myth must be properly laid to rest.

The "death" scene is one of the most suggestive of the play and, in spite of the presence of Nick and Honey, a private conversation between Martha and George. They speak the same language, but never try to explain the contradictions to the others. Nick and Honey will take away what they can absorb; their reaction — like that of the audience — is the measure of their insight. The scene is sober and naturalistic, in keeping with the "tragic" end of the child. The "eulogy" anticipates the straightforward, transparent language of *Tiny Alice* in its sentimental reminiscences, but it is simultaneously an ironic *ritual*.

Albee takes great pains to develop these two distinct voices here, for Martha's "son" — invisible but real — is the most striking paradox of the play. He is the imagination made flesh — or, more precisely, the "word" made flesh, for Martha and George have brought him into the world as talk, as a game between them, in which he arbitrates, comforts, gives strength to his parents. He is clarity, insight, parable. If one were disposed to take on the burden of a polysemous reading, one might trace some interesting religious analogies, such as the "lamb" and the "tree" against which the boy met his death, and the "porcupine" which he tried to avoid, like the crown of thorns in the story of Christ.

One need not labor such analogies, however, to grasp the rich content of the Son-myth. He is Martha's hope, her way of getting psychological relief, her faith that some corner of life remains untouched and pure. Birth came easily, "once it had been accepted"; but his life was not easy, for he bore the burden of his parents' mutual accusations and suffered the agony of their mutual guilt. Innocence and guilt — the divine and human — come together in him. "He walked evenly between us," Martha recalls, "a hand out to each of us for what we could offer by way of support, affection, teaching, even love"; but those same hands held them off, too, "for mutual protection." He ran off periodically, but always returned — just as he was returning that day, the day of his birthday, of his majority. He was expected back; he *did* come back; but in his majority he forced them into a new and unexpected relationship. His death suggests, by way of contrast, a new beginning, a kind of salvation in truth. His sacrifice should be the gift of love.

Such a reading brings to light several hints of a "virgin birth." Martha refers many times to "my" son and George repeatedly tries to correct her; and in one place, at least, she attributes to George a doubt that "deep down in the private-most pit of his gut, he's not completely sure it's his own kid." George's casual remark to Nick that "Martha doesn't have pregnancies at all" strengthens this suggestion: Martha has no pregnancies, but she has nevertheless miraculously given birth.

In this context, the exorcism at the end of the play is the confession which will restore spiritual health. George, the high priest, has already prophesied what must come.

> We all peel labels, sweeties; and when you get through the skin, all three layers, through the muscle, slosh aside the organs (An aside to NICK) them which is still sloshable — (Back to HONEY) and get down to the bone . . . you know what you do then? . . . When you get down to bone, you haven't got all the way, yet. There's something inside the bone . . . the marrow . . . and that's what you gotta get at . . . The marrow.

In his role of prophetic high priest, George hears Martha's "confession," blessing it with his reading of the service for the dead. And like the priest, who in the sacrifice of the Mass becomes once again the figure of Christ, and who in the mystery of the transubstantiation turns ordinary bread and wine into the body and bread of Christ, George too emerges gradually as celebrant of a mystery.

Whether or not he really is the same person that he describes in his story to Nick — the young boy who ordered "bergin" and who killed his mother and father in two separate tragic accidents within several months of one another — can never be decided with certainty. Nor does the *fact* of such an identity really matter. The story, after all, is George's and the boy in it his creation. Some kind of identity does exist, and Martha herself sets up some curious parallels, reminding her audience that there is "something funny" in George's past, insisting that the story George tells Nick is a true one that "really happened," threatening her husband with "before I'm

through with you you'll wish you'd died in that automobile, you bastard."
George sets up psychological reverberations of his own in his account of
how their "son" died — an account strangely similar to the account in the
original story. "He was . . . killed . . . late in the afternoon . . . on a
country road, with his learner's permit in his pocket, he swerved to avoid a
porcupine, and drove straight into a . . . large tree."

The boy in the "bergin" story and the boy in George's book come into
focus in the Son-myth, all of whom are in some way connected with
George himself. He is the double image — both father and son — celebrating in his inspired reading of the Latin service his own death and rebirth.
The parody of transubstantiation is completed in his claim that he ate the
telegram (the only proof of the story he is telling), just as the priest at the
elevation eats the consecrated Host in remembrance of Christ's last supper.
What seems a disjointed, purposeless narrative takes on a providential
aspect even in the manner in which the idea of sunny-Jim's death first
came to him. The chimes had rung — as they do to alert the participants of
the Mass that the elevation is imminent — and had inspired him. Grace —
insight — takes the form of a mystical revelation, a flash of meaning in
which the scattered nonsense of the entire evening suddenly falls into place
and assumes a purpose.

The Son-myth, like Brother Julian's fantasies in *Tiny Alice*, turns out
to be a private indulgence of faith where there is nothing to believe. It is
faith that must try to create from its own wreck the thing it contemplates.
George comes to realize that such faith must be accepted all the way, to
the point of exposure. The Son-myth has come of age; which means,
simply, that it must reveal itself at last for what it is. The agony of the end
is as painful as the labor that brought it into being, but there is no
salvation to soothe the loss. Martha must suffer through it, for there is no
choice left.

> I don't mind your dirty underthings in public . . . Well, I DO mind, but
> I've reconciled myself to that . . . but you've moved bag and baggage
> into your own fantasy world now, and you've started playing variations
> on your own distortions.

Lucidity and purpose are a gain — if that much further loss can be called
"gain." The religious undercurrents and the ironic paradox which is the
result of sacrifice are indeed strangely reminiscent of *The Zoo Story*.

The exorcism culminates in a kind of religious abandonment. Nick —
the scientific skeptic without a trace of sympathy — sees in all this simply
the frustration of a childless couple. Honey senses something of the
mystery and cries out for some small part of the experience. A kind of
religious awe pervades the closing minutes of the play; the coming of dawn
is the paradoxical symbol of exhaustion and death. The mystery is a
dilemma; revelation a trap. The mystical experience is reduced to a
pathetic series of monosyllables.

The existential conclusion is at the same time an assertion. Martha and George find each other in the poverty of their self-hatred. Nick and Honey are properly subdued; but in their tragic awareness of the empti-ness they have created, Martha and George are redeemed. The Son-myth, like a mystical death, is resurrected in the agony of love.

Camping Out: *Tiny Alice* and
Susan Sontag

John Stark*

. . . The best way to begin clarifying *Tiny Alice* is to consider the one point about which the critics agree: that it is obscure. This condition, rather than ending analysis of the play, should begin it. After all, readers have come to accept the creation of obscurity as a literary technique, especially in poetry. One should not be bothered, for instance, by the deliberate ambiguity of the stage directions, which are like those in the Theater of the Absurd. (At one point Albee describes one setting and then another that is "an alternative — and perhaps more practical," and later he says that "maybe" some noise should be made.[1]) After one accepts this kind of obscurity he can concentrate on Albee's reasons for creating it.

Some explanation for this obscurity can be found in Sontag's work. Although she has not written about *Tiny Alice*, her two major essays, "Against Interpretation" and "Notes on 'Camp'," appeared in 1964, just before *Tiny Alice* was first produced. Albee had read Sontag; when an interviewer mentioned that a critic's ideas about *Tiny Alice* seemed similar to some of Sontag's ideas, Albee replied, "this critic . . . what he has done is to misinterpret my attitudes, Miss Sontag's attitudes."[2] So, there is a possibility of influence. But even if there were no influence, the similarity between Sontag's and Albee's ideas is worth exploring because it sheds light on the play.

Three of Miss Sontag's essays are relevant to this play. One is her definitive description of Camp in "Against Interpretation."[3] Robert Brustein has noticed Camp's influence on Albee's play (and undoubtedly is the critic about whom Albee and his interviewer were talking); "*Tiny Alice* is a much more ambitious work than the usual variety of 'Camp,' but it shares the same ambiguity of motive."[4] Brustein, however, does not pursue his insight. It is necessary to go to Sontag's essay and look for ideas that will clarify *Tiny Alice*. She writes that Camp was originally created by homosexuals, and homosexuality — at least in mock form — is evident in *Tiny Alice*. The Lawyer, in the rough and tumble conversation that opens

*From *Players* (April-May 1972):116–69.

the play, imputes homosexuality to the Cardinal and to Catholic clergy-men in general. He refers sarcastically to "their vaunted celibacy . . . among one another," and to the Cardinal's supposed desire for "some good-looking young novice, all freshly scrubbed, with big working-class hands" (p. 4). He also jokingly exchanges a "dearest" and "darling" with Butler (p. 30).

According to Sontag, Camp joking eventually became self-conscious and began mocking modern culture. Much of *Tiny Alice*'s obscurity results from the jocular attitude Albee takes toward some of his most important themes, like sex and religion. The sexual theme provides the play's most spectacular moment, the second act curtain, when Miss Alice opens her cloak, reveals her body to Julian and then enfolds him in the cloak. But sex is also sometimes treated comically — in a Camp manner — in, for example, the erotic puns. Brustein mentions the pun about the unused organ; other puns concern Julian's status as a lay brother and the Lawyer's British title of Solicitor. In her essay "On Style," Sontag explains the attitude of writers who recognize the potential seriousness of certain themes yet treat them comically. This ambivalent point of view will almost inevitably cause obscurity: " 'Stylization in a work of art, as distinct from style, reflects an ambivalence (affection contradicted by irony) toward the subject-matter. This ambivalence is handled by maintaining, through the rhetorical overlay that is stylization, a special distance from the subject."[5]

Albee also treats religion in the ambivalent and obfuscating manner Sontag describes. An example is his failure to clarify the source of Julian's name. It is not clear which of two very different religious persons he is named after: Julian the Apostate, an emperor who abandoned Christian-ity and later persecuted its followers, or Julian of Norwich, a female medieval mystic and author of *Revelations*. Religion is also important in the play's ending, when Julian assumes a crucifixion pose, but even this is burlesqued. He asks for "the sacramental wine" but also for his "cookie," not a wafer (p. 181). The frequent comic reference to wine, especially to the exploding bottles in the cellar, make this image far from serious in the play. The most ironic part of the religious theme is a macabre joke about a woman at the insane asylum who believed her womb contained Christ when it really contained cancer (p. 63). Finally, inside the model and purporting to be a kind of god is Tiny Alice: a mouse, a comic kind of god indeed.

Another essay of Sontag's that is relevant to *Tiny Alice* is "Against Interpretation."[6] In it she argues that art should not be mimetic and that interpretation is therefore an improper response to art: "the modern style of interpretation excavates, as it excavates, destroys; it digs 'behind' the text, to find a sub-text which is the true one" (p. 6). She argues against interpretation because "in a culture whose already classical dilemma is the hypertrophy of the intellect at the expense of energy and sensual capabil-ity, interpretation is the revenge of the intellect upon art. Even more, it is the revenge of the intellect upon the world" (p. 7). These ideas help explain the play's most baffling feature, the model. It is a Chinese box, representing the house, and inside it is a model of the model and so on *ad infinitum*. Art, according to Plato, is just such an indirect representation of reality: "the tragic poet, too, is an artist who represents things; . . . he and all other artists are, as it were, third in succession from the throne of truth."[7] Thus, according to Plato, works of art are part of a Chinese box system. But Sontag and probably Albee disagree with Plato because his theory states that art is mimetic. Albee seems to mock mimetic theories of art by using a schematization of them (the model) as part of his scenery and by placing inside it, as its ultimate representation of reality, a mouse.

In *Tiny Alice* Albee's complaint with the mimetic theories of art is that it argues that art is related to the world, rather than holding that art is self-contained and cut off from external reality. Albee makes his point by presenting a change in Julian's conception of the relation between art and reality. Before the main action of the play Julian had experiences — hallucinations — that should have warned him to be skeptical about believing in a simple relation between reality and representations of it, with the latter mirroring the former. These hallucinations should have suggested to him that it is not always easy to determine precisely what is reality and what is something else, but Julian remains secure in his orthodox conceptions about reality; in fact, he holds to these conceptions throughout most of the play. Near the end he affirms the Lawyer's statement that he, Julian, is dedicated to reality, not to appearance (p. 132). It is the Lawyer who has occasionally been insinuating into Julian's mind another possibility: that non-real things purporting merely to copy reality are not related to everyday reality at all but are themselves an ultimate — perhaps the only — reality. For example, early in the play the Lawyer says: "I have learned . . . Brother Julian . . . never to confuse the representative of a . . . thing with the thing itself" (p. 39). "Representative" is of course a pun on "representation." By the end of the play the Lawyer, with help from other influences, prevails, and Julian decides to forsake other realities for the reality of the model, the representation.

Rather than merely copying part of the everyday world, this play itself, like the model, is in some important respects "about" itself. To be specific, it is a play that examines the validity of representing reality by means of plays. The first thing Miss Alice does is assume the role of an old crone. This role-playing, according to Sontag, is characteristic of Camp: "to perceive Camp in objects and persons is to understand Being-as-Playing-a-Role."[8] Another involution is the play within the play, in which the Lawyer and Butler act out new identities (pp. 100–101). In fact, Julian — along with the more perceptive members of the audience — senses that he is the victim of a troupe of highly skilled actors. Thus the actors in *Tiny Alice* play characters who are actors playing roles. The result is indeed a Chinese box system, with the play moving inward toward a core of dramatic "reality" rather than toward a copy of reality.

Tiny Alice also has the effect of being self-enclosed and separate from external reality because it stresses that to a large extent reality is linguistic. In this it resembles the story of another Alice: *Alice in Wonderland.* In Carroll's book Alice leaves the world of external reality and goes to a world that seems to be linguistically composed (i.e., figures of speech, such as "mad as a hatter," are made manifest). Albee's Alice is reminiscent of Carroll's, particularly late in the play, when her actions become very childish and Albee says that her reaction to Julian is *"surprisingly little-girl fright"* (p. 143). The many puns in the play also emphasize language's role in forming conceptions of reality. Butler indirectly suggests to Julian that this is so when he claims that it was a semantic problem that caused Julian's mental illness (p. 43). Julian's final acceptance of Alice is, among other things, an acceptance of the power of language; he is convinced more by assertion than by evidence. His acceptance is also his validation of drama as not only a representation of reality but *as* reality.

In short, both Albee and Miss Sontag are interested in Camp sensibility and the nature of art. Another way to demonstrate Albee's interest in these matters is to set *Tiny Alice* into its chronological place in his work. The relevant works are *Who's Afraid of Virginia Woolf?* (1962), *Tiny Alice* (1964), and *Malcolm* (1965). *Ballad of the Sad Cafe* (1963), a dramatization of a novella by Carson MacCullers, deals with other themes.) The first of these plays develops the themes of reality, representation and the creation of fictitional alternatives to reality, particularly in its treatment of the fiction about George and Martha's "child." Albee himself mentioned this aspect of *Virginia Woolf* to an interviewer: "and of course, who's afraid of the big *bad* wolf . . . who's afraid of living life without false illusions."[9] *Malcolm* is an adaptation of James Purdy's novel, which is a classic of Camp literature, a peculiar *Bildungsroman* that describes a boy becoming a Camp object, and it is full of Camp characters, rooms, clothes and other trappings. Its Camp theme is recapitulated in the motto of Malcolm's first wife. "Texture is all, substance nothing," which recalls Susan Sontag's statement that "Camp art is often decorative art, emphasizing texture, sensuous surface, and style at the expense of content."[10] Albee's decision to adapt Purdy's novel immediately upon finishing *Tiny Alice* shows his continuing interest in Camp.

One can speculate about Albee's reasons for creating art about art and for treating his in a Camp manner. A probable cause is the large number of critics who turn their attention on the work of contemporary writers. The most striking feature of the interview with Albee in *Paris Review* is his knowledge of the criticism written about him. At one point he says, "about four years ago I made a list, for my own amusement, of the playwrights, the contemporary playwrights, by whom critics said I'd been influenced. I listed twenty-five" (p. 103). Note, too, the strained and uneasy irony of "for my own amusement." His response is certainly understandable, because too much criticism can make any writer uneasy about his work and can even encourage him to fashion what Brustein called a "huge joke on the American culture industry."[11] Once again Sontag has a relevant comment: "a great deal of today's art may be understood as motivated by a flight from interpretation. To avoid interpretation, art becomes parody. Or it becomes abstract. Or it may become ('merely') decorative. Or it may become non-art."[12]

Tiny Alice exemplifies some of the alternatives for art that Sontag proposes. Albee's treatment of the themes of sex and religion is parodic rather than profound, and his development of the theme of art is not immediately clear. The ending, especially in the longer printed version, is ludicrous, probably deliberately so. Julian takes longer to die than a villain in a bad western movie, and his final speech is extremely over-blown. Nigel Dennis' complaint about some other playwrights at first seems to apply also to Albee: "when [Beckett, Ionesco and Genet] got into difficulties . . . they filled up the void with make-believe of meaningless words and stage 'business'. This now has become the approved way, with the difference that as the tradition grows more and more decadent, the firmness of grasp becomes feebler and feebler and the accumulation of meaninglessness greater and greater."[13] Dennis' complaint is over-stated, but he does sound a useful warning. This criticism should not be applied to Albee, however, since he has artistic reasons for the apparent flaws in Tiny Alice.

Tiny Alice should be considered an experiment. As many examples demonstrate, art about art can be great but unfortunately the obscurities and complexities inherent in Camp art-about-art seem to make complete success impossible. Even more unfortunate, this experiment seems to have tainted Albee, for never again has he risen to the heights of his early one-act plays and Who's Afraid of Virginia Woolf? But the fad of the Camp sensibility has waned since Tiny Alice, which leaves hope that Albee (and the other writers who were affected by it) will return to his previous level of accomplishment.

Notes

1. Edward Albee, Tiny Alice (New York: Pocket Books, 1966), p. 22, p. 89. Later references will be to this edition, and will be identified by page number within the text.

2. Paris Review, 10:39 (Fall, 1966), 113.

3. "Notes on 'Camp'," Against Interpretation (New York: Dell Publishing Company, 1967), pp. 275–292.

4. "Three Plays and a Protest," New Republic, 152 (January 23, 1965), 33.

5. "On Style," Against Interpretation, p. 20.

6. Against Interpretation, p. 3–14.

7. *The Republic* (Cornford translation) (Oxford: Oxford University Press, 1941), p. 327.

8. "Notes on 'Camp'," p. 280.

9. *Paris Review*, 10: 39 (Fall, 1966), 103.

10. "Notes on 'Camp'," p. 278.

11. Brustein, 33.

12. "Against Interpretation," p. 10.

13. "Color it Orange," *New York Review of Books*, 9:1 (July 13, 1967), 8.

Toby's Last Stand: The Evanescence of Commitment in *A Delicate Balance*   M. Gilbert Porter*

Common objections to *A Delicate Balance* are that it is a play without a subject or that in depicting tedium tediously it commits the mimetic fallacy. One critic observes of *A Delicate Balance*, for example, that "Albee seems to be stimulated by mere artifice, and the result is emptiness, emptiness, emptiness"; that, like the rest of his plays, it has "no internal validity"; and that, finally, it is "a very bad play."[1] Another charges that the play "is about the nothingness, the bare nothingness of it all — it is a play about nothing. . . . Albee's nothing is as dull as anything"; and the critic asks rhetorically, "why would he [Albee] hurtle into such utter pointlessness?"[2] A third complains that "we have no clear picture of what has been changed by the incidents of the weekend. . . . All we get is the feeling that two houseguests who have been a nuisance are finally going."[3] Among the facts educed to support such negative conclusions are the static nature of the central figures (particularly Agnes), the absence of an integrating principle, and the failure of the play to realize the fear that brings Harry and Edna into the household of Tobias and Agnes.

In the analysis that follows I propose a positive reading of the play to demonstrate that the "emptiness" that many critics have objected to as an absence of subject matter — or boring insignificance — may be regarded as an emotional and moral vacuum that serves as the center of the plot of the drama. Becoming a fully developed existential nothingness, the emptiness at last is both significant and basic to the play's strength. Embodied dramatically in the lives of the characters, such nothingness has resulted from insularity and an attrition of commitment leading to the loss of love, a death-in-life. The static nature of the characters is thus thematically functional.

The integrating dramatic principle is a strategy of circularity in

*From *Educational Theatre Journal* 31 (October 1979):398–408. Reprinted by permission of The Johns Hopkins University Press.

characterization, situation, and language. The circular strategy reflects the play's cycle of emptiness, beginning in the "Nothing" that compels Harry and Edna to the home of Tobias and Agnes and culminating in the loveless void that engulfs them all in the final scene. The central figure is not Agnes but Tobias, whose gradual self-awareness occurs as he sees himself by turns in the lives of the other characters. His dawning recognition of his own emptiness provides the dramatic tension in the play and renders him the hub around which the play's circularity revolves. Thus Tobias is clearly the appropriate focus for critical attention.[4]

The play offers Tobias as the most crucial character because his decent impulses are stunted by his weak will and timorous judgment — and because his confrontation with his flawed self is starker than the similar confrontations of the others. He enlists the sympathy of the audience because he wishes to be better than he is, like Miller's Willy Loman or Bellow's Tommy Wilhelm. To use Tobias as the critical focus of the play is not to ignore or distort the other characters, but simply to see them as satellites moving around him, sharing the same space, the same light and darkness, for their various failures are counterparts to his own. The point is made repeatedly in the play. Agnes declares, "We see ourselves repeated by those we bring into it all, either by mirror or rejection, honor or fault."[5] Harry and Edna are described in the stage notes as "very much like Agnes and Tobias," and Claire characterizes Tobias's friends and former business associates as "your indistinguishable if not necessarily similar friends" (28). Edna warns in the last scene that they must not examine one another too closely "for fear of looking into a mirror" (169). Tobias's relationship with each character, then, reveals a dimension of the weakness or failure in both characters. The following discussion is therefore organized around Tobias: what he learns from each of the other characters about his own shortcomings; how he is at the center of the circular strategies in characterization, situation, and imagery; and why he fails to rise above the void created by his progressive evasion of genuine human commitment.

The most intimate pairing is Tobias with Agnes, a marriage that has lasted at least thirty-seven years and has produced two children. Julia's brother, Teddy, died when Julia was still a child, an event in the antecedent story that severely altered the relation between Agnes and Tobias. Frightened and emotionally scarred by Teddy's death, Tobias began to practice onanism in his sexual relations with Agnes. He sought to prevent conception and thus to protect himself from any further pain connected with paternity. After about a year of such love's labors lost, Tobias moved from *coitus interruptus* to abstinence and slept in a separate bedroom, his sexual withdrawal from Agnes becoming therefore emblematic of his withdrawal from any of life's risks. Tobias let his inaction imply his working creed: nothing ventured, nothing lost. Protesting in vain, Agnes acquiesced in the new circumscribed life and devoted herself to preserving the outward forms of stability. But the price of her adjustment was high: it made her a shrew.

In the action of the play Agnes appears mainly as a "harridan," a "drill sergeant," a "martinet," the most revealing exception being the opening scene of Act 3 in which the ghost of Agnes past appears briefly to Tobias as a loving, sexually responsive, feminine helpmate—her softness here serving to underline her hardness elsewhere. The contrast also calls attention to the role Tobias has played in making Agnes what she is: his fear and effeminacy have called forth her aggressiveness and masculinity as compensation. If he does not like her authoritative manner, and he does not, he must acknowledge that it derives from his abdication of authority. His shamefaced behavior in front of Agnes through most of the play makes this acknowledgement for him.

The tyranny and resigned martyrdom of Agnes are not totally the fault of Tobias, however. He sowed the seeds, it is true, but they fell on fertile ground, and Agnes prides herself on what she considers her indispensable position in the family. With the fixed smile of self-satisfied superiority, she declares herself the "fulcrum" on which the family balance rests and defines her function as a controlling one: " 'To Keep in shape.' Have you heard the expression? Most people misunderstand it, assume it means alteration, when it does not. Maintenance. When we keep something in shape we maintain its shape—whether we are proud of that shape or not, is another matter—we keep *it* from falling apart. We do not attempt the impossible. We maintain. We hold" (88). In the face of a dead son, a disappointing and ungrateful daughter, an alcoholic sister, and a milquetoast husband, Agnes has turned for stability to meal planning, house management, and social ritual, imposing domestic order on internal disorder. In doing so, she exaggerates her martyrdom and intensifies Tobias's guilt.

Agnes is far from guiltless herself. The conditions Tobias offered are the conditions she settled for, and the quality of her life, therefore, is what she has allowed it to be, despite her transparent effort in Act 3 to shift all of the responsibility to Tobias. "We don't decide the route," she says, speaking in her presumptuous manner for all wives. Tobias rightly replies, "You're copping out . . . as they say" (137) and charges her with the refusal to shoulder her part of the guilt for their empty lives. Linked together in their flawed humanity, these two exist in a love-hate relationship typical of Albee's characters. Albee underlines their mutual dependency and estrangement, their diminished capacities, with an allusion to a line spoken by Hamm to Clov in Beckett's *Endgame*: "We do what we can" (19), which Agnes feels should serve as the family motto and be emblazoned on the linens in Latin.

Where Tobias's passiveness has the effect of awakening militancy in Agnes, it curiously abets detachment in Claire, who, like Agnes, has replaced an old self with a new self. Made a member of Tobias's household by her father's dying wish, Claire long indulged herself in alcoholic self pity and a promiscuous search for love. She recalls her condition in the year that Teddy died: "You hate with the same green stinking sickness you feel your bowels have turned into . . . yourself, and *everybody*. Hate, and, oh, God! you want love, l-o-v-e, so badly—comfort and snuggling is what you really mean, of course—but you hate, and you notice—with a sort of detachment that amuses you, you think—that you're more like an animal every day . . . you snarl, and grab for things, and hide things like not-very-bright dogs, and you wash less, prefer to *be* washed, and once or twice you've actually soiled your bed and laid in it because you can't get up . . ." (32). When Teddy's death turned Tobias away from Agnes sexually, he turned briefly to Claire, but his feeling for her culminated in a single instance of sexual intercourse. Since he could not bring himself to leave Agnes or sustain a love for Claire, Tobias discreetly returned to his role of obedient and faithful husband, leaving Claire to carry only a faint ember of love for him in her well-trampled heart. Reminding Tobias of that summer affair which marked the end of her drunken groping for love (and his adventuring), Claire asks about her old self, "What was her name?" "I don't remember," Tobias replies. "No matter," Claire concludes, "she's gone" (30).

Somehow the touch of Tobias—and, perhaps, fatigue—cured Claire of her promiscuity and gave focus to her quest for love, but Tobias's subsequent passiveness has keyed her resigned detachment. The new Claire is a jester-seer, a resident vaudevillian and wise fool who both entertains and criticizes the family. A puckish crowd-pleaser, she tells amusing stories about shopping trips for topless bathing suits, she plays the accordion, yodels, affects regional dialects, and provides captions for the deadly Beckettian waiting game their lives have become: "Waiting. The room; the doctor's office, beautiful unconcern; intensive study of the dreadful curtains; absorption in *Field and Stream*, waiting for the Bi-op-see" (95). And what is the disease Claire sees as "objective observer" from her seat on the fifty-yard line? Fear. Julia's fear of maturity, Agnes's fear of insanity, old age, and death, Harry's and Edna's fear of nothingness, and Tobias's fear of risk, pain, responsibility, life. What she sees and shares is their common silent conspiracy to do nothing, to defer decisions and avoid commitment. She sums up their condition in her description of Tobias's refusal to assert himself with Agnes: "Are those the ground rules? Nothing? Too . . . settled? Too . . . dried up? Gone?" (39).

In the meantime, while Claire waits for Tobias to kill Agnes, or resurrect their adulterous love affair, or carry them all off to a utopian island, she describes for Tobias his plight among his women: "Crisis sure brings out the best in us, don't it, Tobe? The family circle? Julia standing there . . . *asserting*; perpetual brat, and maybe ready to pull a Claire. *And* poor Claire! Not much help there either, is there? And lookit Agnes, talky Agnes, ruler of the roost, and maitre d' *and* licensed wife—silent. All cozy, coffee, thinking of the menu for the week, planning. Poor Tobe" (154). Claire's activities have become surrogate ones: She supplies, unsolicited and ungratified, the eroticism that Tobias no longer seeks in Agnes; she provides the childlike willfulness of Julia while that hoyden is having one of her marriages. Claire is no longer sure she would want Tobias if Agnes were dead, for then she would have to assume the duties of a wife, and Claire has always preferred to be a mistress to "safe" married men, a substitute — irresponsible — wife. "You could find a man," Tobias claims. "Indeed, I have found several, briefly," she replies, "and none of my own" (79). Having dwelt in detachment for so long, she views involvement with mixed feelings, desiring love but fearing its consequences. She is content to bide her time with her humor and her booze and to place her fate, with bemused hope, in the hands of Tobias. She is curious to see if Tobias will ever find the courage to change her into something worthwhile. Like her sister, then, she is culpable for shifting responsibility to another. The half-life Tobias offers is the half-life she has accepted. Instead of wife or lover, she has opted for mistress of the family's elegiac revels. In her weakness Tobias sees his own shortcomings, prounouncing pessimistically, "Once you drop . . . you can come back up part way . . . but never . . . really back again. Always . . . descent" (33).

There is descent also in Tobias's relation with Julia as she describes it: "When I was a very little girl . . . I thought you were a marvel — saint, sage, daddy, everything. . . . And then, as the years turned — poor old man — you sank to cipher, and you've stayed there, I'm afraid — very nice but ineffectual, essential, but not-really-thought-of, gray . . . non-eminence. . . . And now you've changed again, sea monster, ram! Nasty, violent, absolutely human man" (71–72). Tobias takes a ho-hum attitude toward this recital, for he is accustomed to Julia's verbal tantrums. She has chided him about playing golf, baited him about Teddy's probable homosexuality, and flaunted the failure of her four marriages in his face. Yet Julia's taunts are not simply outpourings of hostility; they are forms of engagement, the closest thing to affection Julia will allow herself to show for her father, whose indecisiveness has prompted recklessness in his daughter. Tobias thinks without acting. Julia acts without thinking. Her gesture is the tantrum, his the furrowed brow. Yet in her manner as a "perpetual brat" she loves her father. Her appeal to Tobias for protection against Harry and Edna reveals her childish dependency, as the love scene she enacts with Agnes's bed linens just prior to the gun scene suggests her confused post-pubescent affection for Tobias.

The Freudian overtones here provide a clue to Julia's problem and to Tobias's plight as head of the household. Assuming Agnes's position in bed (clasping the pillow "like a lover," as Tobias reports), Julia indicates her repressed desire for the father — the Electra complex, however faint or far away. Such a feeling also accounts for the frequent and intense hostility between Agnes and Julia, competition for the affection of the father/

husband.[6] Handling and meekly surrendering Tobias's phallic pistol, Julia demonstrates her submissiveness to the momentarily dominating male. Her marriages have ostensibly been searches for the father, but imperfect ones as the father is imperfect. When Agnes tells Julia that Tobias is now sleeping in her room again, Julia comments snidely, "That'll be different" (62). Julia here implies that all her husbands have resembled her father: they have been sexually indifferent, inadequate, or unfaithful. Claire sings a little ditty about it:

> Phillip loved to gamble.
> Charlie loved the boys,
> Tom went after Women,
> Douglas. . . . [41]

Douglas, a liberal, was in Julia's view simply "against everything." Seeking the father, an unworthy model, Julia chooses unsatisfactory husbands. In her bungled marriages, Julia repeats the pattern of Agnes's life: "And when we come to marriage, dear: each of them, the fear, the happiness, the sex, the stopping, the infidelities" intones Agnes as she describes Julia's habitual story to Tobias. And then, lest the point be lost on him, Agnes laments, "my life is gone through more than hers" (116–117).

Like her mother and aunt, Julia wants to shift the responsibility for her unhappiness to Tobias. When he says sarcastically of her husbands, "You do pick 'em," she replies haughtily, "*Do* I pick em? I thought it was fifteen hundred and six, or so, where daughter went with whatever man her parents thought would hold the fief together best, of something. 'Love will come after' " (73). Julia strikes out at Tobias as the author of the soap opera her life has become. She loves him as her father and for the good qualities he once had, and she resents him for what he has become and for what, therefore, she feels he has passed on to her. Faced with an enigmatic daughter whose life is a constant indictment of his own, Tobias can only mumble, "If I thought I might . . . break through to her, and say, 'Julia. . . ; but then what would I say? 'Julia . . .' Then, nothing." (42)

Tobias bears no causal responsibility for what Harry and Edna have become, but their lives mirror his, and the reflection Tobias confronts appalls him. "Our lives," Edna says succinctly, "are . . . the same" (171). Tobias and Harry have been friends for forty years, belonged to the same club, played bridge and golf together, committed adultery separately in the same summer with the same woman (Claire), gradually submitted to impotence at the hands of their wives concurrently and have watched, spectators, as their lives dwindled before their eyes. Harry sums it up: "Edna and I . . . there's . . . so much . . . over the dam, so many disappointments, evasions, I guess, lies maybe . . . so much we remember we wanted, once . . . so little we've settled for . . ." (163). Harry speaks for both of them here, leading up to his admission that if Tobias and Agnes had come to live with him and Edna, reversing the present situation, he would not take them in. He would not want them and "they wouldn't have the right" (164) to so impose on him in the name of friendship. The superficiality revealed by this admission brings Tobias to his feet in a roar of protest, for Harry has given voice to Tobias's own secret selfishness, and he discovers, with fear and trembling, that the selfishness which produces a hollow friendship implies by extension empty family relationships and finally the void of existential nothingness. At the brink of this abyss, Tobias delivers his anguished and belated apologia, which serves as the climax of the play.

The controlling strategy that sets up this dramatic moment places Tobias at the center of a circle formed by his family and friends, each one appealing to him for something which he finds himself inadequate to provide. Julia wants her womb-like room back, her shelter from maturity, and appeals to Tobias, therefore, to eject Harry and Edna. Agnes desires to maintain the quasi-stability she has managed to establish in her household over the years; therefore, she appeals to Tobias to discipline Claire, to restore Julia to Douglas, and to send Harry and Edna home. Claire appeals to Tobias for a rekindling of the love they once shared, which would require him to divorce Agnes, but should he fall short of that — and her hopes are dim — Claire simply desires continued sanctuary from a world in which she has been crazily buffeted about. Harry and Edna also appeal to Tobias for sanctuary, or, as Claire puts it, "Succor. Comfort" (99), for they are afraid and without inner resources to combat their fear. "The helpless are the cruelest lot of all," says Agnes, "they shift their burdens so" (117). Here all burdens fall on Tobias, who is himself helpless to deal with them, and that helplessness becomes an increasing source of frustration to him as the play progresses.

Since every appeal can be granted only at the expense of some other appeal, and since Tobias genuinely desires not to hurt anyone or to be unfair, he practices his characteristic habit of circumspection. His house is full, a crisis is building, he is unable to avert it, but he thinks he at least can defer it, hoping that somehow everything will resolve itself miraculously. For all of Act 1 and much of Act 2, then, Tobias tries to maintain equability in the house. Between Agnes and Claire, he is a mediator and conciliator, urging Agnes to "Be kind, please?" (20) and telling Claire, "Look, now, I think we can do without any of this sort of. . ." (23). Trying to console Claire, he reasons as weak counselor, "Change . . . sometimes . . . no matter what . . ." (35), but Claire only mocks his inadequacy.

He is inadequate, but his motives are decent and honorable. Agnes even perceives a religious impulse animating Tobias (Julia in her childhood had seen him as a "saint"). Agnes describes one of his options for him: "Or get rid of me! That would be easier: rid yourself of the harridan. Then you can run your mission and take out sainthood papers" (147). Agnes may have drawn her image from Tobias's autumnal celibacy as much as from his purity of intention, but her acrimonious tone does not negate the power of her description. Furthermore, Tobias has himself revealed this beatific side of his nature in his guilt over the cat.[7] When Agnes assures him, patronizingly, that he had the cat killed because there was really nothing else to do, Tobias responds as a religious penitent: "I might have tried longer. I might have gone on, as long as cats live, the same way. I might have worn a hair shirt, locked myself in the house with her, done penance. For *something*. For *what*. God knows" (46). Desiring to do good, Tobias did evil. His failure with the cat prefigures his attempt at rectification later with Harry and Edna, where love is again the issue and where, again, Tobias finds himself lacking.[8] Meanwhile, Tobias serves as best he can. As host, he serves drinks around and around; he serves as mediator, compromiser, peacemaker, and comforter, substituting small acts of hospitality for the large act of substantive commitment that he discovers himself ultimately incapable of making. In the religious coloration suggested here, his plight echoes the classical Pauline dilemma: "For the good that I would I do not: but the evil which I would not do, that I do" (Rom. 7:19).

What Claire called the "family circle" in crisis (154) has expanded to include family friends, and all of them are circling around Tobias in a ring of desires that forms the play's basic structural pattern. The issue is love, and all look to Tobias as the hub on which their future involvements turn. Tobias repeats a line from Agnes that serves as a refrain to their collective searches: "If we do not love someone . . . never have loved someone. . ." (46). It is a refrain that comes to full crescendo in his aria with Harry, but Claire points up the circular nature it takes in their relationships: "You love Agnes and Agnes loves Julia and Julia loves me and I love you. We all love each other; yes we do" (47). The love goes around but it is unreciprocated, and it goes, as Claire explains, only to "the depths of our self-pity and our greed" (47). Tobias cannot accept only those two negative motives and offers as a mitigating option, which Claire accepts, "error." A mistake at least mitigates malice, and Tobias needs to cling to that mitigation.

Circular love has its counterpart in circular space in the house. Tobias underlines the shifting of locations when he explains his confusion to Agnes: "I almost went into *my* room . . . by habit . . . by mistake, rather, but then I realized that your room is my room because my room is Julia's because Julia's room is. . ." (131). With only mild irony, Agnes suggests that having his women surrounding him should be a comfort: "But at least you have your women with you—crowded 'round, firm arm, support" (141). (The passage is parodied by Claire's description, cited above, of the "family circle" with "Poor Tobe" at the center of his women.) But Tobias feels that the family "round" him has him encircled, trapped, victimized: "you'll all sit down and watch me carefully; smoke your pipes and stir the cauldron; watch" (141). Playing the witches to his Macbeth, the three women circle Tobias watchfully, casting spells to determine his fate.

The circularity in the play is carried out further by a series of role reversals, one character becoming another and then returning to his original role. Agnes begins these alternations when she tells Julia that "one of the thirty million psychiatrists practicing in this land of ours . . . opines that the sexes are reversing" (65), a report that goes far toward characterizing the marriages of both Agnes and Edna. Agnes then demonstrates the validity of the opinion by becoming Tobias, assuming a "male prerogative," and telling Julia as Tobias enters, "Your mother has arrived. Talk to *him!*" (67). Claire's semi-serious desire for a topless bathing suit (78) is another demonstration of the reversal of the sexes. In part at least, Claire seeks in a man's style suit (and in her earlier sexual adventuring) the freedom of the male, though in her wry detachment all of Claire's desires have become semi-serious. Occupying Julia's room, Harry and Edna become a composite Julia, the frightened child. They need, as Claire explains to Julia, "a special room with a night light or the door ajar so [they] can look down the hall from the bed and see that Mommy's door is open" (99). As they settle in, however, Harry and Edna also become Tobias and Agnes. When Harry takes over at the bar, Tobias feels displaced ("What can *you* make *me?*" [118]), and Julia is driven to the hysterical defense of her own and her father's prerogatives. Edna responds to Julia's outburst by assuming Agnes's role, punishing the daughter and, in the rhythms of Agnes's speech, admonishing Julia in the name of order: "You return to your nest from your latest disaster, dispossessed and suddenly dispossessing; screaming the house down, clawing at order. . ." (121). Seeing themselves enacted by their friends, Tobias and Agnes slip quietly into the background for the remainder of Act 1, as Harry and Edna have done for most of the play. Claire identifies herself as the resident recalcitrant, a Julia figure, in an early exchange with the newly arrived Julia: "Have you come to take my place?" (100). Later, Claire hints that Julia is "maybe ready to pull a Claire" (154). At the end, after some "sibling" rivalry over serving coffee and spilling orange juice — jockeying for position — the interchange is accomplished: "Your daughter," Agnes comments to Tobias, "has taken to drinking in the morning, I hope you'll notice" (173); Claire has done so for years. Even lines come around again: Agnes declares, "If we change for the worse with drink, we are an alcoholic." "And who is to say!" Claire responds. "I!" says Agnes (38). The identical exchange takes place later (73) between Julia and Tobias over the issue of Teddy's possible homosexuality. And Claire coaches Tobias in her role, making him repeat verbatim her humiliating admission: "My name is . . . My name is Claire, and I am an alcoholic" (34). As they move in and out of one another's roles, the characters not only reinforce the circularity of the play but accentuate their essential homogeneity as well, and all of them continue to look to Tobias to resolve their difficulties through any of his several functions: Husband, Father, Lover, Best Friend, Head of the House.

By Act 3 the pressure on Tobias has reached the breaking point. Harry and Edna have come to test the cliché that Claire introduces in Act 1 by way of exposition: "Would you give friend Harry the shirt off your back, as they say?" she queries. "I *suppose* I would," Tobias answers, "He *is* my best friend" (30). As the characters have revolved around Tobias they have trailed a parade of painful memories: Teddy's death, Tobias's sexual qualms, his fainthearted infidelity, his progressive impotence with wife and former mistress, his ineptitude with Julia, whom he has seen hysterical twice in settings that point up his own weaknesses: the bedroom, where he no longer serves, and the bar, where he serves instead. As Act 2 draws to a close, Harry has replaced him at the bar, Edna has become Agnes, Julia has withdrawn in tears with Agnes, and Tobias is left to decline Claire's implied invitation to join her in bed, the symbolic phallic pistol hanging unused by his side—the picture of a man unmanned. He also declines to make love to Agnes during the night (as Harry declines with Edna) and is thus unmanned further by her appearance at the beginning of Act 3 as the soft, sensual Agnes of old, whose sexual willingness is an affront to him in his inability to be both husband and lover. Though he claims to have achieved a "Godlike" detachment in his nocturnal guardianship of the house, the women are not impressed with his "vigil" and quickly reduce him to flunky, calling him "Pop" (147, 148), ordering him to clear away the dishes, and badgering him as he attempts, Polonius fashion, to be profound about their plight. Like picadors, they let his blood, weaken, and anger him. Agnes pushes hardest of all. Though she has blamed Tobias totally for the direction their lives have taken and claims she is leaving the decision to him now, she stacks the deck against Harry and Edna to influence Tobias to execute her will: "It is not Edna and Harry who have come to us—our friends—it is a disease" (156). Agnes reasons here as a sophist, but Tobias does not buy her tricky formulation. With the hint of a backbone stiffening, Tobias refuses to separate abstraction (disease) from embodying concretion (friends): "Oh, for God's sake, Agnes! It is our friends! What am I supposed to do? Say: 'Look, you can't stay here, you two, you've got trouble. You're friends, and all, but you come in here *clean*.' Well, I can't do that" (156).

Tobias's resistance and anger intensify when Harry admits to Tobias that if the situation were reversed, he would not want Agnes and Tobias in his house. In that moment of revelation Tobias sees himself in Harry's eyes and is moved to revulsion and to a final manly but ultimately feeble attempt to rise to the occasion, to salvage something from his misspent years. His aria is heavy with *sturm und drang* but also poignant with honesty and sad with aspiration gone astray. His concluding words came trembling from a torn self: "I DON'T WANT YOU HERE! I DON'T LOVE YOU! BUT BY GOD . . . YOU STAY!" (167). The emotional turmoil evident in Tobias here has sprung from each of his encounters with the specters of failure and loss in the lives of the other characters. In urging their own needs, they have pushed him to this moment of painful anagnorisis in which he approaches the specter of his own emptiness. It leaps out at him from Harry's confession. Tobias's long, impassioned speech grows out of his full awareness that if the friendship has been empty, then all of his relationships have been empty: "if that's all Harry and Edna mean to us, then . . . then what about *us*? . . . When we touch, when we promise, and say . . . yes, or please . . . with *ourselves* . . . have we meant yes, but only if . . . if there's any condition, Agnes! Then it's all been empty" (156).

Despite Harry's acknowledgment in this climatic scene that it *has* all been empty, Tobias tries through a desperate act of will to make it otherwise. He flails his principles to attention, tries to resurrect his will to measure up to his principles, arouses his old inadequacy instead, confronts it in horror, and then bows before it, standing mute until his regressive apology at the end. This scene is the agon of Tobias. He vacillates painfully between his desire for commitment to love and his fear of taking action to achieve it. He has implored Harry to stay to affirm the validity of the principle of love and all its ramifications, but it is, as he knows, lip service only: Harry has already admitted that they are leaving, and Tobias has acknowledged that he does not feel the love the friendship should have grown into — even sadder, that he cannot feel it. In what amounts to a culmination of roads not taken, Tobias rises to defend himself and his own and discovers that there is nothing to defend, and, what is worse, nothing can be done. As he has admitted earlier to Julia, "It's . . . it's too late, or something" (78).

Regaining control, Agnes ends the play and brings it full circle with her second "What I find most astonishing" speech. Both speeches are characterized by similar rhythms, convoluted syntax,[9] and elaborate digressions, and both contain significant parallel circle images. In the initial speech Agnes describes her hypothetical insanity as "sending the balloon adrift" (13) and thus becoming placidly "uninvolved" in the world. Uninvolvement has emerged as a central theme in the play, and the balloon image appropriately captures the shape and character of the "family circle": a globular membrane, highly vulnerable, encompassing nothing. It is the dominant image in the play. In her final speech Agnes invokes the sun, the spherical symbol of the circularity of days, of seasons, of years, as the counterforce to the nightmares of darkness and as the bringer of order. "Come now," Agnes announces, "we can begin the day" (175). The day dawns ironically. Their "order" is a sham, and the sun rises as it does for the final curtain in Ibsen's *Ghosts* — on a blighted family, whose doom here is to continue the vacuous cycle of noncommitment that has diminished them all but has been most terrifying in the lost life of Tobias.

A Delicate Balance begins as an examination of the claims of family versus the claims of friends. Is the blood of family thicker than the bonds of friendship? That initial question leads to others in a spiraling exploration of the quest for love and the various forms of insularity available to disguise the absence of love in contemporary society: wealth, clubs, alcohol, casual sex, shallow friendships, closed families. In a Dantesque dance with the other lost souls in the play, Tobias moves through each of these circles of insularity—and the fears they mask—to the center of the void that engulfs him in the final scene, where Edna provides thematic commentary on his plight and on their collective isolation: "It's sad to know you've gone through it all, or most of it, without . . . that the one body you've wrapped your arms around . . . the only skin you've ever known . . . is your own—and that it's dry . . . and not warm" (169). Through a circular strategy involving plot, space, role-exchanges, and imagery—with Tobias at the center—A Delicate Balance catalogues the price of false values, evasion, and noncommitment; the power of the play grows out of its progression from thematic abstraction to intense presentational immediacy: The intangible "Nothing" or "Terror" that compels Harry and Edna to leave their home becomes the painfully real "Emptiness" or existential "Nothingness" concretely embodied by Tobias and the others as they stand loveless at the end.[10] That they maintain their uneasy balance on the crumbling edge of an abyss comes as news only to Tobias, who learns, sadly and irremediably, that in his own household and in his own character, nothingness has a local habitation and a name.

Notes

1. Robert Brustein, *The Third Theater* (New York, 1969), p. 98. My own reading of *A Delicate Balance* was made possible by funds from the University of Missouri Research Council, whose support I gratefully acknowledge.

2. John Simon, "Theatre Chronicle," *Hudson Review*, 19 (Winter 1966–67), 627, 629.

3. Ronald Hayman, *Edward Albee* (New York, 1973), p. 114.

4. E. G. Bierhaus, Jr. is one of the very few critics who also places Tobias at the center of the play, but he concludes in a quantum leap that the play is a political allegory ("Strangers in a Room: *A Delicate Balance* Revisited," *Modern Drama* 17 [June 1974], 206).

5. Edward Albee, *A Delicate Balance* (New York, 1967), p. 90. Page numbers, referring to this edition, are hereafter placed within parentheses in the text.

6. Allusion also helps to characterize Julia (and the characters who thus allude to her). Claire calls her "Miss Julie" (82), suggesting Strindberg's confused heroine of that name, a victim, among other things, of a domineering "mannish" mother and a permissive father. Agnes twice (16, 43) refers to Lear's "How sharper than a serpent's tooth it is / To have a thankless child," but both times she directs the significance to Claire. The deliberate substitution of sister for child calls attention to itself as a kind of transference, allowing Agnes, without parental guilt, to punish Claire for Julia's shortcomings: her ingratitude, childlessness, and marital failure.

7. For a discussion of other biblical reverberations in the play, see Ruby Cohn, *Edward Albee* (Minneapolis, 1969), pp. 42–43.

8. The story of Tobias and the cat has received several critical readings. C. W. E. Bigsby interprets the story as marking Tobias's recognition "that it is precisely his failure to persevere in love merely because it is not returned which is the source of his guilt" (*Albee* [Edinburgh, 1969], p. 103). According to Richard Amacher, "The elaboration of this story . . . which grows out of the previous talk about friendship and love, serves to symbolize Tobias's feeling about his marriage with Agnes" (*Edward Albee* [New York, 1969], p. 156).

Michael E. Rutenberg, however, sees the relation between Julia and Tobias as the focus of the story: "What Albee wanted, in having Tobias relate the tale, was to have the audience realize Tobias' sense of failure as a father. The thought is so unbearable that he is unable to confess it directly. The narrative implies that, like the cat, Julia once loved and related to her father and that despite his attempt to provide a home for his daughter, she inexplicably withdrew from him until they now no longer communicate" (*Edward Albee: Playwright in Protest* [New York, 1969], p. 150). Other versions abound. Almost everyone notes that Tobias's story of the cat parallels Jerry's story of the dog in "Zoo Story."

9. The language of the play has been the target for much adverse criticism. Ronald Hayman asserted "that Albee has not solved the basic problem of theatrical language" (*Edward Albee* [New York, 1973], pp. 98–115). Robert Brustein considered the language "as far from modern speech as the whistles of a dolphin" ("Albee Decorates an Old House," *The New Republic*, 155 [8 October 1966], 35). Albert Bermel complained of affected dependent clauses and subjunctive moods, "pseudo-Jamesian daintiness with tenses" and concluded: "For all the finicky constructions he draws out of his characters' mouths, for all his archaisms and mock-Anglicisms, his lines are rarely clinched; they appear to be merely unedited" ("Mud in the Plumbing," *The New Leader*, 49 [10 October 1966], 28). Granting the persuasiveness of these arguments, one must also observe that the stylized language seems in final effect appropriate to the urbane pretensions of the characters and is thus one more dimension of their pathetic facades.

10. In what seems to me a serious misreading, Anne Paolucci takes an opposite position: "To top it all, he [Albee] drags in as catalyst—to force the action to a climax— something called the "Terror," which he is inconsiderate enough to leave an uncompromising blank. The mystery—one might be tempted to conclude—is not that grown people like Harry and Edna could be frightened by an empty word, but that a mature and experienced dramatist like Albee should have been satisfied with such a rotten gimmick" (*From Tension to Tonic: The Plays of Edward Albee* [Carbondale, Illinois, 1972], p. 106). My point has been that the "empty word," the abstraction *Terror* or *Nothing*, is defined and concretely presented by the unfolding action of the play, a dramatic progression that serves as the chief source of the play's dramatic impact.

Albee's *Seascape*: Humanity at the Second Threshold
Thomas P. Adler*

In reviewing Edward Albee's *Seascape*—winner of the 1975 Pulitzer Prize for Drama—Clive Barnes concurred with the playwright's own statement that this work should be regarded as "a companion piece" to the play that immediately preceded it, *All Over* (1971), adding the proviso, "but this is an optimistic play, a rose play rather than a black play, as Jean Anouilh would have said."[1] Placing the final curtain lines of the two side-by-side allows one to see readily the basis for the distinction Barnes was making. *All Over*, Albee's much underrated drama about death and egocentrism, about the refusal to commit oneself unselfishly to those one *says* one loves, ends, appropriately enough, with the words "All over";[2]

*From *Renascence* 31 (1979):107–14. Reprinted by permission of the journal.

Seascape, on the other hand, concludes with a challenge: "Begin."[3] Yet the note of pessimism that pervades *All Over* did not signal an abrupt shift in Albee's perspective, for ever since *Who's Afraid of Virginia Woolf?* (1962) — still his greatest critical and popular success — Albee's tone has progressively darkened as he has explored "how much false illusion" man must surround himself with "to get through life."[4] And so one needs to go back farther than *All Over*, specifically to Albee's other Pulitzer Prize-winning drama, *A Delicate Balance* (1966), to find the true "companion piece" to *Seascape*. Indeed, the most fruitful way to approach *Seascape* is to examine it as a reverse image of the earlier play.

Whereas the central couple in *All Over* are in their seventies, Agnes and Tobias in *A Delicate Balance* are, like Nancy and Charlie in *Seascape*, in their fifties. Furthermore, the concluding line of *Delicate Balance*, Agnes's ironic "Come now; we can begin the day,"[5] provides a more subtle and telling juxtaposition with *Seascape*'s "Begin." Since both these dramas about people in their mid-middle-age concern themselves with the effects of time on human choice and the possibility for change, it seems that Albee (himself now middle-aged) is in his latest full-length drama intentionally going back and giving his characters a second chance to not make such a muddle of their lives, as if to say things need not be so bleak. Though separated by nearly a decade in production, *Delicate Balance* and *Seascape* thus form an Albee diptych, in much the same way that *Ah, Wilderness!* and *Long Day's Journey Into Night* do for O'Neill.

Almost the entire first act of *Seascape* is a "two-character play," taken up with Nancy's and Charlie's diametrically opposed viewpoints on where they go from here — a conflict so basic and yet so shrouded by an aura of ordinariness as to seem like no conflict at all, which several critics claim is the case. But it is typical of Albee's later dramas that the outward action has become more sparse while the language has become increasingly more poetic rather than naturalistic and colloquial. Yet here the battle lines between the urge to ever fuller life and the opposing urge to death are drawn early and in no uncertain terms. As Charlie languishes on the seashore after a picnic lunch, he revels in the prospect of gradually and painlessly easing out of the picture by withdrawing from all purposive activity: "I don't want to do . . . anything . . . I'm happy . . . doing . . . nothing" (9). Faced with Charlie's desire to spend his waning years calmly wasting away, Nancy chides him, "all *you* want to do is become a vegetable. . . . a lump" (42). Lying just beyond the sand dunes in the stage set is the sea, archetype at one and the same time of both life and death; once symbolic of Charlie's life-wish, it now symbolizes his willed movement towards inertia and death. He has confessed to Nancy that as "a little boy" he "wanted to live in the sea," and recounts with great nostalgia that in his more adventuresome adolescence he

> would go into the water, take two stones, as large as [he] could manage, swim out a bit, tread, look up one final time at the sky . . . relax . . .

begin to go down. Oh, twenty feet, fifteen. . . . You can stay down
there so long! . . . one stops being an intruder, finally—just one more
object come to the bottom, or living thing, part of the undulation and
the silence. It was very good. (18)

Yet if this "game" once served as a confirmation of life, implicit in it
all along was the pull towards death: We rise from the sea at birth only to
return to it at life's end. Like the persona in Robert Lowell's "For the
Union Dead," Charlie now "sigh[s] still / for the dark downward and
vegetating kingdom / of the fish and reptile,"[6] a vision of a place where life
goes on without burden and responsibility. A place where one can retreat
into a pre-moral condition, Charlie thinks, free from the terror that is an
inescapable part of life, which Albee here symbolizes by a recurrent sound
effect: four times "a jet plane is heard from stage right to stage left—
growing, becoming deafeningly loud, diminishing" (3, 14, 53, 130).
Feeling existential man's *angst*, terrified by "deep space? Mortality?
Nancy . . . not . . . being with me?" and the possibility that even life
itself might be just "an illusion," Charlie yearns for "Death [as a] release"
since he has "lived all right" (85, 129). So the sea becomes for him a
thanatopsis.

If Tobias in *Delicate Balance* has as his motto, "We do what we can"
(19)—attesting to his refusal to go that extra distance, if necessary, to love
instead of just being loved—Charlie in *Seascape* has adopted as his
watchword "We'll see," which is essentially another way of saying that
something is "then put off until it's forgotten" (29–30). Such delaying
tactics in answering the call to action harbor within them, however, the
potential for finally stultifying the very ability to act. As Agnes in *Delicate
Balance* wisely perceives: "Time happens, I suppose. To people. Everything becomes . . . too late, finally. You know it's going on . . . up on the
hill; . . . but you wait; and time happens. When you *do* go, sword,
shield . . . finally . . . there's nothing there . . . save rust; bones; and the
wind" (169). Life is a matter of diminishing possibilities; the "road not
taken" can never be traversed. Every choice one makes limits all of one's
future choices, for each time one chooses A over B, one's options at the
next moment of choice are automatically halved: If one chooses A, the
possibilities that would have opened up if he had chosen B instead are lost
forever, and vice versa. Eventually, with the passage of time, the pattern
has been so firmly fixed that man becomes locked in it, and it is then "too
late" to break from it.

Albee shares with O'Neill this notion of man's possible choices
becoming fewer and fewer with the passage of time and as finally
determining his fate. In one of the central passages in *Long Day's Journey*,
Mary Tyrone's words presage Agnes's: "None of us can help the things time
has done to us. They're done before you realize it, and once they're done
they make you do other things until at last everything comes between you
and what you'd like to be, and you've lost your true self forever."[7] In

Virginia Woolf?, George poses much the same question about time's effect on human choice in an evolutionary metaphor that is a particularly apt gloss for *Seascape* as well: "man can put up with just so much without he descends a rung or two on the old evolutionary ladder. . . . and it's a funny ladder . . . you can't reverse yourself . . . start back up once you're descending."[8] It is at this decisive point—poised between going onward into the unknown or succumbing to the urge to descend (metaphorically) back down into the sea—that Charlie finds himself.

Nancy insists that they not spend what time they have left, however long or short it might be, in a retreat from life; she refuses to vegetate in a period of inactivity that would be like condemning themselves to a "purgatory *before* purgatory," demanding instead, "We will do *something*" (10–11). She believes that man must create his own happiness, must make a Kierkegaardian leap of faith and find some positive value in life. The gift of life is precious in and of itself and, in fact, is all that any of us have a right to ask for. Simply by having lived as long as they have, they "have earned a life" and the time to "*try* something new" (43–44). Whereas Charlie, afraid of change, desires stasis, Nancy accepts flux as a part of life, as, indeed, the necessary precondition for progress and growth. Life, according to her, should never be in the "past" tense. Her motto, were she to formulate one, would be something like: Experience as many new things as possible, in one's fantasies if not in reality. Such a philosophy has helped her weather and turn to a positive advantage the rough times of loneliness within her marriage, for when Charlie lost all interest in sex during his "seven-month decline," she thought of something she had never imagined before, not even in her dreams, and that, without his "inertia" and inattention, might have been lost to her forever: "A child at thirty, I suppose. Without that time I would have gone through my entire life and never thought of another man, another pair of arms, harsh cheek, hard buttocks, pleasure, never at all" (24–25).

Nancy has hardly completed her admonition to Charlie that they "do something" when the opportunity to respond to "something new" startlingly present itself with the appearance of "two great green lizards" (120). Without pursuing the point any further, in his review of the original production Howard Kissel detects in *Seascape* a continuation of the recurrent pattern in Albee's dramas of a person or persons arriving at the home—or territory—of someone else, with one or other of the parties then subjecting the other to a potentially salvific test, "prodding the others into a traumatizing outburst of emotion and violence."[9] In *The Zoo Story* (1959), for instance, Jerry arrives in Central Park and accosts Peter on his comfortable bench; in *Virginia Woolf?* Nick and Honey come for an early morning round of "fun and games" at the home of George and Martha; in *Tiny Alice* (1964), Brother Julian arrives for his "dark night of the soul" at the Gothic residence of Miss Alice; in *Delicate Balance*, Harry and Edna come to Agnes's and Tobias's demanding to be given shelter from the terror; and now in *Seascape*, Leslie Lizard and his wife Sarah arrive on the beach to confront Charlie and Nancy about admission to the human race.

The parallel between *Seascape* and *Delicate Balance* is, however, the most emphatic, for in these two cases the couples who arrive are designed more as allegorical personages than as fully-dimensioned characters, which contributes to the distinctive parable-like quality of the two plays. Leslie and Sarah exist at some pre-human stage on the evolutionary scale, while Harry and Edna are, as the List of Players indicates, "very much like Agnes and Tobias" (9). They thus function as mirror images so that Agnes and Tobias can see themselves as they never have before. Brought face-to-face with the existential void ("We were frightened . . . and there was nothing" [55]) and now in need of "succor" and "comfort" (99), Harry and Edna bring "the plague" and "terror" (155) of self-knowledge into the home of Agnes and Tobias, who can see reflected in their hesitancy to assuage their best friends' needs the failure of their own existence.

In *Seascape*, Leslie and Sarah, instead of functioning as mirror images of what Charlie and Nancy now are, serve as recollections of what the older couple once were, for, as Charlie says, "there was a time when we *all* were down there" before one of our ancestors "came up into the air and decided to stay" (138, 145). Like Harry and Edna before them, Leslie and Sarah are afraid, but whereas the former couple was frightened by the prospect of the nothingness after death, the latter couple is terrified by "what [they] don't know" (85), by the challenge of a more highly developed — which is to say, more fully human — life on earth. If life in the sea was unterrifying because a known quantity, it was also restrictive and limiting; as Sarah points out, they outgrew what was down there, and "didn't feel [they] *belonged* there any more" (136). They experienced, as Nancy would put it, the dissatisfaction which can be redirected in either a positive or a negative way. In a very basic sense, every living creature must be "dissatisfied" with the way things are, or there could be neither movement nor progress in human history. The condition of stasis, of "delicate balance" in a comfortable routine that Tobias and Agnes nurture and cling to, can have as its result only death-in-life. So Leslie's and Sarah's predicament — faced as they are with the attractive temptation of "making do down there" (137), of taking comfort in passively settling in and thus settling for less than a full life — exactly parallels Charlie's.

Significantly, it is Charlie, himself afraid, who convinces Leslie and Sarah to remain up on earth rather than return to their familiar habitat. And in the moment of convincing them, he himself undergoes a regenerative epiphany, moving from his customary stance of "put off" and "make do" to beginning again. Walter Kerr confesses some mystification over exactly what occurs at the climactic point in *Seascape*, feeling that Albee somehow misses his chance to connect the fate of the humans with that of the lizards:

But there is at last an issue, a crisis, and it seems, as issue and crisis, very much related to Mr. Nelson's [Charlie's] earlier urge to surrender. Why is that now not picked up, toward one end or another? Since the very problem so much *concerns* Mr. Nelson, why does he not engage himself, as devil's advocate, as newly enlightened human being, as something? His very boyhood games seem to make him a lively participant in the struggle — to advance or not to advance — and we wait for connections, for a door to be opened that will disclose whatever futures humans and lizards choose. But with the key in his hand and a carefully built-up promise, Mr. Albee will not use it. . . . neither she [Nancy] nor the new arrivals have any [effect] on the man in the case — or on the relation between man and wife — and the encounter comes out lopsided, lopsided and rather bland.[10]

Yet the connection is there, and it is precisely the same kind of connection as in Albee's earlier plays. The pattern of saving-others-in-order-to-save-oneself that recurs here should be familiar to students of Albee's work: in *Zoo Story*, Jerry (at least in Rose Zimbardo's widely-known and influential interpretation)[11] sacrifices himself, Christ-like, so that Peter might be redeemed from his vegetable-like complacency; in *Virginia Woolf?*, George and Martha destroy the sustaining illusion of the child so that Nick and Honey can see the sterility of their own marriage — and, in the process, George and Martha achieve a firmer communion within a marriage now rebuilt on a stronger foundation;[12] in *Delicate Balance*, Harry and Edna offer Tobias and Agnes a chance to be "good samaritans" and thereby redeem their "empty" existence, but the chance for salvation is rejected.

At the climactic point in *Seascape*, Charlie, like George and Jerry before him, hurts Sarah (and Leslie) in order to help them. Like Jerry — and this may well be the key line for understanding what happens in Albee's dramas — Charlie realizes "that neither kindness nor cruelty by themselves, independent of each other, creates any effect beyond themselves," and that oftentimes "we neither love nor hurt because we do not try to reach each other."[13] Recognizing that what separates man from beast is precisely man's "aware[ness that] it's *alive*, [and] that it's going to die" (149), Charlie sees that to complete the transformation from beast to man that Leslie and Sarah embarked on with their sense of uneasiness in their old life in the sea, he must make them experience truly human emotions: playing on Sarah's fear of Leslie leaving her and "never coming back," he deliberately makes Sarah cry, which, in turn, makes Leslie so defensive and angry at Charlie that he hits and chokes him. Having tasted these dark human emotions of sorrow and wrath, Sarah and Leslie want more than ever to return to the pre-human security of the sea. The only thing that quenches their fear is Nancy's and Charlie's pleading with them not to retreat, and extending their hands in a human gesture of compassion and solidarity — a clear visual echo of the dramatic gesture which also ends

Virginia Woolf?. In helping Leslie and Sarah to cross the threshold from animal to man, to take the mythic journey from the womb into the world that, however traumatic, must sometime be taken, Charlie simultaneously leaves behind his earlier attempts to escape from life and asserts once again his will to act, to live. And if one views Charlie as not only an individual but also as a representative, middle-aged Everyman who has fallen prey to ennui and despair, then Leslie's "Begin" on which the curtain falls is an act of faith and hope uttered not just for himself and Sarah and for Charlie and Nancy, but for all humankind who, with the passage of time, must be periodically rescued from the temptation of being "half in love with easeful death" and inspired to continue its arduous journey despite the inherent dangers.

Reportedly, it was Thornton Wilder who first suggested to Albee that he take up playwriting, and *Seascape*, Albee's most optimistic drama so far, might be seen as his homage to Wilder, since it contains not only verbal echoes to Wilder's plays but is likewise imbued with his positive tone and philosophy.[14] In his review of *Seascape*, Brendan Gill succinctly capsulizes its theme—"Boldly and simply, it asserts that, at no matter what age and in no matter what time and place, acts of discovery remain to be undertaken"—and likens it to "some superb long poem."[15] Certainly, one does find in it the repetition of imagery and verbal motifs, particularly of the words "wondrous" and "adventurous" or some form thereof (7, 31, 46, 54, 91, 118), that one expects to find in poetry. Interestingly enough, Wilder designates one of these concepts as "the moral" of his delightful farce, *The Matchmaker*, with Barnaby saying in his curtain speech to the audience, "I think [the play's] about adventure. . . . we all hope that in your lives you have just the right amount of — adventure!"[16] Nancy displays a childlike enthusiasm for "every bit" (5) of the world and wants to be immersed in it. Leslie and Sarah share Nancy's capacity for awe; he punctuates his language with phrases like "My gracious" and "Wow" (93, 98) in response to even the ordinary facts of life usually taken for granted, revealing that he already possesses the insight that Emily in Wilder's *Our Town* can reach only in death: "Oh, earth, you're too wonderful for anybody to realize you. . . . Do any human beings ever realize life while they live it?—every, every minute?" (62). Nancy's reaction of "great awe" and "infinite wonder" (53–54) at first setting eyes on Leslie and Sarah reminds one of "stout Cortez" in Keats's poem; the empirical-minded and prosaic Charlie (he has, Nancy claims, "no interest in imagery" [17]) long ago "decided that wonders do not occur" (123) and so concludes that they must be dead — as he metaphorically is — in order to see such creatures. Finally, however, Charlie perceives that he cannot spend the rest of his life on the plain or in the valley; he must dare "the glaciers and the crags" (54). Most of all he learns, like the Antrobuses in Wilder's *The Skin of Our Teeth*, about man's capacity for achieving progress in the long run if he only has the courage and confidence to always begin anew, often in the face of what seem like insurmountable odds. As George Antrobus, representative of mankind, expresses it at the end of that play: "Oh, I've never forgotten for long at a time that living is a struggle. I know that every good and excellent thing in the world stands moment by moment on the razor-edge of danger and must be fought for — whether it's a field, or a home, or a country. All I ask is the chance to build new worlds and God has always given us that" (135–36). Nancy's words quoted earlier, about being given the time to "try something new," might be seen, therefore, as Albee's measured confirmation of the philosophy Wilder put forth through Antrobus.

Notes

1. "Albee's *Seascape* is a Major Event," *The New York Times*, 27 January 1975, p. 20.

2. *All Over* (New York: Atheneum, 1971), p. 104.

3. *Seascape* (New York: Atheneum, 1975), p. 158. Further references are to this edition and will be cited by page number within parentheses in the text.

4. Edward Albee, "Critics are Downgrading Audience Taste and Have Obfuscated Simple *Tiny Alice*," *The Dramatists Guild Quarterly*, 2, 1 (Spring 1965), 14.

5. *A Delicate Balance* (New York: Pocket Books, 1967), p. 175. Further references are to this edition and will be cited by page number within parentheses in the text.

6. *For the Union Dead* (New York: Farrar, Straus & Giroux, 1964), p. 70.

7. Eugene O'Neill, *Long Day's Journey Into Night* (New Haven: Yale University Press, 1956), p. 61.

8. Edward Albee, *Who's Afraid of Virginia Woolf?* (New York: Atheneum, 1962), p. 51.

9. "*Seascape*," *Women's Wear Daily*, 27 January 1975, reprinted in *New York Theatre Critics' Reviews*, XXXVI, 2, pp. 370–71.

10. "Albee's Unwritten Part; McNally's Missing Joke," *The New York Times*, 2 February 1975, Sect. 2, p. 5.

11. "Symbolism and Naturalism in Edward Albee's *The Zoo Story*," *Twentieth Century Literature*, VIII, 1 (April 1962), 10–17.

12. See my article, "Albee's *Who's Afraid of Virginia Woolf?*: A Long Night's Journey Into Day," *Educational Theatre Journal*, 25, 1 (March 1973), 66–70.

13. *The Zoo Story* (New York: Signet, 1961), pp. 35–36.

14. In a conversation with me (Morgantown, West Virginia, September 23, 1977), Mr. Albee confirmed my suspicions about the influence of Wilder's philosophy on *Seascape*.

15. "Among the Dunes," *The New Yorker*, 3 February 1975, p. 75.

16. Thornton Wilder, *Three Plays* (New York: Bantam Books, 1966), pp. 224–25.

A Monologue of Cruelty: Edward Albee's *The Man Who Had Three Arms*

Matthew C. Roudané*

The most conspicuous element in Edward Albee's *The Man Who Had Three Arms* is its blatant assault on the audience. Whereas in *The Zoo Story*, *Who's Afraid of Virginia Woolf?*, *A Delicate Balance*, and *Seascape* Albee created a certain objective distance between the actor and the audience, the playwright banishes the fourth wall altogether in *The Man Who Had Three Arms*. "Himself," the protagonist fixed behind the podium, lectures his invisible audience for two acts, presenting his own ethical conflicts directly to both an imagined and real audience. Himself launches a verbal attack, not on an unsuspecting Peter or a Nick and Honey or an anesthetized Tobias or a retiring Charlie, but on his audience. It's a Pirandellian audience, of course, for the audience is both the imaginary group of listeners attending the "Man on Man" lecture series and the actual theatergoer or reader. Except for the Man and the Woman, whose repartee with Himself is minimal, we the audience ineluctably become central participants in the drama.

The largely negative critical reception to the play may be understandable.[1] Between the play's antimimetic texture, its alleged autobiographical nature (which Albee denies), and Himself's adamantine monologue of cruelty, critics found little to praise. Further, within the play's two-act structure, as Beckett scholar Vivian Mercier would say, nothing happens, twice. But what does occur — Himself's hostile account of his sudden rise to the top of fortune's wheel and his pathetic descent to the bottom — invites us to explore Albee's purpose. I would like to suggest that we may gain insight into Albee's dramatic theory and technique by considering the play's relationship with its fictional and actual audience.

Albee's Pirandellianism permeates the play. The stage directions, for instance, signal the multiple roles the Man and the Woman will assume, allowing them to complement or disagree with Himself's narrative when decorous. At one point the Man and the Woman become, respectively, a physician and a nurse, aiding Himself's account of the medical world's reaction to his third appendage. Earlier, when Himself mocks the Catholic Church, the Man suddenly appears in clergy garb and accuses the speaker, "You are a freak of nature."[2] Also, like Pirandello before him, Albee embellishes scenes with a deliberate self-consciousness, as evident when, for example, the Man and the Woman call attention to the rhetorical gallantries — and artificiality — of their introductory exchange:

---

*This essay was written for this volume and is published by permission of the author.

> WOMAN: . . . Dear friends, we *have* been fortunate over the years, being witness, as we have, to those who have made our history and shaped our culture, men and women whose accomplishments have wreaked their order on our havoc.
>
> MAN: Oh! What a very nice phrase!
>
> WOMAN (*Genuinely pleased*): Thank you, *thank* you! (*To her notes again*) . . . their order on our havoc and identified our reality by creating it for us.
>
> MAN: Even better! (*Begins applauding*) My goodness. (12)

Albee's Pirandellian technique, one employed in *The Lady From Dubuque*, functions on two important levels. First, such a technique invites the audience to question its willing suspension of disbelief. By calling attention to the very nature of theatricality, Albee experiments with the illusion of dramatic mimesis, challenging traditional responses to the theater. *The Man Who Had Three Arms* testifies to Albee's willingness to examine, in C. W. E. Bigsby's words, "the nature of theatrical experiment . . ." and his refusal "to accept conventional notions of theatrical propriety."[3]

Second, like *Six Characters in Search of an Author*, *The Man Who Had Three Arms* forces the audience to break down its barrier between itself and the actors. In *The Man Who Had Three Arms* Albee minimizes the barrier radically, however, involving the audience directly as participants throughout the action. At one point Himself talks to the audience, with the stage directions and dialogue suggesting the intimacy between the actor and spectator:

> (*To someone in the front*): Do you remember what I said? Before we broke? Remember I said that if you came upon me sobbing in a corner, not to disturb? That it was a way I had and not to worry? Do you remember? (*Note: If the person says "yes," say: "You do!" If person says "no," say: "You don't!" If person fails to respond, wing it, choosing what you like*)   (59)

Albee does not direct Himself to start fighting with the actual audience, as Julian Beck had members of The Living Theatre do with his audience. Still, Albee creates an overly aggressive text, expanding the boundaries of theater as collective, communal spectacle. Albee discussed this point, observing the relatedness of the actors and audience within his theory of drama:

> In nine or ten of my plays, you'll notice, actors talk directly to the audience. In my mind, this is a way of involving the audience; of embarrassing, if need be, the audience into participation. It may have a reverse effect: some audiences don't like this; they get upset by it quite often; it may alienate them. But I am trying very hard to *involve* them. I don't like the audience as voyeur, the audience as passive spectator. I want the audience as participant. In that sense, I agree with Artaud:

that sometimes we should literally draw blood. I am very fond of doing that because voyeurism in the theater lets people off the hook. *The Man Who Had Three Arms* is a specific attempt to do this. It is an act of aggression. It's probably the most violent play I've written.[4]

The play's audience, for better or worse, stands as the recipient of the violence.

Himself puts into concrete voice Albee's Artaudian dramatic theory. By drawing "blood," Himself supports the use of cruelty as a means of purging oneself of demons, of effecting a sense of catharsis, two factors which seem germane to Artaud's theater of cruelty.[5] Moments into the play, Himself chides the audience, but the sarcasm quickly transforms to the opprobrious verbal assault:

> (*Looking across the front row*): Where is she? Where is she, I wonder; the lady, the girl, usually, who sits there in the front row, almost *always*, wherever, whenever I speak—not the *same* girl, woman, you under-stand, but of a certain type: plain, more than a little overweight, smock top, jeans, sandals, dirty toenails—sits there in the front row, and, as I lecture, *try* to lecture, try to fill you in, so to speak, make you understand, sits there and runs her tongue around her open mouth, like this, (*Demonstrates*) hand in her crotch, likely as not, bitten fingers, lascivious, obscene, does it over and over, all through my lecture, my expiation, my sad, sad tale, unnerves me, bores, finally wearies me with her longing. . . . (15)

Act Two begins with a tale that escalates Himself's attack on the audience. Claiming a female journalist hounded him during intermission, Himself physically assaulted her, although Albee presents the account ambiguously enough that we are never sure of its occurrence:

> "You're good," she said, "you're really good." There was a loathing to it, a condemnation that I dare be articulate, coherent. "You're really good." "So are you," I said. "You've got balls."
>
> The energy of the hatred here, the mutual rage and revulsion was such that, had we fucked, we would have shaken the earth with our cries and thumps and snarls and curses: a crashing around of Gods—chewed nipples, bleeding streaks along the back. Had we fucked . . . Oh, Jesus! what issue! *But* . . . but the only issue was the issue of me, the . . . dismemberment of me. "You've got balls!" I said. And I crashed my hand into her crotch like a goosing twelve-year-old. "Get your hands off me," she said. "Get your filthy hands off me." I withdrew my hand: it had hit rock. "If you'll excuse me," she said, ice, shoving past me. She *is* an impressive lady. (56–57)

In his monologue of cruelty, then, Himself not only chronicles the growth of his third arm and its enervating effect on his world, but implicates the audience throughout for contributing to his present condi-tion. To be sure, his sudden fame had its positive points: he hobnobbed with British royalty; earned $25,000 an hour for public appearances; visited the White House; starred in ticker-tape parades; graced the covers of *People, Newsweek,* and *Time;* in brief, Himself became "the most famous man in the world" (86–87). But the public, people like the omnipresent journalist he (may have) attacked, the fame, the wealth conspire, according to Himself, to undermine his sense of self-balance. Unable to deal with the decadence of celebrity-hood, Himself loses sight of objective reality: his marriage dissolves, his own agent hornswoggles him, and, after his mysterious arm disappears, the public discards him. That is why he stands as a last minute substitute speaker in this play, his last pathetic connection with a public he both needs and abhors.

On a thematic level, *The Man Who Had Three Arms* thus exposes the monstrous effects of stardom on the individual's spirit. The play addresses, for Thomas P. Adler, "contemporary America's almost ghoulish need for culture heroes. . . ."[6] Within this context, the public, the sycophants accentuate Himself's internal as well as external freakishness, canonizing him one moment, abandoning him the next, even though by his own admission he has *no* talent, has done nothing exemplary to achieve social accolades. As the third arm dissipates, so Himself's fame diminishes, reducing him to a pathetic figure consumed with self-pity. Like the unnamed hero in Pirandello's *When One Is Somebody,* Himself becomes a prisoner completely trapped within his (post)celebrity-hood. In Albee's own assessment, the play thematically charts "the specifically American thing called 'hype': the creation of celebrity. The play is about the creation of celebrity and the destruction of celebrity-hood, because his third arm starts going away . . . So *The Man Who Had Three Arms* is about that particular kind of hype and celebrity: undeserved, unearned, and how we need it and how we destroy the person once we created him."[7]

Albee explores the corrupting and transitory effect of "celebrity-hood" on the Great, the near-Great, and the pseudo-Great. On top of fortune's wheel one moment, relegated to the bottom the next moment, Himself experiences financial as well as spiritual bankruptcy. This is why near the close of the play he specifically reflects on the loss of his self (90–91). Himself's hostility towards the audience measures the intensity of such loss. His anger, his directly involving the audience in his world, is apparently his form of expiation. Disassociated from his self and the other, the hurlyburly of his life now producing a new form of freakishness, Himself closes the play with a loving plea to stay, a hateful cry to leave, a pitiful gesture to understand. Throwing over the podium, Himself thus begs:

> No one leaves until you apologize to me!! I want an apology for all the years!! For all the humiliation!! (*Sudden change of tone; abrupt realization of futility; a great weariness*) Nah! You don't owe me anything. Get out of here! Leave me alone! Leave me alone! (*Curtain Starts; Himself notices.*) (*Off*) No! Don't do that! Don't leave me alone!

(*Out*) Stay with me. Don't . . . leave me alone! Don't leave me! Don't
. . . leave me alone. (*Curtain completes itself*) (102–3)

The ambivalence of Himself's closing lines reflects Albee's larger
thematic concerns in the play. Himself does not wish to banish all people
and institutions who have exacerbated his freakishness. Rather, he insists,
without success, that those people and institutions not dismiss the private
individual beneath the public facade. Himself's aggressive assault of the
audience belies his inner need for sympathetic understanding of his
humanness. It's a plea to be recognized as an individual, one consigned to
an ordinary existence:

> (*Out; pleading alternating with hatred*) I'm no different from you; I'm
> just like everyone you know; you love *them*: you love *me*. Stop treating
> me like a freak! I am *not* a freak! I am *you!* I have always *been* you! I
> am you!!! Stop looking at me!! Like that!! (102)

Himself's social devoir seems so irreverent, his angry monody so relentless,
of course, that he can never gain the audience's sympathy.

Many of Albee's past heroes protest honestly, what the existentialists
would call authentically, against an absurd cosmos. Himself protests
against a commercialized universe that divests him of self-freedom,
understanding, and love. And Albee implicates the audience for its
support of a Madison Avenue mentality promoting Himself's entrapment.
As such, he represents the latest Albee hero who has the courage to face
life without absurd illusions. As Albee remarked, "The entire structure of
what happens to Himself is based totally on absurdity; and it is precisely
the absurdity that he's railing against."[8]

In theory and structure, in language and theme, *The Man Who Had
Three Arms* boldly attempts to extend the conventions of the contemporary theater. Perhaps Richard Schechner's following observations about
contemporary theater will prove helpful in coming to critical terms with
Albee's play:

> The poison of the commercial theatre has so soaked into our ways of
> thinking about theatre that even in experimental work a production is
> regarded as a success or a failure. . . . This is a stupid way of advancing
> theatrical thought: for why can't a work in the theatre be neither a
> success nor a failure but a step along the way, an event that yields some
> interesting data? In other words, though values of entertainment are
> truly important in the theatre, they are not the only values. And those of
> us devoted to experimentation in the theatre need to be particularly
> rigorous in separating out from each of our works what is useful,
> regardless of the overall "success" of the project.[9]

Albee exhibits an artistic courage to experiment, without regard to the
play's commercial impact. However, I would like to conclude, but cannot,
that the play succeeds in shocking the audience into self-awareness, in
producing the catharsis we experience at the closure of *The Zoo Story* or

Who's Afraid of Virginia Woolf?. *The Man Who Had Three Arms* never matches the multivalency of a Pirandello play, never achieves the cleansing effect of cruelty Artaud envisioned. This play may "yield some interesting data," but it remains to be seen if it stands as "useful" material for future experiments.[10]

Notes

1. The following are representative samplings of initial responses to Albee's play. Those reviewing the Chicago performance (October 1982) submitted mixed findings: Glenna Syse praised the play because "It looks at pity for self and for others, it conjures up Job and divine justice and it pushes us to examine our absorption with fame and what happens to the celebrated and the celebrating" (" 'Man Who Had Three Arms' Absorbing, Commanding," *Chicago Sun-Times*, 5 October 1982, 51–52); For Richard Christiansen, Albee's "attack is brutal, obscene, always intense, often eloquent" ("Albee's 'Arms' is an Eloquent Ordeal," *Chicago Tribune*, 6 October 1982, 7, 9); see also Christiansen, "Edward Albee: 20 Years After 'Virginia Woolf,' " *Chicago Tribune*, 26 September 1982, sec. 6, 5. Bury St. Edmund voiced an ambivalent assessment of the production: "Albee's too insightful to be bland, too eloquent to be dull, but with *The Man Who Had Three Arms* he's too desperate to be dramatic" ("The Man Who Had Three Arms," *Chicago Reader*, 15 October 1982, 43). Even Thomas P. Adler conceded, "Albee can still pen those wonderful arias for which he's always been noted, yet even for an Albee aficionado, this isn't much of a play, even in any non-traditional sense of the term" ("The Man Who Had Three Arms," *Theatre Journal* 35 [March 1983]:124). Those reviewing the New York production (April 1983), however, registered damning responses: Michael Feingold argued that Albee composed "a text so restrictive, so flat, so full of evasions and trivialities and circumlocution" that we experience merely a "prospectus" of a play ("Small Craft Warnings," *Village Voice*, 19 April 1983, 106). Similarly, Brendan Gill called the "dry, anguished text" of the drama "not so much a play as a literary exercise that happens to take place in the theater" ("Bellyacher," *New Yorker*, 8 April 1983, 130–31). And Jack Kroll concluded that what Albee's "written is not a play at all but a nasty and embarrassing display of bad manners" ("Edward Albee's Hymn of Self-Disgust," *Newsweek*, 18 April 1983, 54).

2. Edward Albee, *The Man Who Had Three Arms* (New York: Atheneum, 1987), 25. All further references are to this edition and will be cited parenthetically in the text.

3. C. W. E. Bigsby, "Introduction," *Edward Albee: A Collection of Critical Essays* (Englewood Cliffs, N. J.: Prentice-Hall, 1975), 8–9.

4. Matthew C. Roudané, "Albee on Albee," *RE: Artes Liberales* 10 (Spring 1984):1–2.

5. See Antonin Artaud, *The Theater and Its Double*, trans. Mary Caroline Richards (New York: Grove Press, 1958); for further discussions of Artaud's theories and the audience response which may prove useful in understanding Albee's play, see Peter L. Podol, "Contradictions and Dualities in Artaud and Artaudian Theater: *The Conquest of Mexico* and the Conquest of Peru," *Modern Drama* 26 (December 1983):518–27 and Una Chaudhuri, "The Spectator in Drama/Drama in the Spectator," *Modern Drama* 27 (September 1984):281–98.

6. Adler, "Man Who Had Three Arms," 124.

7. Roudané, "Albee on Albee," 2.

8. Personal Interview with Edward Albee, 12 February 1985.

9. Richard Schechner, "Genet's *The Balcony:* A 1981 Perspective on a 1979/80 Production," *Modern Drama* 25 (March 1982):82.

10. I would like to thank Edward Albee, who kindly provided galleys of *The Man Who Had Three Arms* so that I could write this essay.

ALBEE ON ALBEE

A Playwright Speaks: An Interview with Edward Albee
Matthew C. Roudané*

The interview took place near Miami, Florida, on 12 February 1985, where Albee vacationed after concluding a month-long stint teaching playwriting at Johns Hopkins University. Having interviewed Albee in Berkeley in 1980 and in his New York City home in 1983, I wasn't sure how he would respond to yet a third conversation. When one interviews Albee, one always has to be on guard: one moment he responds with an adamantine commitment to serious issues of the contemporary theater, but the next moment, I sometimes sense, he plays games, providing puckish responses to certain questions. I was soon relieved, however, for Albee appeared as enthusiastic and opinionated as in our earlier conversations. Moments after a brisk work out at the gym, Albee voiced his opinions, not only about his artistry, but about the function of the playwright and the contemporary theater.

Albee, like Arthur Miller, is a much-interviewed playwright. And although Lawrence's reminder — that we should never trust the artist but the tale — is important, scholars nonetheless may gain useful insight into a writer's vision by listening to his conversations. Albee's interviews allow scholars to trace parallel developments between his plays and dramatic theories. Albee's once scathing attacks on critics he considered myopic appear less frequently. Albee no longer "defends" his transition from Off-Broadway to the Great White Way; his more experimental pieces; his willingness to take aesthetic risks. This is not to imply, of course, that Albee's rage and anger have diminished. Albee's protests against various crimes of the heart appear as intense as the days when he was labeled the new Angry Young Playwright. But recent interviews reveal a more mature, thoughtful Albee. Now he simply tries to explain, precisely, his convictions.

During interviews, Albee persistently discusses his views on dramaturgy, theory, and the civic dimension of drama. More specifically, however, he talks about what, for him, stands as his most compelling

*This interview was conducted for this volume and is published by permission of the author.

subject: *consciousness*. Self-awareness, suggests Albee in both the plays and interviews, not only produces better social, economic, political, and aesthetic choices, but seems essential if the individual is to remain alive. In the following conversation, finally, Albee again gives definition to the play as equipment for living.

Q: Why is it so vital for you to break down the actor / audience barrier during the performance? And on what levels do you wish to engage your audience?

A: First of all, you have to discover what audience you're talking about. The ideal audience I'd like to reach is the audience that brings to the theater some of the same attention and work that I do when I write a play. The willingness to experience the play, if the play is successful, on its own terms, without predetermining the nature of the theatrical experience. Someone who's seeing a play should be seeing the first play he has ever seen. I am referring to a state of innocence in which our theater is most ideally approached; the key is for one to have no preconceptions, as if it's the first theatrical experience that person has ever had. If people approach the theater that way, viewing the spectacle becomes an experience of *wonder* for them rather than saying that, "oh, I can't relate to this" or "the play is 'difficult' and therefore I can't take it!" If one approaches the theater in a state of innocence, sober, without preconceptions, and willing to participate; if they are willing to have the status quo assaulted; if they're willing to have their consciousness raised, their values questioned — or reaffirmed; if they are willing to understand that the theater is a live and dangerous experience — and therefore a *life-giving force* — then perhaps they are approaching the theater in an ideal state and that's the audience I wish I were writing for.

However, that is not the way everybody approaches theater. It's not even the way I approach the theater all the time, although I wish I did. But we should all approach the theater in this state of innocence. But the one thing a playwright can't do is write for an "audience" at all successfully. If you're writing for a group of intellectuals, then you're leaving other people out, proving only how smart you are. If you're trying to reach a larger audience than your work would normally reach, you're probably telling half-truths rather than total Truth; you're probably oversimplifying that which by its very nature is incredibly complex! There are some plays I write that are difficult, some that are easy, some that will reach more people than others, even in that ideal audience. But the basic, the essential thing is to let the play happen on its own terms the way it wants to happen. And then assume there will be enough people who are willing to let it happen on its own terms. That's about all one can do.

Many people at the colleges I visit ask me over and over again, "Why do you ask such tough questions and why do your plays seem so difficult or depressing?" Or "Why don't you write happy plays?" About what, happy problems? But I keep reminding them that drama is an attempt to make things better. Drama is a mirror held up to them to show the way they do behave and how they don't behave that way any longer. If people are willing to be aided in the search for total consciousness by not only drama but all of the arts — music and painting and all the other arts give a unique sense of order — then art is life-giving. Art gives shape to life; it increases consciousness.

Q: Death pervades your theater. Why your preoccupation with death?

A: As opposed to the slaughter in Shakespeare, the tuberculosis and consumption in Chekhov, the death-in-life in Beckett? Is that what you mean? There are only a few significant things to write about: life and death. I am very interested in the cleansing consciousness of death; and the fact that people avoid thinking about death — and about *living*. I think we should always live with the consciousness of death. How else can we possibly participate in living life fully?

Q: What influence has Artaud had on your dramaturgy?

A: Undoubtedly he's had a lot of influence on me, especially since we live in a postexistentialist world as a result of World War II, Sartre, and Camus. We also live in a post-Artaudian world as a result of his theories and accomplishments. He has clearly influenced several generations of dramatists, all of whom influence me, and of course I'm influenced by him. I imagine he opened a few doors as well as a few chasms. All drama goes for blood in one way or another. Some drama, which contains itself behind the invisible fourth wall, does it by giving the audience the illusion that it is the spectator. This isn't always true: if the drama succeeds the audience is *bloodied*, but in a different way. And sometimes the act of aggression is direct or indirect, but it is always an act of aggression. And this is why I try very hard to involve the audience. As I've mentioned to you before, I want the audience to participate in the dramatic experience. In this sense, I agree with Artaud. Voyeurism in the theater lets people off the hook. Sometimes the playwright should draw blood.

Q: Such playwrights as Arthur Miller or David Mamet explore the myth of the American Dream, the myth embracing the work ethic as a means to material success and so on. Could you comment on this?

A: I'm quite in favor of hard work, something I do a lot of myself! There's nothing wrong with the notion of making your own way. What is wrong with the myth of the American Dream is the notion that this is all that there is to existence! The myth is merely a part of other things. Becoming wealthy is O.K. I suppose, but it is not a be all to end all. People who think that the acquisition of wealth or property or material things or power; that these are the things in life; the conspicuous consumption of material things is the answer; this creates a problem. The fact that we set arbitrary and artificial goals for ourselves is a problem, not the hard work ethic *per se*.

Consider *The Man Who Had Three Arms*. It concerns the way we have, especially with movie stars, rock stars, politicians, created artificial gods for ourselves. In this play I have very carefully created a monster, Himself, who rose to incredible fame without any ability of his own, besides the fact that he grew a third arm, which is hardly a talent, an accomplishment. It's merely something that happened. And he is taken up by the press, by the media, and is built into this false god. I was examining the way in which we worship that which is wrong; the way we worship that which is empty and artificial; and the way we devour and spit out.

So the myth of the American Dream, if you're an American writer, is not only your cultural background but your set of paints and brushes. The picture you create is indeed colored by your environment and what you experience, live through.

Q: As a playwright, do you see yourself as a social critic?

A: Directly or indirectly any playwright is a kind of demonic social critic. I am concerned with altering people's perceptions, altering the status quo. All serious art interests itself in this. The self, the society should be altered by a good play. All plays in their essence are indirectly political in that they make people question the values that move them to make various parochial, social, and political decisions. Our political decisions are really a result of how we view consciousness. Plays should be relentless; the playwright shouldn't let people off the hook. He should examine their lives and keep hammering away at the fact that some people are not fully participating in their lives and therefore they're not participating with great intelligence in politics, in social intercourse, in aesthetics. It's something that I dearly hope runs through all of my plays. You can find it specially in *The Death of Bessie Smith*, *The American Dream*, *Seascape*; it's certainly there in *The Man Who Had Three Arms*. You find it in its approach to death in *All Over* and *The Lady From Dubuque*. The politics in my plays is mostly indirect because politics is a result of how my characters function. It does not cause how they function; it is a product of how we think and how we respond. If a playwright examines the total consciousness and tries to make the individual aware of how he is not participating in living fully, then he is going to awaken the spirit, and political and social consciousness will be one of the results. Think of *The Zoo Story*.

Q: So you're speaking about the civic function of the theater, right?

A: Yes. All art is useful in this context; it's not decorative. All my plays try to readjust our vision, to reorder our values.

Q: In *Counting the Ways*, He talks about "loss"; and loss seems to be a dominant characteristic of your theater. Could you talk about the function of loss within this play or others?

A: The play concerns the loss of time, the loss of innocence, loss of opportunity, loss of freshness. Loss happens, time happens. This is also what Agnes says near the close of the third act of *A Delicate Balance*: "Time happens I suppose. To people. Everything becomes . . . too late, finally. You know it's going on . . . up the hill; you can see the dust, and hear the cries, and the steel . . . but you wait; and time happens. When you *do* go, sword, shield . . . finally . . . there's nothing there . . . save rust; bones; and the wind." And during the precious time of our lives, we suffer losses, injuries, some of which are self-inflicted, others of which come from outside. We're aware of these events happening to us. We gain and we lose simultaneously. Theoretically we gain wisdom just in time to lose everything. I guess that is one of the awful ironies of the human condition.

Q: In your earlier plays, the typical Albee family had a domineering mother, an emasculated father, and the critics made a great deal about the hostility between the sexes in an Albee production. What do you think?

A: Well, now this is true in *The American Dream*; this is only one play within the early canon. It doesn't happen in *Who's Afraid of Virginia Woolf?*, where George and Martha are equal combatants, are equal to each other. I don't examine marriage in *The Death of Bessie Smith* or *The Zoo Story*, but the kind of "family" relationship you're referring to does appear in *A Delicate Balance*: Tobias is a fully conscious man, he's simply made certain choices; he is not a weak or emasculated person. But as I think more about it, this happens, really, in one play, *The American Dream*. But people pretend it happens in all the others. You know, one of the things I get so tired of is that things happen in one play and critics extend these particular events into all of my plays, when they're not really there! It's a distortion. Look at it this way. I write about imbalances within many relationships. My goodness, if I came upon a totally balanced and content situation, where's the drama in that? What would I write about? All drama is about people not getting along with each other. All drama embraces imbalance, discontent. It has to be or there's no dramatic experience.

Q: When you were first struggling to become a playwright in the 1950s, did Thornton Wilder or W. H. Auden encourage or inspire you?

A: Well, I met both of them, but Auden told me I wasn't a very good poet and so did Wilder. Wilder suggested that I should write plays, but I didn't take his advice for eight years. But were they encouraging? How can you tell someone who thinks he's a poet that he should not write poetry but plays? (*Laughs*). Thornton was gentle about it. I wasn't so much inspired by them as I was copying them; I suppose that's a certain inspiration.

Q: Your vision seems to deal with certain profound crimes of the heart: the individual's inability to deal honestly, or what the existentialists would call authentically, with the self and the other. Is this accurate?

A: Yes, I suppose it is. After all, what else is there to deal with? The single journey through consciousness should be participated in as fully as possible by the individual, no matter how dangerous or cruel or terror-filled that experience may be. We only go through it once, unless the agnostics are proved wrong, and so we must do it fully conscious. One of the things that art does is to not let people sleep their way through their lives. If the universe makes no sense, well perhaps we, the individual can make sense of the cosmos. We must go on, we must not add to the chaos but deal honestly with the idea of order, whether it is arbitrary or not. As all of my plays suggest, so many people prefer to go through their lives semiconscious and they end up in a terrible panic because they've wasted so much. But being as self-aware, as awake, as open to various experience will produce a better society and a more intelligent self-government. This notion is even present in *The Man Who Had Three Arms*, which, by the way, I've always found very very funny. This play is a ludicrous, absurd play. If any play that I've written that is linked to the Theater of the Absurd, it may very well be *The Man Who Had Three Arms*. The entire structure of what happens to Himself is based totally on absurdity; and it is precisely the absurdity that he's railing against.

Q: Why do so many of your characters in, say, *Box and Quotations From Chairman Mao Tse-Tung, All Over, Counting the Ways*, and other plays have only generic, functional names?

A: In *Quotations From Chairman Mao Tse-Tung*, nobody can talk to each other, so they didn't have to address each other, communicate with anyone, and therefore they didn't need names, did they? I gave them the names that describe them. The Long-Winded Lady in *Mao Tse-Tung* didn't even say hello to the others. They didn't need names! My characters have names only when they need them. When they don't, why should they have them? These names aren't meant to suggest universal or symbolic things or that these particular characters stand as symbols; this is also why I don't give my characters last names.

Q: Looking back on twenty-five odd years of playwriting, which characters hold fond memories for you?

A: A lot of people ask me that and I have absolutely no way of dealing with it. Each experience, each creative process, each character is interesting while I'm completely involved in it, but then each experience also fades.

Q: What's the value of a playwright directing his or her own plays? I ask because you've directed a number of your own over the years.

A: When I write a play, I see it and hear it on a stage. I therefore have the closest vision of what I the author want the play to hear and sound like. Why not share that with an audience? No other director can come as close to my original intention; whether that's the best for the play or not doesn't matter. But I am interested in people seeing as precisely as possible what I meant, and so why not have the person who best knows the play direct it? It seems so simple, doesn't it?

Q: Could you discuss the role of communication within your theater?

A: So many of my characters deal with the refusal or the inability to communicate honestly. People are capable of a great deal more communication than they usually engage in. There's a problem in all this because communication is dangerous. It may open people up, which is terrifying to many. Again, this all ties in to the importance of raising one's consciousness. The function of a good play is to communicate. All art, unless it's useless, decorative, attempts to communicate. It's there in *The Zoo Story*: Peter's made too many safe choices far too early in his life and Jerry has to shock him into understanding the tragic sense of being alive. George and Martha realize the importance of communication all through *Who's Afraid of Virginia Woolf?* It's clearly there in *Seascape*.

Q: Do you consider yourself an eclectic playwright?

A: I think one should have as many arrows in one's artistic quiver as possible. If you make all these things your own, you're not eclectic, you're diverse. I rather think of myself as being a diverse, not an eclectic, playwright. If you're eclectic, you go around copying other people. I hope I have the ability to learn from what others have accomplished; I hope I've been influenced by my peers and my betters; but I hope I've absorbed sufficiently, so that while I am diverse, each experience is pure Albee.

Q: How do you answer the charge that you're a nihilistic, pessimistic writer?

A: If I were a pessimist I wouldn't bother to write. Writing itself, taking the trouble, communicating with your fellow human being is valuable, that's an act of optimism. There's a positive force within the struggle. Serious plays are unpleasant in one way or another, and my plays examine people who are not living their lives fully, dangerously, properly.

An Annotated Bibliography of Albee Interviews, with an Index to Names, Concepts, and Places
Lea Carol Owen*

During the last twenty-five years, Edward Albee has written, directed, and produced plays from the Broadway stage to college theaters. The 1962 premiere of *Who's Afraid of Virginia Woolf?* placed him firmly among America's most acclaimed playwrights. Though he has never again encountered such critical or commercial success, Albee continues to be a prolific writer and outspoken critic of the American stage. His frequent interviews with both scholars and journalists provide a remarkable commentary on Albee's career, elucidating not only his writings and development, but also his aesthetic theories and views on the theater world.

Although several of Albee's major interviews have been reprinted (see entries 11, 22, 25, 27, 45, and 70), they have not been collected in one volume. This bibliography has been prepared to identify major interviews by listing, annotating, and indexing them. Brief, topical newspaper interviews are included, as well as in-depth scholarly discussions. Although many articles include narration by the interviewer, these have been considered "interviews" when they contain significant quotations from Albee. Items are alphabetized within each year, and Albee's comments are indexed by entry number in an appendix. His comments on plays are generally indexed under the author's name.

ABBREVIATIONS

AD	*The American Dream*
AO	*All Over*
BOX	*Box-Mao-Box*
BSC	*The Ballad of the Sad Cafe*
CW	*Counting the Ways*
DB	*A Delicate Balance*
DBS	*The Death of Bessie Smith*
EG	*Everything in the Garden*
FAM	*FAM and YAM*
L	*Listening*
LFD	*The Lady from Dubuque*
LOL	*Lolita*
M	*Malcolm*

---

*This bibliography was compiled for this volume and is published by permission of the author.

MWHTA   *The Man Who Had Three Arms*
QUO   *Quotations from Chairman Mao*
SBX   *The Sandbox*
SEA   *Seascape*
SUB   *The Substitute Speaker*
TA   *Tiny Alice*
VW   *Who's Afraid of Virginia Woolf?*
ZS   *The Zoo Story*

BIBLIOGRAPHY

1960

1. Gelb, Arthur. "Dramatists Deny Nihilistic Trends." *New York Times*, 15 February 1960, 23. Albee and Jack Gelber discuss their current Off-Broadway works, ZS and *The Connection*. Albee denies the interviewer's charges: " 'The Zoo Story' is neither nihilistic nor pessimistic. . . . My hero is not a beatnik and he is not insane. He is over-sane." Both playwrights lament Broadway's state of malaise, as Gelb provides their biographical synopses and describes their works-in-progress.

1961

2. Booth, John E. "Albee and Schneider Observe: 'Something's Stirring.' " *Theatre Arts* 46 (1961):22–24. Albee and Schneider (director of *AD*) reject Booth's suggestion of a "new theatre," blaming middlebrow audiences and staid playwrights for theater's current stagnation. Albee hopes to revitalize the art by breaking down conventions and involving his audience in the experience.
3. "King of Off-Broadway." *Newsweek*, 13 March 1961, 90. With the opening of *DBS* (which joins *AD* on a twin bill), Albee celebrates his vitality and that of Off-Broadway theater. Anticipating productions of *VW*, *BSC*, and *A Separate Peace*, he compares drama to music ("[in both] there is a statement of theme, and variations, largo, allegro") and reflects on his new-found financial stability.
4. Kosner, Edward. "Social Critics, Like Prophets, Are Often Honored from Afar." *New York Post*, 31 March 1961, 38. Albee's biting social comments — displayed in *AD* and ZS — are not part of his self-satisfied demeanor: "I write angry plays, but I don't come on angry." He explains *AD* as concerning "the substitution of artificial values for real values, the acceptance for content, the slow drift of accommodation." The playwright reviews his adolescence and early adulthood, anticipating the debuts of *VW* and *BSC*. "I think I'm doing my part by writing plays," he says.
5. Lask, Thomas. "Dramatist in a Troubled World." *New York Times*, 22 January 1961, sec. 2, 1. Albee describes artistic anomie and self-consciousness in America, citing European productions as on the frontier of today's theater. He compares this work to the agitprop plays of the 1930s. Lask recounts Albee's prep school problems.

6. Ross, Lillian. "Albee." *New Yorker*, 25 March 1961, 30–32. Interviewed in his Greenwich Village apartment, Albee gives extensive autobiographical information, focusing on his education and former jobs. Influential contemporaries and changes in his lifestyle since *ZS* are explored, as well as the effects of Brecht, Genet, and Shaw on Albee's work.

1962

7. "Avant-Garde Theatre—Real or Far Out?" Audiotape. American National Theatre and Academy, Greater New York Chapter, Matinee Theatre Series. 2 April 1962. T3602. Following the presentation of Ionesco's *The Shepherd's Chameleon* and Albee's *FAM*, Albee participated in this symposium with David Brooks, Richard Coe, Henry Hewes, Arthur Kopit, and Jack Richardson.

8. "Talk with the Author." *Newsweek*, 29 October 1962, 52–53. The long-awaited opening of *VW* evokes Albee's comments on artistic influence: "I've been influenced by everybody, for God's sake. Everything I've seen, either accepting or rejecting it." The selective reality demanded by "realistic" theater and his upcoming adaptation of *BSC* supplement these reflections.

9. Tallmer, Jerry. "Edward Albee: Playwright." *New York Post*, 4 November 1962, 10. Albee remembers the decade from ages twenty to thirty as a "fog in which I didn't know what I was doing." But the 1959 production of *ZS* in West Berlin launched Albee's career as a playwright. Considered by many the "new Eugene O'Neill," Albee differs from his forebear in two major respects, according to Tallmer: whereas O'Neill dramatized his life quite literally, Albee writes metaphorically; he handles language more eloquently than the ponderous O'Neill. Both writers, however, share a powerful vision: "a primal concern over man's capacity for deluding himself; his hunger to believe that things are not what they are."

10. Zindel, Paul, and Loree Yerby. "Interview with Edward Albee." *Wagner Literary Magazine* 3 (1962):1–10. Albee resents his bourgeois audience and its sensationalistic tastes, but cites other problems as more basic to Broadway: besides "rising costs and timid producers and greedy theater owners and megalomaniac actors," he blames "the desire on the part of almost everyone concerned with the commercial theater, to bring it down to the easiest level of audience acceptance by a rather lazy audience." He defines commercial theater as "obscene," outlines his creative process, and explains his drama.

1963

11. Diehl, Digby. "Edward Albee Interviewed." *Transatlantic Review* 13 (1963):57–72. Rpt. as "Edward Albee." *Behind the Scenes: Theater and Film Interviews from the Transatlantic Review*. Ed. Joseph McCrindle. New York: Holt, Rinehart, and Winston, 1971, 223–42. Albee tentatively outlines current work on *BSC* and *SUB*. He discusses the problems inherent in "adaptation," and differentiates "pity" and "compassion" with regard to his writing process. Maligning the placid American audience, Albee lauds Off-Broadway experimentation and anticipates the rejection of naturalism.

12. Lask, Thomas. "Edward Albee at Last." *New York Times*, 27 October 1963,

sec. 2, 1, 4. Occasioned by the opening of *BSC*, this interview focuses on the methods and purposes of both original and adaptive writing. Albee has bought the rights to Purdy's *Malcolm*, and plans to have it developed by some other able playwright.

13. Lukas, Mary. "Who Isn't Afraid of Edward Albee?" *Show*, February 1963, 83, 112–14. Albee has emerged from a "clutter of old newspapers, beer cans, records and books" into one of America's leading dramatists. Lukas profiles his unhappy family life and his Greenwich Village years, recording Albee's comments as well as those of his close friends.

14. "The Problems of Literary Creativity." Audiotape. Princeton Symposium on World Affairs, 19–21 April 1963. T4073-1–4. Albee's discussion with Arnold Gingrich, Bernard Malamud, and Robert Penn Warren is recorded.

15. "Problems of the Contemporary Artist." Audiotape. Princeton Symposium on World Affairs, 19–21 April 1963. T4073-12. Another discussion involving Albee, Arnold Gingrich, Bernard Malamud, and Robert Penn Warren.

16. "Soviet Writers Found Unafraid." *New York Times*, 4 December 1963, 54. Interviewed in Moscow, the final city of his thirty-day Soviet tour, Albee is distressed by suppression in the U.S.S.R. Writers there are culturally isolated, he reports — unexposed to most modern Western literature. Albee concludes, "A couple of hours every day I felt like killing myself. . . . I was a homesick boy."

1964

17. Gardner, R. H. "Albee Asks and Albee Answers." *(Baltimore) Sun*, 25 October 1964, sec. d, 34. This article, passed to Gardner by a press agent, was written by Albee himself. Albee assumes the personae of interviewer and interviewee, asking salient questions and providing pertinent (and impertinent) answers. Broaching the topic "How 'Who's Afraid of Virginia Woolf?' Has Changed My Life," Albee promotes the Off-Broadway theater and stresses that "people should be more interested in a writer's work than in the person of the writer."

18. Meehan, Thomas. "Edward Albee and a Mystery." *New York Times*, 27 December 1964, sec. 2, 1, 16. The Broadway premiere of *TA* occasions Meehan's meeting with Albee. The playwright focuses his comments on an upcoming play, hinting that "it's a mystery play, in two senses of the word. . . . That is, it's both a metaphysical mystery, and, at the same time, a conventional 'Dial M for Murder'-type mystery."

19. Ross, Lillian. "Albee Revisited." *New Yorker*, 19 December 1964, 31–33. As Ross accompanies Albee to a *TA* rehearsal, the playwright reviews recent international openings of *VW*. He reiterates assertions that "the play exists in its total and real form on the typewritten page," and that " 'naturalism,' 'stylism' — those terms don't mean anything to me."

20. Smith, Michael. "Edward Albee in Conversation with Michael Smith." *Plays and Players*, March 1964, 12–14. On the eve of *VW*'s London opening, Albee predicts its success. "I go . . . every time for my London disaster. I always have disasters in London." Dramatic censorship in England and the U.S.S.R. disturbs Albee. He elaborates on playwriting methods, and discusses the Edinburgh Theater Festival.

21. Wager, Walter. "Playwright at Work: Edward Albee." *Playbill* 1 (1964). Albee describes his cultural exchange mission with four Iron Curtain countries, praising theatrical productions in Moscow, Leningrad, and Warsaw. He cites Russia's repertory system as a key to "an integration of performance we don't get on Broadway," yet notes that Soviet theater is propagandist. Albee recounts his writing process and mentions his work-in-progress, *SUB*.

1965

22. Flanagan, William. "Edward Albee: An Interview." *The Paris Review* 9 (1965):93–121. Rpt. in *Writers at Work: The Paris Review Interviews*. Ed. George Plimpton. New York: Viking, 1967, 321–46. Also rpt. in French as "William Flanagan interroge Edward Albee." Trans. Claude Clerge. *Cahiers de la Compagnie Madeleine Renaud-Jean Louis Barrault* 63 (1967):3–10. From his decision at age six to be a writer, to his recent disaster *M*, Albee recounts his career. He condemns critics and directors, and discusses his playwriting method. He is pleased with the film *VW*, and maintains that his script was written about heterosexuals. In addition, Albee articulates the link between "a dramatic structure, the form and sound and shape of a play, and the equivalent structure in music."

23. Gardner, Paul. " 'Tiny Alice' Mystifies Albee, Too." *New York Times*, 21 January 1965, 22. Interviewed at the New School for Social Research, Albee and director Alan Schneider elucidate their controversial, confusing *TA*. Breaking precedent, Albee discusses conscious and unconscious symbolism, disowning any attack on the church. Rather, he says, *TA* attacks "the way people use religion."

24. "Is the American Youth in a Vacuum?" *Dorothy Gordon Youth Forum*, 25 November 1965, WNBC. Note: The Zimmer Reporting Service could not provide a transcript.

25. Narducci, Michael, and Walter Chura. "Playwright Edward Albee: An Exclusive Interview." *Beverwyck* (Siena College) 20 (1965). Rpt. in *The Playwrights Speak*. Ed. Walter Wager. New York: Delacorte, 1967, 26–67. Condensed as "Edward Albee: An Interview." *The Times of India* (*The Bombay Times*), 28 September 1969, 5, 8. The interviewers probe for Albee's interpretation of *TA*, launching discussions of world politics, New York theater, and the playwright's works-in-progress. Albee encourages audiences to "stop thinking and react emotionally" in order to understand his writing, which tears at the social fabric they need. "You've got to *raze* something before you can *raise*." In the reprint, Wager provides a detailed chronology of Albee's life and work.

26. Rutenberg, Michael E. "Two Interviews with Edward Albee." *Edward Albee: Playwright in Protest*. New York: Avon, 1969, 229–44 (interview took place 17 March 1965). Rutenberg gleans details about Albee's intuitive "musical" theory of dramatic composition, as well as the playwright's own writing process. Albee reflects on *AD, ZS, VW, TA, BSC,* and *DBS*, and on misinterpretation of these plays. Assaulting Broadway's "destructive" atmosphere, he expounds upon the dramatist's position as "a man out-of-step with his society. A man who feels primarily that his play should not have had to have been written."

27. Steward, R. S. "John Gielgud and Edward Albee Discuss the Stage Today." *Observer*, 18 April 1965. Rpt. as "John Gielgud and Edward Albee Talk about the Theater." *Atlantic Monthly* 215 (1965):61–68. Rpt. in *Edward Albee: A Collection of Critical Essays*. Ed. C. W. E. Bigsby. Englewood Cliffs, NJ: Prentice-Hall, 1975, 112–23. Collaborators on *TA*, Albee and Gielgud discuss their production, stressing connections between avant-garde and classical theater, as well as the inadequacy of American actors. Albee laments the Broadway / Off-Broadway dilemma: "it's ironic and unfortunate that once [the actors] have gotten their training in excellent plays, they're encouraged to go on to . . . plays that aren't so good." He elaborates upon the unconscious evolution of his works, and stresses audience involvement as critical.

28. "Who's Afraid of Success?" *Newsweek*, 4 January 1965: 51. On the eve of his *TA* opening, Albee explains, "It's a mystery . . . [and] a morality play, about truth and illusion, the substitute images we create . . . easy virtues, easy Gods." Albee foretells writing *SUB*, adapting *M*, and seeing the filmed *VW*.

1966

29. Lester, Elenore. "Albee: 'I'm Still in Process.' " *New York Times*, 18 September 1966, sec. 2, 1, 6. Partners Albee, Barr, and Wilder publicize their dramatic endeavors: Cherry Lane, Van Dam Street, the Playwrights Unit. Each emphasizes the view that "plays should be literature," as opposed to "productions," citing the Living Theater and "happenings" as undesirable.

30. Newquist, Roy. "Interviews with Edward Albee." *Showcase*. New York: William Morrow, 1966, 17–29. Reviewing Albee's career through the production of *TA*, this interview begins with his prep school dramatics. It covers the Gielgud / Albee conflict (*TA*), the Hollywood / Albee conflict (*VW*), and the Odets / Albee conflict (agitprop, didacticism, thesis plays vs. organic, musical writing). Albee comments on theater as art and as diversion, audience / playwright responsibilities, and America's theater heritage.

31. Thompson, Howard. "Albee's 'A Delicate Balance' Goes into Rehearsal." *New York Times*, 16 August 1966, 35. Albee's fifth Broadway play in five years, *DB* begins rehearsal with an optimistic, big-name cast. Albee explains his plot with confidence, comparing its naturalism to that of *VW*.

1967

32. Clarkson, Adrienne. "Private World of Edward Albee." *Montrealer* 41 (1967):42–49. This article is an edited transcript of Albee's interview on CBC's *Take Thirty*. Conducted at the Playwrights Unit, the interview first concerns this theater, then Albee's own writing. Albee focuses on himself, not his audience, when writing, and he advises writers to assume that "what fascinates you is going to involve the rest of the world." Denying that he creates "monstrous" women, Albee concludes by defining himself as "an American playwright." Though ambivalent towards geopolitics, he pragmatically states, "One has to live somewhere."

33. Downer, Alan S., ed. "An Interview with Edward Albee." *The American Theater Today*. New York: Basic Books, 1967, 111–23. Washington: U.S.I.S.,

1967, 123–36. Albee surveys his career, from age six to the present, assessing the many foreign productions of his plays and explaining that America's commercial theater imports serious drama rather than premiering it. Although Albee supports the Playwrights Unit, he admits that, "I don't think playwrights can ever be trained." More optimistic about audiences, he hopes that greater education in the arts will raise popular expectations among Americans, while honing their perceptions.

1968

34. Rutenberg, Michael E. "Two Interviews with Edward Albee." *Edward Albee: Playwright in Protest*. New York: Avon, 1969, 244–60. Albarr Productions has contracted to film *DBS*, giving Albee his first experience in that medium. Current work on *BOX* prompts his note that "anybody could put whatever symbolism they want" to his plays. Rutenberg probes into critical interpretation—and misinterpretation—of *DB*, *M*, *TA*, and *VW*.

1969

35. Wardle, Irving. "Edward Albee Looks at Himself and His Plays." *(London) Times*, 18 January 1969, "Arts," 17. Having completed twelve plays and three adaptations, Albee is in London for the opening of *DB*. As the "dramatist of Western cannibal customs," he discusses the peculiar problems of adapting another writer's work, as well as his desire for dramatic catharsis: "I think it should take place in the mind of the spectator some time afterwards—maybe a year after experiencing the play. One thing I don't like about the naturalistic theatre in general is that it usually gives answers instead of asking questions."

36. Zasurskii, Y. Ustrecha. "A Meeting with Edward Albee." *Literaturnaia Gazeta* (Moscow), 24 December 1969, 13. Interviewed in his New York home, the playwright comments on the sexual revolution in theater: "Nudity prevents us from listening. It distracts our attention from the most important thing, namely the meaning of the play." Albee reemphasizes the writer's purpose as "to transform facts into truths." Expressing little admiration for most twentieth-century drama, Albee specifically praises Chekhov, O'Neill, Beckett, Williams, and Kopit; he opts, however, to control his own film and theater projects, putting authorial intent before nonliterary theatrical creation.

1970

37. Clurman, Harold. *Ideas on the Theater* (videotape). New York: University at Large, Chelsea House, 1970.

1971

38. Bosworth, Patricia. "Will They All Be Albees?" *New York Times*, 18 July 1971, sec. 2, 1, 3. This interview profiles the William Flanagan Center for Creative Persons, a colony of artists sponsored by Albee in a former stable near Montauk, Long Island.

39. Flatley, Guy. "Edward Albee Fights Back." *New York Times*, 18 April 1971, sec. 2, 1, 10. Albee's penchant for literary drama has pervaded *AO*, a

production attacked for its static wordiness. The playwright protests his critics as being tasteless, unqualified judges and is pessimistic about the future of "serious" commercial theater. For responses to Albee's comments, see editorials in the *New York Times*, 9 May 1971, sec. 2, 6. Also note the "Drama Mailbag," 18 April 1971, sec. 2, 7—"Albee—Again a Controversy."

40. Glover, William. "Albee: A Peep Within." *Houston Post Spotlight*, 25 April 1971, 21. "Is Albee death-obsessed?" queries Glover. Albee thinks not, explaining, "Almost any play I can think of that I've any respect for, from Sophocles to Beckett, concerns death. But at the same time I think the subject of my plays is life and the degree to which people are willing to live it fully."

41. Gussow, Mel. "Albee's New 'All Over' in Rehearsal." *New York Times*, 9 February 1971, 32. Albee gathers cast, producers, and reporters for his initial *AO* rehearsal. He reveals that *AO* is "a serious play about how people get through life," and he forecasts *SEA* and discusses man's sense of mortality.

1973

42. Donnelly, Tom. "Albee on the Real Thing (Theater) Versus a Film." *Washington Post*, 28 October 1973, sec. L, 1–2. The filming of *DB* for the American Film Theater series occasions Albee's comments on the film medium, and on experience as metaphor. His goal in writing is that his plays "encourage people to participate in their own lives more."

43. Kramer, Carol. "Albee: A Case Against Compromise." *Chicago Tribune*, 28 October 1973, sec. 6, 13. Albee discusses the American Film Theater's production of *DB*, including Katherine Hepburn's portrayal of Agnes. He reasserts his desire to awaken people to life, not through short-lived agitprop theater, but through metaphor: "I don't write about specific problems but about the states of mind that allow problems to exist."

1974

44. Ross, Lillian. "Theatre." *New Yorker*, 3 June 1974, 28–30. As students from Brearley and St. Bernard question Albee about his life and work, he describes the "unconscious process" of writing, the importance of Samuel Beckett, and his efforts to instruct his audience.

45. Schneider, Howard. "Has the Tarantula Escaped?" *Pittsburgh Press*, 3 February 1974, 6–7. Rpt. in *Biography News*, March 1974, 246–47. Schneider reviews Albee's turbulent childhood, meteoric theatrical origins, and current artistic plateau. Albee cites waxing public taste, but laments an entrenched mediocrity in public theater. He reasserts that his plays are political metaphors of our national psyche, though they are not topical in the agitprop mode.

1975

46. "Albee: 'I Write to Unclutter My Mind.'" *New York Times*, 26 January 1975, 1, 7. The long-awaited premiere of *SEA*—Albee's first Broadway show in four years—occasions this interview. Albee speaks of being "with play," and expands this metaphor for his writing process. Relating drama to music, he

applauds the American public's improving critical eye, but regrets that commercial theater offers little to discerning audiences.

47. Gussow, Mel. "Recalling Evolution of 'Seascape' Play, Albee sees Tale Not of Lizard, but Life." *New York Times*, 21 January 1975, 40. Questioning our assumptions of "evolution," *SEA* has been written, directed, and coproduced by Albee. He traces the evolution of this play from conception to out-of-town tryouts, citing one's need to "have a tragic sense of life to see the humor of the absurd."

48. Salveson, Veronica. "In a Small Quiet Room Back Stage" [*Santa Monica College*] *Corsair*, 16 April 1975. For the first time, with *SEA*, Albee is directing the first production of his own play. In this interview with 20 college journalists, Albee and actress Deborah Kerr discuss their collaboration on this project. Explaining *SEA* as "about the beginning of awareness," Albee describes the writing, directing, and rewriting of this show.

49. Schneider, Howard. "Albee: Hard Act for Himself to Follow." *Los Angeles Times*, 23 March 1975, "California Arts and Leisure," 1, 50. Suffering a critical decline since *DB*, Albee hopes to redeem his reputation with *SEA*. Denying that he has mellowed with age, the playwright explains, "People talk softer in some of my more recent plays, . . . but they say angrier things." Admitting his political bent, he states, "Specifics never interest me. . . . I'm more interested in the overtones." These are reflected in his recurrent dream of Armageddon.

50. Sysa, Glenna. " 'A Great Play Can Change the World.' " *Chicago Sun-Times*, 20 April 1975, "Arts," 2. Interviewed during the Chicago run of *SEA*, Albee admits being unable to survive on American productions of his works alone. Comparing *AO*'s New York run (of 30 performances) to its London season (of 120), he exclaims, "The play wasn't a failure. It was a commercial failure." Thus the escapist / artistic dichotomy of the theatre world is reiterated, with Albee's desire being a theater which "changes in some fashion how you view reality." Declaiming Joseph Papp and agitprop productions, Albee looks forward to his first major directing job, *Sweet Bird of Youth*.

1976

51. Kelly, Kevin. "Edward Albee on Albee: The Superstar of Drama." *Boston Globe*, 14 March 1976, "Focus," A9, A14. Noting the influence of Beckett and Ionesco on his own writing, Albee discusses *AO* and *SEA*, new works *L* and *CW*, and future projects *SUB* and "Atilla the Hun" (sic). As background to this interview, Kelly provides a biography of the writer from birth through theatrical career, a personality profile (noting Albee's "aura of dark moodiness" and "ironic turn of speech"), and an overview of contemporary playwrights Shepard, Rabe, and Kopit.

52. Long, Mary. "Interview: Edward Albee." *Mademoiselle*, August 1976, 230. "Audiences prefer reaffirmation of their own values," Albee attests. "They don't want to be upset or disturbed." The playwright's job is to fight this tendency towards illusion. With the revival of *VW*, Albee reaffirms his belief in the writer's duty to be a "demonic social critic."

53. Oakes, Philip. "Don't Shoot the Playwright. . . ." *(London) Sunday Times*, 12

December 1976, 35. The London opening of *CW* precipitates Albee's comments on criticism. "I never mind a bad review if it has something to do with what I intended to write." Considering commercial theater and author / audience responsibility, Albee reveals that his current backlog of plays is "about indifference, apathy, waste, communication, lack of communication. The usual spectrum."

54. Stern, Daniel. "Albee: 'I Want My Intent Clear.'" *New York Times*, 28 March 1976, sec. 2, 1, 5. Directing the Broadway revival of *VW*, Albee considers the playwright as director: "If you can remember what you intended when you wrote the play . . . you can probably, if you're somewhat objective, end up with a fair representation of what you intended. . . . You won't necessarily end up with the most effective production." Gazzara and Dewhurst, appearing as George and Martha, comment on Albee's direction, and Albee again refutes any homosexual interpretation.

1977

55. Blake, Jeanie. "Tulane Speakers Write for Selves." *New Orleans Times-Picayune*, 20 March 1977. Edward Albee, Melvin Van Peebles, and Truman Capote commune at Tulane University's Direction '77 program. Albee emphasizes the restrictions which audience apathy places on theater.

56. Glover, William. "Albee Not on a Soap Box, But. . . ." *New Orleans Times-Picayune*, 30 January 1977, sec. 2, 11. Bringing *L* and *CW* to the Hartford stage, Albee introduces these "intimate studies of ambiguous personal relationships." He reviews their British production histories, and reiterates his preference for "intentional" directing.

57. Von Ransom, Brooks. "Edward Albee Speaks." *Connecticut*, February 1977, 38–39. Albee explains choosing Hartford for the American premieres of *CW* and *L*. "I don't have to be subject to that make-or-break commercial situation that exists even in the Off-Broadway theatre in New York. These are not ideal plays for the Winter Garden Theatre. . . . They are intimate, difficult, avant-garde plays." Albee's dislike of television ("it's misused," "it invades one's privacy") and film ("it's synthetic," "it's George Orwell time") supplement this discussion of commerciality.

1978

58. Connolly, Patrick. Supplementary material from the *New York Times* and the Associated Press. *New York Times*, 4 October 1978, "Magazine," 68. Interviewed during the Seattle stop of a lecture tour, Albee contrasts the ideal artistic climate with that of modern America. His proposal to star Helen Hayes in a television version of *SEA* was rejected; he suggests that "maybe Farrah Fawcett-Majors . . . could rescue the venture."

1979

59. Arthur, Thomas H., Steven Snyder, and Theresa Beal. "Edward Albee: Auto If Not Biographical." *The [James Madison University] Breeze* 1979. Rpt. in *Dramatics* 51 (1979):3–4. The interviewers question Albee about his life as transformed by *VW*. He stresses the importance of self-education and

suggests television as a new field for dramatists: "it's an entirely new kind of drama. . . . It should be developed, since it's what the majority of people spend their lives with."

60. Cavett, Dick. *The Dick Cavett Show*, filmed 18 April 1979 (aired 31 May 1979 and 1 June 1979), WNET. New York: Daphne Productions.

61. Shirley, Don. "An Audience with Albee." *Washington Post*, 2 February 1979, sec. K, 1, 14. Albee's revival tour of seven one-acts is visiting college campuses, giving him occasion to lecture and to be interviewed. Here he discusses directing, his school and work history, and the upcoming *LFD*.

62. Wallach, Allan. "Edward Albee: 'If the Play Can Be Described in One Sentence, That Should Be Its Length.' " *New Orleans Times-Picayune*, 19 January 1979, 4. At the beginning of his national tour of one-act plays, Albee profiles the upcoming *LFD*: "It's a fairly devious play with a fairly easy-going surface to it." He compares his latest plays to earlier ones, tracing recurrent themes — love, religion, anomie.

1980

63. Adam, Peter. "Edward Albee: A Playwright Versus the Theatre." *Listener*, 7 February 1980, 170–71. In this BBC interview, Albee synopsizes his 20 years as a poet, then describes his playwriting process. He reiterates his view that "a first-rate play can only be proved, not improved, by production"; delineates the constraints of commercial theater; and expresses pessimism towards future artistry in the theater: "We are the only animal who attempts metaphor. . . . If [our society] is unwilling to use the metaphor . . . then we are this curious kind of society which is on its way downhill without ever having reached the top."

64. "Edward Albee: An Interview." *Edward Albee: Planned Wilderness*. Ed. Patricia De La Fuente. Edinburg, Tex.: Pan American UP, 1980, 6–17. Albee theorizes that all serious art "is an attempt to modify and change people's perception of themselves, to bring them into larger contact with the fact of being alive." He celebrates the optimism inherent in writing and chastises regional theater for succumbing to commerciality. Discussing his own trend to "adaptation" Albee lauds Latin America's theatrical sophistication, and decries Neil Simon's commercial "pornography" — an escapist insult to serious drama.

65. Woggon, Bob. "The Writing Life: Avant-Garde Albee." *Writer's Digest*, October 1980, 18, 20. Northern Illinois University is the scene for this discussion of Albee's writing technique and upcoming plays. Commercial television bears the brunt of Albee's criticism as he fears Americans are "in danger of *losing the metaphor*, and of becoming hopelessly mired in escapist entertainment." Critics nourish this problem, Albee claims, with their incorrect and insipid interpretations.

1981

66. Berkvist, Robert. "Nabokov's 'Lolita' Becomes a Play by Albee." *New York Times*, 1 March 1981, sec. 2, 1, 4. In response to charges that *LOL* is

pornographic, Albee contends that he has faithfully translated Nabokov's prose into dramatic form.

67. Krohn, Charles S. and Julian N. Wasserman. "An Interview with Edward Albee." *Edward Albee: An Interview and Essays*. Ed. Julian N. Wasserman. Syracuse, N.Y.: Syracuse UP for the University of St. Thomas, Houston, 1983, 1–27. A discussion of "serious drama" and "true comedy" begins this interview, which soon turns to American education. Albee suggests that "our colleges are cluttered with people who don't need to be there." He impresses upon his audience the necessity of "engagement rather than escapist" entertainment to achieve Art. Furthermore, he rejects social instruction as a substitute for aesthetic experience. Differentiating "translation" from "adaptation," Albee uses *AD*, *SEA*, *L*, *LOL*, and *ZS* to illustrate his point: "In a utopian society, we'd have no literature, no art, because there would be no need for any, because all art is corrective."

68. Rubin, Stan Sanvel, Adam Lazarre, and Mark Anderson. "Edward Albee." *Brockport Writers Forum*, 5 February 1981. Brockport, NY: SUNY-Brockport.

1982

69. "The Playwright as Curator." *Art News* 81, no. 5 (1982):17–18. Curator of an Edward F. Albee Foundation exhibit, Albee explains his efforts to support young artists and discusses his own art collection.

70. Richards, David. "Albee After the Plunge." *Washington Post*, 24 January 1982, sec. K, 1, 5. Rpt. in *San Francisco Chronicle*, 28 March 1982. Richards observes that, if Albee depended on the kindness of critics, "he would probably be lying in some dark alley, semi-comatose and caked with dried blood." The struggle to surmount his own successes — notably *ZS* and *VW* — has indeed been difficult. But Albee has introduced to his audience the idea that "people invent their own illusion to give themselves a reality," and that they "are aware they're creating the illusion themselves." He recapitulates his views on middlebrow theater, his writing process and work-in-process *MWHTA*.

1983

71. Anderson, Teresa H. "Students Learn Disdain from Albee." *New Orleans Time-Picayune*, 2 March 1983, sec. 4, 6. During a month-long residency at Southwestern University in Georgetown, Texas, Albee holds a press conference in which he reiterates his "ardent dislike of critics and a festering dislike of the theater-going public." Attacking the "big business" which theater has become, Albee asks that audiences demand art which will "change your views and your perceptions of reality."

72. Roudané, Matthew C. "An Interview with Edward Albee." *Southern Humanities Review* 16, no. 1 (1983):29–44. Albee makes an artistic distinction — "Everything in a good play is inevitable, everything in a bad play is arbitrary" — and asserts that "creative people have perceptions . . . different from other people's." Discussing the boldly complex *L*, the vaudevillean *CW*, and *AO* with its air of loss, Albee contrasts these to the more traditional *ZS*,

DBS, and *VW*. Allying himself with Sontag and Artaud, Albee agrees that "the most interesting drama always releases the collective unconscious . . . the primordial demons."

1984

73. Roudané, Matthew C. "Albee on Albee." *RE: Artes Liberales* 10, no. 2 (1984):1–8. Having finished *Finding the Sun*, Albee is drafting *Another Part of the Zoo* and *Walking*. Each play encourages communication through audience "participation," reflecting Albee's "optimistic existentialism." Rejecting commercial theater, he lauds Chekhov, Beckett, Sophocles, and Genêt as "authentic" inspiration for his own work: "Write as much truth as clearly as you can. . . . Don't pander, don't sell out. . . . If there's nobody listening there's nobody listening."

1985

74. McNally, Terrence. "Edward Albee in Conversation with Terrence McNally." *Dramatists Guild Quarterly* 22 (Summer 1985): 12–23. Then vice president of the Dramatists Guild Project Committee, playwright McNally asks Albee about his boyhood in Larchmont, his early works, his views of the theater of the 1960s, his "famous flops" (especially *Breakfast at Tiffany's*), and his interests in directing. Albee claims that of all his plays *MWHTA* "is the one for which I received the most enthusiastic and favorable response from people in the arts — my peers."

1986

75. Roudané, Matthew C. "A Playwright Speaks: An Interview with Edward Albee." *Critical Essays on Edward Albee*. Eds. Philip C. Kolin and J. Madison Davis. New York: G. K. Hall, 1986. Albee encourages a "state of innocence" in his audience, a willingness to dismiss preconceptions. For both audience and playwright, "the essential thing is to let the play happen on its own terms." Of his role as social critic, Albee notes: "I am concerned with altering people's perceptions, altering the status quo." He cites Artaud, Sartre, and Camus as inspiring his "aggressive" dramas and encourages living fully conscious ". . . no matter how dangerous or cruel or terror-filled" that might be.

INDEX TO NAMES, CONCEPTS, AND PLACES
FOR THE BIBLIOGRAPHY OF ALBEE INTERVIEWS

INDEX

Note: Lea Carol Owen's bibliography of interviews is indexed separately in the preceding pages.

DATE			